FLY ON

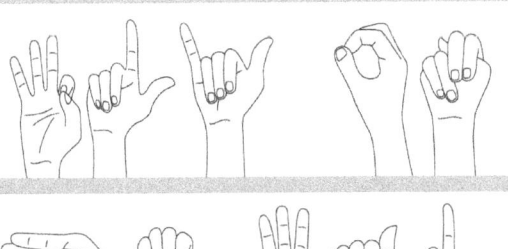
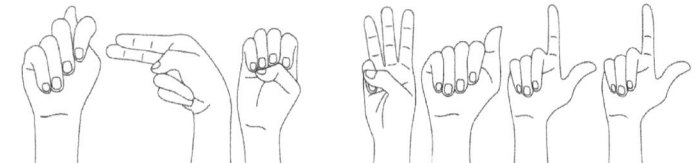

THE WALL

BILL PUGIN

This book is dedicated to two important women in my life.

My sister, Mary Anne Pugin, for putting me on my path.

My friend and mentor, Janet Bailey, for helping me stay there.

Foreword

It is rare to come across someone who has truly dedicated their life to bridging worlds, making communication not only possible but meaningful. Bill Pugin is one such person. For fifty years, he has stood at the intersection of two languages, two cultures, and two communities, facilitating understanding and connection between the Deaf and hearing worlds. But this memoir is not simply a chronicle of his career—this is a story of passion, perseverance, and an unyielding commitment to the art of interpretation.

As a sign language interpreter, Bill's hands have spoken volumes—carrying stories, emotions, and even the silence between words. His journey has not been without challenges, but Bill has always faced them with grace, humor, and an unwavering belief in the power of communication. He has seen the world through the lens of two languages, both of which carry their own unique beauty and richness. Yet, as you read these pages, you will discover that the language of connection—of truly understanding each other—is what has driven him above all else.

Over the years, Bill has become a fixture in the Deaf community, earning the trust of countless individuals and working alongside organizations to ensure that access to communication is never a barrier. But what sets him apart is not only his technical skill as an interpreter but his deep empathy, his ability to make people feel seen, heard, and valued.

As for me, Bill is my friend. He's also a work colleague and we have worked and played together for many years. As my interpreter on set of whatever I'm filming, Bill has always been able to keep me calm and has always known how to keep me in the right frame of mind. It's hard to explain, but when I know Bill is there, I know I'll be okay. At ease. Safe.

This memoir is more than a collection of stories—it is an invitation into the world Bill has navigated with such purpose and dedication. It's a glimpse into the challenges, joys, and rewards of a profession that requires a rare combination of intellect, intuition, and compassion.

As Bill reflects on his journey, I hope readers will see not only the man who helped others understand each other but also the human being who gave so much of himself to make sure that no one was ever left without a voice.

This is the story of a man who gave meaning to silence and whose work continues to speak far beyond the boundaries of words.

— **Marlee Matlin**

Author's Note on Terminology

Throughout this book, you will see the terms Deaf and deaf used in different contexts. This distinction is intentional and meaningful.

When I use Deaf with a capital "D," I am referring to individuals who identify as members of the Deaf community—a rich cultural and linguistic group that uses American Sign Language (ASL) as their primary means of communication. Being Deaf in this sense is not solely about hearing level; it is about shared language, values, and identity.

On the other hand, deaf with a lowercase "d" is used to describe the audiological condition of hearing loss or to refer to individuals who do not identify with the ASL-using Deaf community. This may include people who communicate primarily through spoken language, use hearing aids or cochlear implants, or simply do not participate in Deaf culture.

In some cases, you may notice the term deaf used even when the exact cultural identity of the individual was unclear to me. Out of respect and a desire for accuracy, I chose the lowercase d unless I was certain the person identified as part of the capital-D Deaf community.

This distinction matters. It reflects the diversity within the broader deaf and hard-of-hearing population and honors the lived experiences of those who belong to the vibrant Deaf community.

Thank you for reading with awareness and care.

— Bill Pugin

Table of Contents

Beginnings & Family Roots

In The Beginning

I remember the place and situation very clearly. At my current age of 67, this is not always the case. My memory has never been great, which, I think, has benefited my interpreting. But more about that later.

It was after dinner at my family home in Eastman, GA. We were sitting around the dining room table with Dad at the head of the table, Mom clearing the table, sister Evelyn already up and gone, and my other sister, Mary Anne, sitting directly across from me. Mary Anne was home for Christmas… or maybe Easter. See what I mean about my memory? It was one of those holidays when I was a senior in high school.

I had skipped my junior year and found myself suddenly a senior. It wasn't that I was a brilliant kid (though I may have been!), but in my junior year, I realized I had satisfied all my courses, and my senior year would have been a full year of electives and senior English. I did not want to waste a year of my life in this small town just to take English.

So, I made an appointment to meet with the principal to discuss my idea of taking two English courses in one year so that I could graduate and get out! He said it had never been done before, and he understood my concern. He asked if I thought I could handle two English classes in one year. I could have taught English in this school, so I said, "Yes, sir... I think I can handle it."

Now, it's Christmas (or Easter), and I'm having a discussion with Mary Anne and Dad about my future. Graduation was approaching, and because I was a year earlier than expected, I hadn't applied to any colleges. Mary Anne made a suggestion.

My sister, Mary Anne, is eight years older than I and is Deaf. She lost her hearing around the age of 2 or 3 (still a bit of a mystery with lots of theories up for discussion) and started her life with Mom, Dad, and our oldest sibling, Welby (two and a half years older than Mary Anne). Dad was in the Navy, and the family moved a lot. Mary Anne was placed in regular public schools and "did her best" to keep up with her hearing peers.

As time passed, school became more challenging, and sitting in the front row trying to lipread the teacher just wasn't cutting it. When Mary Anne was six, our sister Evelyn was born. Two years later, I came to be. Dad was stationed at Barbers Point, Ewa Beach, Hawaii, at the time, and Mary Anne and Welby were attending the local school on base. Ev was a toddler, and I was goo-gooing in my crib.

Mom was 37 when I was born, Dad was 41, and he was thinking about retiring from the Navy after achieving his Commander rank. Mary Anne had been deaf six years at this point, so I only knew her as "my deaf sister."

Two years after I was born, Dad retired and took a job in the aluminum business, courtesy of a Naval buddy. From the islands to the Midwest, our family ping-ponged across the country a couple of times before finally settling in South Bend, Indiana. It was here that my memories started to take root, and, unsurprisingly, center on me.

One of my earliest memories involves my mother taking me to the local WSB-TV station for a week on Romper Room. Yes, Romper Room, where children were groomed for a life of stardom, or so I assumed at the time. My shining moment came when I managed to walk around with a basket balanced on my head like I was auditioning for The Sound of Music: The Early Years.

Miss Kathy, the teacher, and the producers were so impressed that they asked me to come back for a second week. My mother was beside herself with pride, though I suspect she also just wanted five more days of someone else keeping me entertained. It was my introduction to the world of production, and let me tell you, I felt destined for greatness. (The basket was just the beginning.)

While I was wowing the local TV station with my exceptional basket-balancing skills, Welby was starting high school, and Evelyn was climbing the social ladder of second grade. I, meanwhile, was taking my first cautious steps into kindergarten at John Marshall Elementary, just a short walk from our house.

But Mary Anne? She wasn't with us. By then, she'd been sent to the Lutheran School for the Deaf in Detroit.

Her grades had been slipping, and my parents made the difficult decision to send her away. Back in the 1950s, "expert" advice on raising deaf children was as progressive as a rotary phone. Doctors insisted that using American Sign Language (ASL) would somehow stifle Mary Anne's ability to read, write, and speak. "A crutch," they called it. A crutch. To this day, that philosophy lingers in certain circles, and I can tell you with full confidence that it's absolute nonsense.

Here's the thing: Deaf people gather information visually. If you don't sign, you're left trying to lipread, a Herculean task that requires guessing at context more often than not. Some letters and words look identical on the lips: "p," "b," and "m" are indistinguishable, and don't even get me started on "sixteen seconds" versus "sixty-six socks." Imagine spending your entire life puzzling out the difference between "I love you" and "island view." It's exhausting just thinking about it.

Eventually, my parents enrolled Mary Anne in Detroit. Mom, a lifelong Lutheran, took comfort in knowing the school shared her values, which softened the blow of the separation. For Mary Anne, though, it was a game-changer.

I'll never forget our first visit to her school. My five-year-old eyes widened as I watched kids talking to each other with their hands. Their movements were fluid and expressive, like a secret language that everyone but me had cracked. Mary Anne didn't know how to sign yet, but she picked it up as though it had been waiting for her all along. Watching her was like watching a flower bloom, like someone had finally turned on the sunlight.

She excelled at school. For the first time, she wasn't the kid stuck in the front row struggling to keep up. She was thriving. But when she came home for the holidays, it was back to lip-reading. Back to struggling through every conversation. Back to being the first one done at the dinner table, excusing herself to bury her nose in a book.

She loved her family, of course, but being surrounded by people who didn't sign was isolating. She missed her friends, her real community, the ones who "spoke" her language.

That's when it hit me. Watching Mary Anne, I became fascinated, curious even, about this gap in communication. Why didn't we, her family, learn to sign? Why did we make her carry all the weight of bridging that gap? It wasn't fair, and for the first time, I started to see that.

Of course, I was five years old, so my contribution to the solution was probably limited to a half-hearted attempt to mimic her fingerspelling the alphabet. But that curiosity? That sense of wanting to understand her world? That stuck with me. And it would come back to me in ways I didn't fully understand yet.

Mary Anne would always teach me some signs when she visited, and I never forgot them. I learned to cobble together simple sentences, filling in the gaps with fingerspelling for the signs I didn't know. She taught me the 26 handshapes of the alphabet early on, and I practiced obsessively, like a kid rehearsing for a spelling bee, except with my hands.

When she brought a friend from school, I would sit in the room silently, mesmerized by their conversations. I never understood a word, but oh, how I wanted to. I wanted to know what was just said that made them laugh. What was the secret? Watching them was like witnessing a beautiful dance, their hands choreographed in a rhythm I couldn't quite follow. It felt oddly familiar, like the tap-dancing lessons I'd started when I was six, a little musical, a little mystical.

Except instead of shuffle-ball-changing across the stage, they were weaving entire conversations out of thin air.

When our church in South Bend, Hilltop Lutheran, announced sign language classes, Dad didn't hesitate to sign us up. It was thrilling, for me, at least. Dad gave it his best shot but would shrug after every class with his favorite old-dog-new-tricks line.

Mom, bless her heart, was a lost cause. Fingerspelling was completely out of her league. As for signing, forget it.

"I don't need to learn sign language," she'd say. "Mary Anne and I communicate just fine." That was true as long as the conversation didn't extend beyond breakfast options. Their exchanges were cordial, pleasant even, but never deep. Never philosophical. Over time, as happens in so many hearing families with deaf children, they grew apart, two people who loved each other but lived in different worlds.

Not me.

I wanted more. I wanted real conversations with my sister on her terms. I didn't want our relationship to stall at "pass the salt" or "how was your day?" I wanted to understand her world and meet her there.

Then, at eight years old, everything changed again. We left the snowy winters of South Bend, Indiana, and headed west to Riverside, California. Until then, the Midwest was all I'd ever known, friends, family, and my grandparents. But California! I mean, it had movie stars and swimming pools! I'd seen The Beverly Hillbillies, and I thought we were heading straight for Hollywood.

Well, Riverside is not Hollywood. But at eight years old, "close enough" was good enough for me.

Dad rented a house on Elsinore Road that had the biggest swimming pool I'd ever seen. We moved in January, and by February, I was dog-paddling my way through mornings while Mom and Dad sipped coffee on the patio. It was the kind of life a Midwestern kid dreams about during those endless snow days. California had me hooked almost immediately.

Evelyn and I started school, though, for the first time, we weren't in the same building. She was off at the junior high while I joined the 4th grade at Louisa May Alcott Elementary. This was a new experience for me, being "the new kid" after the school year had already started. I'll never forget the way everyone stared when the teacher introduced me to the class. I felt like an alien who'd just landed from another planet, and for the first few days, I was convinced I'd die of embarrassment.

But I learned how to make friends quickly, mostly because I had no other choice. And while I missed my friends and family in South Bend, California started to grow on me. Between the endless sunshine, the pool, and my best girl, our dog Pandy, life didn't seem so bad. Oh, and I had a rabbit named Smokey, who was a new addition to the family. Living in his cage by the pool, life was good for him, too! This new adventure was starting to feel like home.

Mary Anne graduated from the Indiana School for the Deaf in Indianapolis and was now a student at Gallaudet College, the world's only liberal arts college exclusively for people with hearing loss. That summer, Mary Anne and several of her friends came to visit our home on Elsinore Road, and suddenly our backyard turned into a kind of adventure park. They would all splash and laugh in the pool, their hands flying in a symphony of signs that I watched with a mix of fascination and excitement from my perch on a lounge chair.

I'd try to keep up, squinting like Sherlock Holmes as though lipreading might unlock the secrets of their hand ballet. My curiosity eventually boiled over into a full-blown case of sign language envy. Why weren't my parents desperate to decode this world? Mom and Dad, it seemed, were content to stick to their roles as summer hosts, keeping things breezy and transactional. "Did you sleep okay?" or "Orange juice or Apple juice?" formed the linguistic high notes of their interactions with Mary Anne and her friends.

But I wanted more. I was the pesky younger brother, relentless in my questions and determined to know what every single flick of Mary Anne's wrist or arch of her brow meant. I wanted in. Their language felt like an exclusive club, and I was tired of being the outsider craning my neck from behind the velvet ropes.

Soon after this summer vacation with Mary Anne and her friends, Dad decided it was time to uproot us again, this time into a subdivision called "Canyon Crest." Our new digs on Via Tioga came with some upsides (a pool with a slide!) and one memorable downside: an uphill bike ride to my new school, Castle View Elementary. There I was, red-faced and pumping furiously on the way there, then a triumphant blur tearing back down in the afternoons. Why "Castle View," you ask? It had a view of an honest-to-goodness castle, which I was told belonged to a Catholic monastery. Nuns had always scared me. Good thing I wasn't raised Catholic.

By the summer of 1969, both Mary Anne and our older brother, Welby, were back at the new Riverside house. I can't remember if Mary Anne brought friends this time. It's possible she decided a younger sibling tugging on her arm 24/7 was sufficient company. What I do remember is savoring every moment with her. With a few new signs and an alphabet of fingerspelling at my command, I started to piece together conversations, feeling more like an insider than ever before. When Mary Anne signed back something that showed she actually understood me, it was like hitting the jackpot. You could've floated me on a cloud of smug satisfaction. "Yes," I would think to myself. I think I'm getting better at this!

But all good things must come to an end, and the dreaded goodbyes would roll around when she returned to Gallaudet. I always felt a pang of loss, not just because I missed her, but because it meant the next chapter of my signing adventures was on indefinite hold.

Just as life started to feel settled, Dad, once again, threw a curveball. "We're moving to Atlanta," he announced one ordinary afternoon, casually dismantling our lives like he was folding a game of Monopoly.

Wait, what? We had just gotten here. The pool and the tetherball had hardly been used, and now we had to leave? Poor Mom sighed under the weight of yet another mountain of boxes, and off we went again.

This time, we landed in the then-tiny town of Peachtree City, Georgia. It wasn't just small, it was microscopic. A grocery store, one lone church, a golf club, and a school. My sixth grade was spent at Peachtree City Elementary, where every kid who was anybody cruised the streets... in a golf cart. Golf carts were the mode of transportation, and yes, we got one, too.

Today, Peachtree City is apparently thriving, a full-blown suburb of Atlanta, bursting with life and, presumably, fewer golf carts on the streets. Back then, it was simpler. I, a sixth-grader determined to learn more about signing and a golf cart commute to navigate whatever new adventures life decided to hurl my way.

Mom had the foresight of a seasoned time traveler. She never unpacked all the boxes because, surprise!, another year, another move. This time, we landed in Eastman. By this point, Evelyn and I had developed a sort of well-oiled system for our perpetual reinventions as "the new kids." It wasn't so much that we rolled with the punches; we practically choreographed them. Sure, the stares were inevitable, as were those hesitant introductions, where kids would size us up as if we were auditioning for a role in their carefully curated childhoods. But our philosophy was simple: "To know us is to love us, and you will. Eventually."

One thing all the moving did give me (besides the ability to pack and unpack endless boxes) was the uncanny ability to read a room and win it over. Evelyn shared the same knack, though hers leaned more toward charm, while mine involved a sort of "class clown who knows when to rein it in" energy. Between the two of us, it wasn't long before any new town felt like ours, until, of course, we packed up and did it all over again.

Spring 1971

Spring brought a fresh adventure. We took a train from Georgia to Washington, D.C., to watch Mary Anne graduate from Gallaudet. Riding the train felt like stepping into an old Black and White movie. The tiny compartment somehow fit Mom, Dad, Evelyn, and me, and yes, there was a single bathroom for all of us to share. Not that I minded, I was having the time of my life.

One moment that stuck out was this mysterious little cupboard with a door that opened to the hallway on the other side. Dad told me to stash my fancy graduation shoes in there before we went to bed. "Why?" I asked. He just shrugged and said, "You'll see."

The next morning, I swung open that little door, and voilà, my shoes were polished to a military shine. Magic. It was like something out of a fairy tale. If that service still exists, I'm willing to take a train every chance I get. I wonder what they'll do with my sneakers?

Arriving on Gallaudet's campus was like stepping into another world, a buzzing hive where every hand was in motion. The flurry of graduation prep brought out a kind of joyful chaos. Posters hung from dorm windows, family members crowded campus paths, and everywhere I turned, people were signing. To me, it wasn't noise, it was music.

One standout moment: Mary Anne's roommate appeared at her dorm window, spotted me gawking below, and waved. She motioned for us to "come up" using simple gestures anyone could understand, like charades. I immediately signed back, "CAN-WE?", the first two words I had ever signed to someone other than Mary Anne. When she signed "YES!" back, I felt like I'd unlocked the secret handshake to the universe.

It's funny the things that stick with you, how a tiny triumph like that can linger for decades.

The Blur of Adolescence

The years after that seemed to blur together, like flipping through a scrapbook on 78 RPM. By the time I hit 10th grade, I'd learned how to settle in quickly, make friends faster, and establish a kind of charisma that came from being an outsider. Eastman was a town where most kids were practically born on the same block they grew up on. They all had southern accents, called their elders "Ma'am" and "Sir," and couldn't have picked me, a Yankee, out of a lineup if it weren't for my voice.

Oddly enough, the whole "Ma'am" and "Sir" thing worked to my advantage. Evelyn and I were so baffled by it at first that the locals gave us a pass. Even our teachers excused us from using the titles, probably because they liked us. I wasn't just another face in the classroom; I was "that northern kid who got all the jokes but never said 'Yes, Ma'am.'"

Dad being retired in the military seemed like it would demand "Sir"-filled formality at home, but nope. He ran a tight ship without requiring the theatrics, so Evelyn and I grew up in a loving, relaxed home and not a boot camp.

Those early years in Eastman left their mark. I learned how to adapt, connect, and maybe even thrive, but mostly, I learned how to exist as someone who might show up in a new town and say, "To know me is to love me… and you will."

So there I was, almost seventeen, sitting at the dining room table, somewhere between a Christmas ham and an Easter roast, staring into the abyss that was the question, "What are your plans for the summer?" I hadn't thought much about it. My grand plan for life at that point was simply to graduate and stay out of trouble. Lofty goals, I know.

That's when Mary Anne came up with a great suggestion. She said to Dad, "Why doesn't Billy come to DC, live with me for six weeks, and take an ASL class?"

I froze, sneaking a glance at Dad. "Sounds like a great idea," he said. "Bill?"

Just like that, my summer plans went from a question mark to a full-tilt adventure.

At seventeen, I graduated high school, threw one last wave at Eastman in the rearview mirror, and headed off to Washington, DC, in my 1972 Ford Pinto. Ah yes, my Pinto. Possibly the least glamorous vehicle in history, but to me, it felt like a chariot of independence, even if it rattled a little too much on the highway.

Mary Anne, always the protective big sister, flew down to join me for the drive. In hindsight, it was probably less about family bonding and more about ensuring I didn't veer off into parts unknown. Either way, I was stepping into adulthood, or at least I hoped so.

Mary Anne had graduated from Gallaudet a full four years before, and she hadn't just graduated, she'd thrived. That place was her kingdom and her home. I was stepping into her world, and as her little brother, I wasn't about to screw it up.

Gallaudet offered summer ASL classes at various levels, and while I expected to start as a total beginner, they evaluated me, and, surprise!, I was shuffled into Beginning II. Apparently, years of pestering Mary Anne to teach me signs had paid off.

My instructor was Jackie Roth. Let me tell you about Jackie. She was dazzling in that effortless way some people are, with dimples that could melt the iciest soul and an eye twinkle that said, I see right through you, and I like what I see. As a theatre major, Jackie was theatrical in the best possible way. When she signed, it was like watching poetry come to life. Naturally, I had a massive crush on her.

Jackie had a habit of asking questions in class, and here's the thing, I was the only one who could consistently answer her. That earned me some serious street cred, and, in my mind, a fighting chance at making her notice me as more than "student number whatever."

But of course, life being the cruel teacher that it is, Jackie pulled me aside the first day and said I was too advanced for Beginning II. She suggested I move to Intermediate I. I wanted to argue. What do you mean, "too advanced"? I liked being the star pupil! And also, I liked Jackie. Leaving her class felt like a breakup.

Still, I switched, and it turned out to be the right move. Intermediate I was challenging. And by challenging, I mean I no longer felt like the best dancer in the room. Mary Anne, bless her heart, also became part of my experiment. I made a solemn declaration.No more speaking to me. Only signing.

This, I realized later, was as much of an adjustment for her as it was for me. Up until then, our sibling dynamic had been the typical big-sister-little-brother routine. She'd speak, I'd respond, and somewhere in there, she'd throw in some lip-reading magic. Now, I was asking her to abandon all that for pure signing, a tall order.

Despite the rocky transition, it worked. By the end of the summer, I was immersed in a whole new world. Signing had become second nature, and receptive skills, the Achilles heel of any language learner, began to sharpen. I was hooked. Not just because I could now communicate with people like Mary Anne, but because I discovered I was actually good at this.

Fast forward a bit less than a year, and I was interpreting. Me. Interpreting. From awkward teenage brother to fluent sign language user in a matter of months.

Turns out, when you mix sibling love, a Ford Pinto, pure determination, and a knack for language, you don't just learn, you excel. That summer didn't just change my plans. It changed me.

Discovery at Gallaudet

Gallaudet

That summer of 1975 was a whirlwind of discovery, most of it revolving around Gallaudet's kaleidoscopic culture. I had arrived a slightly awkward teenager with a few clumsy signs in my pocket and left feeling like I'd stumbled into the heart of a vibrant, beating world where language danced in the air.

One highlight of that magical summer was Mary Anne taking me to a performance of Good Vibrations. It was like nothing I'd ever seen before, a dynamic troupe of Deaf, hard-of-hearing, and hearing performers signing songs. Imagine a concert with the sound turned up really loud, where the lyrics soared not only through speakers but through hands, faces, and movement. And for someone like me, who'd always loved to sing and dance, it was as if someone had hand-delivered my life's purpose on a platter.

The show was a performance and a revelation. Every song pulled me deeper into the experience, and I could barely sit still. The packed theatre pulsed with energy. When one of the performers, a dazzling redhead named Janet Bailey, signed My Boyfriend's Back, I grabbed the program and mentally tattooed her name onto my brain. Janet Bailey. The way her signs flowed and her long red hair seemed to shimmer under the stage lights. She and the whole show was magic.

I left the theatre electrified, more determined than ever to become part of that world. Not the audience, the stage. It was all the things I loved wrapped into one glittering package- the creativity, the movement, the connection. By the time the curtain closed, I'd made a decision, even if I wasn't yet sure how to make it happen.

The six weeks at Gallaudet flew by. My ASL class was wrapping up, and I found myself preemptively mourning the end of what had been the best experience of my short life. Through Mary Anne, I'd met an incredible group of people, students, performers, instructors, who welcomed me into their orbit despite the fact that I was just a 17-year-old tagging along. Somehow, I fit. I felt I belonged.

It wasn't just the friends or the thrill of learning something new. I could feel my signing skills improving by leaps and bounds. Gallaudet was more than a college campus; it was an incubator, and I was hatching into someone new, someone with confidence and a voice that spoke without sound.

Even ordinary moments became small victories. On Saturday, Mary Anne and I went to see Jaws. It had just opened, and the line to get into the theater snaked around the building.

While we waited in line, Mary Anne leaned over and asked, "Can you interpret what the people are saying behind us?"

"Wait, what?" I said.

"I've always wondered what it's like for hearing people to just... overhear things," she said. "You know, random conversations."

That was my first stab at interpreting, and let's just say Spielberg's shark wasn't the only thing biting off more than it could chew. I strained to listen and pieced together what I could.

It wasn't perfect. In fact, it was a bit clumsy. If I didn't know a sign, I'd fingerspell, and Mary Anne would either figure it out or teach me on the spot. It wasn't glamorous, but it worked. By the end of that Jaws line, I wasn't just interpreting conversations. I felt like I was interpreting my future.

Mary Anne was impressed. I was surprised by how much I could do. Sure, it was consecutive interpreting, I'd listen, process, and then sign back, but still. It was a small but thrilling taste of what it felt like to bridge two worlds.

For the rest of the summer, I soaked in every ounce of language, culture, and community Gallaudet could give me. It was heady stuff for a 17-year-old whose world had been, until now, one of small towns, bike rides, and bouncing between schools. By the time I drove my Pinto back to Georgia, one thing was clear. I didn't just want this world, I was already a part of it.

And this world fit me better than anything I'd known.

Gallaudet Round Two

Leaving Gallaudet at the end of the summer was like pulling yourself out of the warmest pool on the coldest day—you're dripping and shivering, and all you want to do is dive right back in. My brief stint in D.C. had been a revelation, and returning to Eastman felt like stepping back into a pair of shoes that had suddenly shrunk two sizes. It wasn't Eastman's fault, but I'd outgrown it. Still, there I was, home again, sitting on the couch like a sad sack of post-adolescent angst, not sure what was next.

And then, just a few days later, Mary Anne's letter arrived, waving a tiny, metaphorical flag of hope. Inside was a job listing for a Faculty Secretary/Clerk Typist position at Gallaudet. Apparently, the long-time person in that position was retiring, and the slot was wide open for, as Mary Anne put it, me.

I could hardly believe it. Sorting mail? Easy. Operating a Xerox machine? Done that. Running mimeograph copies? Child's play. Typing letters? I was at the top of my high school typing class. But interpreting? Gulp.

And leaving home, at 17, to live in the actual city of Washington, D.C., for a year? That was a whole other level of adulthood I wasn't sure I was ready for, assuming my parents would even sign off on the idea.

The Sell Job

Mary Anne could be very convincing. She walked them through her pitch, armed with every logical and emotional reason they couldn't say no.

"Look," she said, laying it all out. "He's mature. He found his thing at Gallaudet. He's making himself crazy just sitting here in Eastman with nothing to do. And… the job pays seven thousand, six hundred and twenty-five dollars a year."

To me, that number was jaw-dropping. In Eastman, I'd been toiling away at the local weekly paper for twenty dollars a week. This felt like Rockefeller-level wealth. Practically Mega-millions of money. I imagined myself waltzing into my first day at Gallaudet and being handed the whole sum in a single fat envelope. What did I know?

Turns out life doesn't work like that. Dad had to sit me down for a sobering crash course in grown-up finances. "You get paid twice a month, you're going to have rent, food, bills…"

Taxes are deducted from my paycheck? That felt incredibly unfair! Still, the thought of going back to D.C., to that exhilarating world of signing, learning, and possibility, overrode any trepidation I had about the logistics.

Striking the Deal

Of course, my parents didn't let me get away without a trade. They agreed to let me take the Gallaudet job, but only if I promised to return after a year and enroll at Georgia Southwestern College in Americus. Mom really played up Evelyn's attendance at Southwestern. It'll be great! You'll be in the same school again! She'll be a senior and can show you the ropes!

Secretly, I figured I'd cross that bridge when I got to it. Dad was notorious for forgetting promises made months earlier. Mom? Not so much. But I was the youngest, the golden child with a black-belt-level ability to sweet-talk her into anything. If push came to shove, I was confident in my schmoozing skills.

Dad and my siblings would ask me how I've got Mom wrapped around my little finger. It's a gift. I'm the baby. Her favorite. What can I say?

And just like that, at the tender age of 17, I packed up my dreams and whatever essentials would fit in my Pinto, ready for round two with Gallaudet. Eastman might have been my hometown at that point in my life, but Washington, D.C., was where my heart, and apparently my future, was waiting.

After all, who could turn down $7,625 a year?

Leaving home this time felt like the big leagues. I wasn't just hauling my duffel bag for a summer adventure, I was packing for an entire year, armed with my Pinto and a mix of excitement and a healthy dose of terror. This wasn't going to be Mary Anne with a safety net for me. No, I was moving in with Hoke and Willie Sisk, my dad's old Navy pal, and his wife, who now lived in a brownstone mansion on Massachusetts Avenue. It was the kind of house that made you lift your jaw off the floor as you walked through the door.

The Sisks didn't just let me crash in the corner of some broom closet, they handed me the entire top floor. That meant a bedroom, a bathroom, and… my own staircase. I wasn't just moving to D.C.; I was moving up in the world. I was handed the penthouse suite, courtesy of adulthood.

Driving in Circles (Literally)

Mary Anne and her friend and work colleague, Anne Wilson, another star in my growing constellation of favorite people, flew down to Georgia to help me drive back to D.C. Anne was hearing and fluent in ASL, so between the three of us, the trip was a smorgasbord of signs, jokes, and me repeatedly apologizing for being a less-than-confident driver.

Driving in D.C. was a different kind of chaos. In Eastman, traffic was a couple of farmers waving at each other while dragging tractors down Main Street. Washington, D.C., on the other hand, had roundabouts, spinning death traps designed to expose my nerves and embarrass my little Pinto. Massachusetts Avenue had one right near the Sisk's house, and let me tell you, that circle and I did not bond well.

Picture me in that Pinto, white-knuckling the steering wheel while my foot hovered over the brake. My first couple of attempts found me stranded on the inner ring of the roundabout, going around and around like an extra in National Lampoon's European Vacation. After many attempts, I inched my way to the outer part of the circle so I could finally exit. No roundabouts in Eastman! We had only one stop light!

Baptism by Fire

My first day at Gallaudet was nothing short of a collision between naïveté and the deep end of the grown-up pool. I wasn't just a wide-eyed small-town kid anymore, I was the Faculty Secretary at Gallaudet College. Professors were depending on me. These weren't kindergarten teachers waiting for glue sticks; they were grown adults expecting professionalism, competence, and fluent sign language.

It didn't take long for my trial by fire to begin. My first moment of panic came when a professor, Dr. Bushnaq from The Kingdom of Jordan, asked me to make a phone call on his behalf. I felt every molecule of oxygen leave my body. My six weeks of ASL classes hadn't covered what Dr. Bushnaq would be talking about on the phone. His signs were a mix of something uniquely his, and I had to lean heavily on my powers of observation and desperate politeness.

At Gallaudet, students and faculty hailed from all over the world, carrying with them their own versions of sign language, signs steeped in culture and whatever traditions they brought from home. That first phone call with Dr. Bushnaq was equal parts comedy and terror, with a sprinkle of I hope he doesn't ask to fire me.

The Learning Curve

Despite the shaky start, I threw myself into the role with the kind of reckless determination that can only come from being 17, starry-eyed, and too stubborn to quit. If I didn't know a sign, I learned it. If I didn't understand an accent, I asked questions until I did. And if I didn't know how to professionally Xerox something... well, okay, that one I nailed right away.

The truth was, Gallaudet was teaching me in ways no classroom ever could. I wasn't just there to help; I was there to learn. Every interaction, every misunderstanding, every moment of sheer "fake it 'til you make it" panic felt like another step up a ladder I didn't even know I was climbing.

Plus, as daunting as it was, I'd made it through the first fire. It wouldn't be the last, but in those moments, I learned something critical. You never get out of life's roundabouts by sitting in the inside lane. You steer, you signal, you inch your way forward, and sometimes, you floor it.

Dr. Bushnaq's departure left me standing in the quiet office, catching my breath and wiping sweat off my brow. It wasn't just nerves, I had practically marinated in self-doubt and fear, but somehow, I'd done it. My first interpreting attempt hadn't ended in disaster, and that tiny flicker of success fueled me. I didn't let myself bask for long; there was mail to sort, machines to run, and letters to type on actual typewriters. These weren't the keyboard-and-backspace days; they were the Wite-Out-and-start-over days. A single mistake near the end of a page meant ripping it out and starting fresh. For some professors, mistakes were shrugged off. For others, they expected nothing less than perfection.

Each day, I learned new things like how to adjust margins without screaming, how to sort mail like a well-oiled machine, and, most importantly, how to navigate the delicate art of forging ahead even when everything felt like a first draft. And then, there was mail delivery by Mike Atchison.

First Steps on Stage

Good Vibrations Redux

Mike wasn't just a regular mail guy; he was a living, breathing star in my eyes. I'd recognized him immediately from the summer's "Good Vibrations" show, where I sat in the audience like a spellbound moth drawn to the spotlight. Mike was another performer who made poetry with his hands. So, every time he walked into the office to drop off mail, I internally rehearsed all the things I wanted to say to him. Your signing is incredible. I want to do what you do!

One day, the words tumbled out, awkward but genuine. I told him how much I admired the show, how deeply it inspired me, and how I hoped to someday be good enough to audition. To my shock, Mike didn't just thank me politely and leave. No, he casually dropped the single most thrilling sentence of my young life: "We're having a meeting soon, you should come."

He said it so matter-of-factly, but to me, it was monumental. I immediately accepted, vowing to attend and be a silent sponge soaking up the brilliance of the Good Vibrations cast. I didn't think I could sign well enough to hold my own in a room full of performers, but that wasn't the point. Just being there, observing the magic, I was already living my dream.

Apartment Hunting with Surrogate Dad

As the excitement of the meeting buzzed in my head, the Sisks and I broached another subject. It was time for me to find my own place. Staying at the Sisk Mansion had been an incredible gift, but we all knew it wasn't permanent. At 17, I couldn't rent a place on my own, so Hoke stepped in as my guardian angel slash co-signer. He took on the official role of "responsible adult" for the leasing process. As we visited potential apartments, he eyed each one with a discerning, Navy-trained eye for safety.

Me? I was mostly concerned with whether the place had a working bathroom and somewhere to park my Pinto without it spontaneously combusting.

Eventually, we found a modest little apartment that felt just right, my first real space of independence. Hoke signed the lease, and we shook on it with an unspoken agreement that I would do my absolute best not to ruin this opportunity. If something went wrong, financially or otherwise, it wasn't just my future on the line. Hoke had put his reputation and trust in me, as had my parents back in Georgia.

Walking the Tightrope

The stakes were high, and I knew it. Dad wasn't the type to tolerate failure disguised as teenage drama. If something went awry, whether late rent, a failed work obligation, or even a speeding ticket, he wouldn't hesitate to haul me back home faster than you could say, "Pack your bags." And the thought of leaving Gallaudet, my job, and the intoxicating whirlwind of signing was too painful to even imagine.

So, I made a silent pact with myself. I would walk the line, pay my bills, and continue growing in ways that felt monumental at the time. Every time I typed a letter flawlessly, learned a new sign, or interpreted a phone call without passing out, I gained a tiny sliver of confidence.

It wasn't just about proving myself to everyone else, though that mattered, too. It was about proving to me that I belonged here in this fast-paced world of spinning circles and signs that flowed like rivers. That world was quickly becoming home.

Hoke spotted an ad for an apartment at Fairlington Villages in Arlington, Virginia, just a hop, skip, and a Potomac away from D.C. At the time, I didn't have the faintest clue where anything was, geography was just a vague suggestion to me, so I simply followed along, trusting Hoke's instincts.

The apartment was a two-bedroom relic in a sprawling community of similar relics, charmingly marketed as "vintage" but more accurately described as "old." A guy, whose name escapes me, and let's be honest, it's probably better that way, had posted the ad looking for a roommate. Hoke, ever the practical one, thought I needed an adult around. He was absolutely right. I was essentially a child with a slightly more developed vocabulary.

The guy seemed pleasant enough at first glance, like someone who wouldn't steal your stuff or murder you in your sleep. The bar was low, but he cleared it. Hoke signed the lease, and before I knew it, I was moving in with my bed (a lovely parting gift from the Sisk family), my record player, my records, and a smattering of clothes. It was a minimalist lifestyle, though not entirely by choice.

And then, like any good sitcom setup, things took a turn. It turned out my roommate had done some, shall we say, creative subletting. Enter Donna. This little detail, her impending arrival, had not been mentioned during the initial apartment tour. Donna came with a full set of living room furniture, which is more than the other guy and I had. What's-his-name failed to mention that having Donna there - with all her furniture - would be a financially savvy move. I realized something wasn't right. How was this arrangement supposed to work?

My roommate's solution was both practical and wildly inappropriate. "Well, since Donna's a girl, she'll get her own room. You and I will share the other one." That wasn't the deal. The deal was two bedrooms, two people. What he was proposing sounded suspiciously like a plot twist I wanted no part of.

Donna moved in anyway, and to my surprise, I liked her right away. She was a classic girly girl, frilly dresses, meticulous makeup, and, as it turned out, a passion for collecting dolls. She was also a lesbian with a girlfriend also named Donna. Donna #2 was Donna #1's polar opposite. A no-nonsense telephone pole-climbing lineman with a low voice and a penchant for men's jeans. They were madly in love, and their dynamic was as fascinating as it was endearing.

So now we had two Donnas and one increasingly awkward living situation. I was crammed into a room with my pot-smoking, party-loving roommate, a lifestyle I did not and could not partake in, and felt like a ticking time bomb. All I could see was my carefully laid plan of working at Gallaudet unraveling if this guy's antics led to, say, a police visit. My gut was screaming at me. Get out while you can!

And so, armed with my trusty record player and a growing sense of self-preservation, I started plotting my escape.

Luckily, Donna #1 came home one day with news that could only be described as divine intervention. She and Donna #2 had decided they wanted to live together (imagine that!) and had found a two-bedroom apartment in the same complex that was fully renovated and, by all accounts, far superior to our current setup. Then came the kicker. Donna #1 asked if I wanted to join them as their roommate. My own room. Same rent. No pot-smoking stranger lurking nearby. I practically leaped into her arms and shouted, "YES!"

I don't even remember if I told the Sisk family about the move. For all I know, they thought I was still unpacking. But within days, I was lugging my sparse belongings down the block, feeling like I'd hit the jackpot.

Around this time, I started carpooling to Gallaudet with a colleague, Penny Shoup. Penny was sharp, polished, and ever-so-slightly intimidating because she worked in the Dean's Office and reported to Millie, the very woman who had hired me. Naturally, I was determined to make the best impression possible. I wanted her to see me not as the baby of the office (though I absolutely was) but as a responsible, capable 17-year-old with my act together. This took a huge effort, given that I was still figuring out what exactly my act was.

Our carpooling arrangement was functional but far from glamorous. My '72 Pinto was a temperamental beast that came with no air conditioning, no heat, and a vendetta against human comfort. Winters had us shivering like Jack Nicholson at the end of The Shining; summers turned the car into a rolling sauna. Penny hated it. I hated it. But I also kind of loved it. Every morning, I'd barrel across the 14th Street Bridge, dodging D.C. traffic like I was in a high-stakes action movie. It felt thrilling. Grown-up. Each stoplight, each reckless merge, was a little victory in my ongoing transformation from small-town kid to competent city dweller.

Meanwhile, my excitement was building to a fever pitch because the day of the Good Vibrations meeting had finally arrived. I was so giddy I could barely focus at work. All I wanted was for these people, these magical, larger-than-life performers, to like me, laugh at my jokes, and welcome me into their fold with open arms.

When I walked into the meeting, I was greeted by a room full of familiar faces, the same people I'd watched on stage last summer, larger than life, immensely talented. Even though I was grinning, my nerves got the better of me, and instead of intro-ducing myself, I froze. I sat quietly, absorbing every word, too scared to approach anyone.

At the head of the table sat Cynthia Saltzman. If you lived in D.C., you knew Cynthia. She was on TV every morning, deliver-ing the news in ASL with a grace that made signing look like an art form. I'd watched her religiously, hanging on her every ges-ture, desperate to soak up more sign language. She was beautiful, with a cascade of curly hair, and she exuded confidence in a way that made everyone else in the room seem slightly dimmer by comparison.

Even her name sign was iconic, a combination of the signs for "curly hair" and "popular" because, of course, she was. She was magnetic, drawing people to her effortlessly, and when she signed, I was mesmerized. Her most famous performance was Melissa Manchester's Midnight Blue, and to this day, that song is forever tied to her in my mind.

I sat there, trying to keep my cool while silently willing my-self to be as impressive as I could. I just wanted to be a fly on the wall and take it all in.

I took a seat at the far edge of the U-shaped table, trying to blend into the furniture. At Gallaudet, I'd learned that seating arrangements were always thoughtfully designed. Traditional rows? Useless. Everyone needed a clear line of sight, so rooms were arranged in circles or U-shapes, ensuring no one missed a thing. This was functional brilliance but terrible news for some-one trying to be invisible.

From my spot, I scanned the room, starstruck. I mentally cataloged each person, matching their faces to the songs they had performed over the summer. These were the people that made me first on my feet for the standing ovation. I was in the same room with them. The whole thing felt surreal like I'd stumbled into an exclusive club where I was not on the guest list but somehow still got past the bouncer.

The meeting was supposed to start at 5 p.m., but I was so busy basking in my own excitement that I didn't realize we were already running late. Cynthia eventually stood and signed while using her voice for the lawyer, the guest of honor, announcing that we'd wait a few more minutes because the interpreter hadn't arrived. This was a very important meeting with a lawyer to discuss the possibility of incorporating Good Vibrations. The lawyer was hearing, of course, and needed an interpreter for all his remarks.

And then, it happened. Cynthia scanned the room, her eyes darting from face to face until they landed on... me.

"YOU!" she signed and said, pointing with the kind of authority that could part a crowd. "Come up here. You're hearing! Come and interpret so our guest can begin!"

Me? Surely, she didn't mean me. There had to be some other poor, hearing soul in this room who had been hiding better than I was. But no, Cynthia's gaze didn't waver.

I froze. Every nerve in my body screamed This is not what I signed up for! I had a plan, and it did not involve interpreting in front of all these people I wanted to impress with my charm and wit. My plan was simple: slip in unnoticed, casually introduce myself to a few people and fade into the background. But now, thanks to Cynthia, I was being thrust into the literal spotlight.

Mike Atchison, seated a few chairs away, motioned for me to get up there, his face saying, Don't make this weird. Geez!

With knees that were knocking so loud a deaf person could hear, I shuffled to the front of the room. Cynthia looked at me expectantly, and the lawyer gave me a polite smile that screamed, Good luck, kid. I leaned down to the attorney and whispered, "Please talk slowly. I'm new. Like, really new. I've had six weeks of class. Please."

The lawyer nodded, but the look in his eyes told me he wasn't holding out hope for a stellar performance. And honestly, neither was I.

As I straightened up and turned to face the room, my mind raced. This was it. My big moment. Not the one I wanted, but the one I got. It wasn't a stage, and I wasn't performing a Top 40 hit, but all eyes were on me. And if I messed this up, I could kiss my Good Vibrations fantasy goodbye.

The lawyer proceeded to speak in legalese at a speed akin to the chocolate conveyor belt scene in I Love Lucy when the woman yelled, "Speed it up a little!" This was NOT what I had planned. He spoke too fast, and though I was trying my best to keep up, I was failing miserably. At one point, a member named Harry Horton raised his hand and said, "I don't understand."

The lawyer asked, "You don't understand what I'm saying?"

Harry replied, "I understand you because I'm reading your lips. I don't understand the interpreter!"

At that very moment, a tornado-like wind blew open the door, and a force of nature flew into the room with speed and determination, her red hair flying in the air. Janet Bailey.

The room erupted in applause, including the attorney! I slumped back to my chair with my tail between my legs, feeling humiliated and completely defeated. I had wanted to impress them and be asked to join the group. I was determined not to cry in front of these people.

"Sorry I'm late," said Janet. Then, she started interpreting.

I never took my eyes off her. She was incredible. Smooth, confident, clear, everything I dreamed of being. It was at that moment I knew what I wanted to do.

Soon afterward, Janet took me under her wing. She understood I had been placed in an impossible situation. She became my friend, my interpreting partner, and my mentor. To this day, 50 years later, she's still my mentor. I call her when I have an issue because I know she'll steer me in the right direction. That day and that experience changed my life.

I dove headfirst into practicing my interpreting. Having Janet as my friend and mentor helped me get involved with all sorts of things that improved my skills. Janet also got me into Good Vibrations! By this time, I was doing well at my job and making friends left and right. My office was in the Hall Memorial Building (HMB), and the Registrar's Office, where Mary Anne worked, was right down the hall. She would pop in from time to time to check on her "baby brudder," and it was comforting having her so close by. She was, and still is, my cheerleader.

I realized soon after I started working at Gallaudet that my signing style was so much like hers. Genetics, right? I also realized that my burgeoning interpreting style was like Janet's. I learned from the best.

I was a part of Good Vibrations, but there hadn't been a show produced since the one I saw in the summer of '75. Cynthia and the others wanted to put together a new show, and I desperately wanted to be a part of it.

One weekend, for reasons that remain as confusing as the New Jersey Turnpike, I found myself driving Cynthia and Mike Atchison to New York City in my perpetually unreliable '72 Pinto. How a 17-year-old ended up as the designated chauffeur for two Deaf friends on a road trip to the Big Apple is anyone's guess, but there we were, hurtling toward adventure at approximately 45 miles per hour.

Somewhere in New Jersey, Pinto and I engaged in our usual routine of getting lost, but nobody seemed to mind. Cynthia and Mike spent the drive chattering in ASL about the upcoming show, their hands flying with a kind of grace and energy that almost made me forget the unnerving clunking sounds coming from the engine.

Cynthia, ever the visionary, turned to me at one point and said, "You know what song you should do? Bridge Over Troubled Water. You'd be perfect!"

Mike piped up from the backseat with an enthusiastic agreement. And just like that, the seed was planted. The idea lodged itself in my brain like a catchy tune you can't shake.

When we got back to Gallaudet, rehearsals for the new show kicked into gear. I was cast as the background for Jesus Christ Superstar and The Night Chicago Died. Not exactly the spotlight I dreamed of, but I was thrilled just to be part of the magic. Then, true to her word, Cynthia handed me the opportunity of my young lifetime. Bridge Over Troubled Water.

Our first performance was scheduled at the Hilton Hotel's ballroom in Maryland, a glamorous venue that felt impossibly grand to my small-town self. I was a bundle of nerves. Not only was this my first time performing a song in sign language on stage, but it was also my chance to prove I belonged among these incredible performers. No pressure.

Cynthia, in her typical show-biz savvy, had choreographed backup signers to visually represent the sound of crashing waves during the song. When they got into position, the overture began. I stood backstage, counting my breaths and my blessings, and timed my entrance just right.

Three steps up. Center stage. Spotlights.

And then the opening lyrics hit. When you're weary...feeling small...

Something magical happened. It was like slipping into another dimension where fear didn't exist. I was completely in the zone, signing my heart out to one of the most emotionally charged songs of the era. My backup signers swirled around me, their hands mimicking the crashing waves of the music as I let the words guide me. Every movement felt deliberate, powerful, and alive.

When the final note approached, I raised my arms high, holding the last sign as though reaching for the heavens. The music ended. I froze, holding the pose.

The room fell silent for a beat, and then erupted. The crowd leaped to their feet, cheering, clapping, and waving their arms. It was surreal. I felt like I'd just nailed the Olympic routine of my life.

Out of the corner of my eye, I caught sight of Cynthia and Janet standing together offstage, clapping and smiling. They weren't just supportive, they were proud.

At that moment, I knew this wasn't just a dream; it was a dream I'd worked for and one I'd keep chasing.

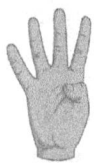

Roots & Departure

Free to Be... You and Me

After the Hilton Hotel performance, Good Vibrations hit its stride. For about a month, we were everywhere. Malls, parks, cozy little theater spaces, and, of course, Gallaudet. We were like the Rolling Stones of the sign language performance world, where groupies gathered and waved.

As the performances started to wind down, Janet unveiled her next big idea. "Free to Be... You and Me".

For the uninitiated, Free to Be... You and Me was a groundbreaking show and album Marlo Thomas had produced a couple of years earlier. It was a love letter to individuality, tolerance, and the idea that boys and girls didn't have to be boxed into stereotypical roles. Boys could cry, girls could climb trees, and everyone was free to dream big, truly radical stuff for the mid-'70s. Janet's genius was in realizing how beautifully this message would translate into sign language. She imagined a full production with a cast bringing Marlo's whimsical, empowering stories to life.

Thankfully, she asked me to be a part of it. Janet had this way of making you believe you could do anything, even if you had no clue what you were doing.

Janet handpicked me and then opened auditions for the rest of the cast. Before long, our little troupe was assembled. Janet, Skee, Barbara P., Hank, Gina, Barb G., Ward, and yours truly. Rehearsals began almost immediately, and the energy was electric.

May 12, 1976, rolled around, and with it, my 18th birthday. Mary Anne, in all her big-sisterly glory, decided to throw me a party. By "party," I mean she packed her condo to the rafters with people, Free to Be castmates, Good Vibrations members, and a mix of Gallaudet students and staff. It was like being at the center of my own little universe, surrounded by people who had somehow become my family in this strange, wonderful city.

For the first time in my life, I felt like I was exactly where I was meant to be. My days were filled with work, friends, and rehearsals, performing the way I'd always dreamed of but never thought possible. Back in Eastman, I'd been president of the Drama Club in high school. This was more of a title than an actual activity. We never mounted any productions because no one else was interested, but the school insisted we have a club. I was the entire club. It was like running a lemonade stand in a town that didn't drink lemonade.

Deep down, I always knew I wasn't meant for Eastman. It wasn't the town's fault, it just didn't have the kind of opportunities I craved. Moving to D.C. was like stepping into a Technicolor version of life. Suddenly, there were people who got me, who shared my passion for the arts, and who believed in lifting each other up.

Turning 18 felt like crossing a finish line I didn't even know I'd been running toward. It wasn't just an age; it was a declaration. You're here. You've made it. And you're just getting started.

Not long after my 18th birthday, I decided it was time to bid farewell to the two Donnas. I was officially an adult now, at least in theory, and I wanted to try living on my own. Well, as "on my own" as you can be while still needing to borrow furniture. Moving was a breeze; my worldly possessions could fit into a Pinto and still leave room for a hitchhiker.

I ended up living in a big, creaky, old Victorian house in the NE section of Washington, D.C. It was the kind of place that looked like it might be haunted but also had a comforting charm. The neighborhood, on the other hand, was... less charming. Walking from the car to the house felt like a scene from an action movie, where you keep one hand on your keys and the other on your imaginary weapon. But I loved it.

Gina Mullen, one of my castmates from Good Vibrations and Free to Be…, and her husband, Steve, had invited me to join their housing adventure. Everyone in the house was either deaf or connected to the Deaf community, which made it the perfect crash course for improving my signing and interpreting skills. It was a full immersion experience, and I soaked it up like the eager sponge I'd become.

In keeping with my newfound adulthood, I decided to embrace some personal reinvention. I got a perm.

It was the 1970s, after all, and perms were all the rage, right up there with Earth Shoes and clogs. Until then, my haircutting experiences had been limited to barber shops, where the options ranged from "short" to "shorter." But in D.C., I discovered something revolutionary. Hair salons. On a referral, I went to a place called Bananas, a name that felt appropriately daring, and got my very first perm.

When it was done, I looked in the mirror and barely recognized myself. My hair, still a very pale blond at the time, had transformed into a fluffy halo that screamed albino Angela Davis. I even carried a pick in my back pocket, just for the flair. Opinions on the look varied (to put it mildly), but I thought it was hip. Every time I caught my reflection, I reassured myself. All the rage. Totally all the rage.

The summer of 1976 was a whirlwind, and not just because of the hair. Evelyn came to Gallaudet for a six-week sign language class taught by Will Madsen, a beloved figure on campus. She stayed with me in the big Victorian, and for the first time in ages, three siblings, Mary Anne, Evelyn, and I, were together in the same city.

That summer was also America's Bicentennial, and it felt like the whole country had turned into one big birthday party. Mom and Dad came to visit, and they stayed with us, too. When I say the house was big, I mean big. It was the kind of house that could comfortably fit your family, your friends, and maybe a small marching band.

Having everyone there was incredible. I got to show Mom and Dad my office in the Hall Memorial Building (HMB), and the pride on their faces was enough to make me float for days. It was a surreal moment because less than a year ago I'd been fumbling my way through my first sign language class, and now I was working on campus, interpreting for actual Deaf people in actual situations.

My skills were still a work in progress, but I was good enough to meet the needs of my consumers. And let's be honest, most of them knew me, or, more accurately, they knew Mary Anne, and were probably cutting me some slack. I think a lot of folks asked for me as their interpreter just to help me gain experience. It was an act of kindness that I appreciated more than they probably realized.

Working at Gallaudet felt like moving to Paris to learn French. Sign language was everywhere, on the walls, in the air, in every conversation, and I was drinking it like it was water and I'd been wandering in the desert. Every day brought new challenges, new opportunities, and new connections.

The kid from Eastman, Georgia, was finding his way.

When it came time for Mom and Dad to head back home, they trotted out that promise I'd made them like it was a contract signed in blood. I still had a couple more months at my job, but then, yes, I was supposed to come home, too. They weren't clueless; they could see my life in Washington, D.C., and they could see how much I loved it. I mean, it wasn't subtle. It radiated off me like I was lit from within. I didn't want to leave, and they knew it.

But Mom, God bless her, was determined. She was the architect of this so-called deal and the enforcer, too. She wanted me to enroll in the same college as Evelyn and "get on with my life." As if I hadn't already been doing that. I thought I was getting on just fine, thank you very much. But a deal's a deal, and if I had one thing, it was a stubborn commitment to follow through, even when it felt like jumping off a cliff with no parachute.

Meanwhile, life in D.C. kept dazzling me. Janet and I were tearing it up, performing together in our own act. We built this eclectic repertoire, Barry Manilow, Barbra Streisand, The Manhattan Transfer, and Broadway hits, that had something for everyone. I'm telling you, we were a sensation! People had lost their minds over "Supercalifragilisticexpialidocious," and honestly, who could blame them? We didn't make up a sign for it; we fingerspelled it!

Beyond the music gigs, we had another claim to fame as the resident interpreters at the Folger Shakespeare Library. It was a dream job, though let's not pretend I had any clue what the Bard was actually saying half the time. My little 18-year-old brain was drowning in Elizabethan English. Thankfully, Janet was brilliant, an actress ten years my senior, with wit and wisdom to spare. She'd break it down for me, translating Shakespeare into modern English and then into ASL gloss. I couldn't have done it without her.

For Shakespeare productions, we worked with scripts perched on music stands. (Because, let's face it, there was no way I could just wing iambic pentameter in another language.) Janet was my guide through it all, a rock I clung to in the middle of this exhilarating chaos. I trusted her implicitly.

Years later, when I finally left Washington for Los Angeles, Janet stayed and started her own business, Sign Language Associates. It took off like a rocket. I mean, she built the biggest, most successful interpreting agency in the country, maybe even the world. And no, that didn't surprise me one bit.

When I started my own business, Janet was still there, the same beacon of advice and support she'd always been. But more about that later. Let's not get ahead of ourselves.

Georgia

I arrived back in Eastman a couple of weeks before the fall quarter began at Georgia Southwestern College, dragging behind me a funk the size of the Washington Monument. The previous year had been nothing short of transformative, a Technicolor dream where I lived, acted, and worked as a bona fide adult. I wasn't just existing; I was contributing. My interpreting mattered. It mattered to the people I worked with, and it mattered to me.

And now I was back in a one-stoplight town, staring down the barrel of a promise I made to Mom, preparing to enroll at a small college I hoped, hoped, would make me happy because it had Evelyn. Let me tell you, "hope" turned out to be just another four-letter word.

Americus, the college town, was far enough from Eastman to justify dorm living. I figured, why not? A fresh start, right? Wrong. The first time all the guys in the dorm were called to a meeting in the TV room, I knew I was a fish not only out of the water but possibly in the wrong aquarium altogether.

The meeting kicked off with introductions, such as name, hometown, and intended major. What followed was an unrelenting parade of Physical Education majors. I mean, it was like every guy in the room was auditioning for the role of future high school football coach. When my turn came, I said, loud and proud, "Theatre Arts." And let me tell you, if they'd handed out medals for silence, that room would've swept the Olympics. The looks I got made me feel like I'd just announced plans to major in interpretive macramé.

"Uh… isn't anyone else majoring in Theatre Arts?" I asked. Rookie mistake. The answer was an obvious no.

During Frat Week, I was "rushed." Me. Mr. Theatre Arts. Friendless, apathetic, and entirely uninterested in joining any group that required me to be in a group. I turned down every fraternity because I'm not a joiner. Never have been. The whole campus felt like the 13th grade of high school anyway, with everyone toting small-town life experience as their badge of honor. Meanwhile, I'd tasted the forbidden fruit of city life, an apartment, a job, friends, purpose. And now I was here, clutching a bag of laundry, waiting for something to make sense.

On my first weekend home, I vented to Mom and Dad. "I'm miserable," I said, plopping my laundry basket down as proof of my return to dependence. "I don't belong there. I'm not learning anything, and I don't want to stay." I laid it all out. The square-peg-round-hole dynamic, the lack of connection, the suffocating smallness of it all.

They seemed sympathetic. "Give it more time," they said in that parental tone that's both reassuring and maddening. "The three months will fly by. You'll make friends. You'll settle in. You'll look forward to going back after Christmas."

I did not look forward to going back.

I gave it the old college try, pun intended, but every day was its own unique form of torture. Evelyn was busy with her senior year, so I barely saw her. Classes wrapped up early in the day, leaving me with hours to kill in a dorm room that felt more like a holding cell. Every moment, I was wishing, aching, to be any-where else.

When a few people found out I knew sign language, they clued me in about a local church with a deaf congregant who faithfully parked herself in the front pew every Sunday. No interpreter, just her, sitting there like a one-person silent protest. Suddenly, I had something to do! I reached out to the church, and before I knew it, I was showing up every Sunday to volunteer as the service interpreter.

Now, this was before the ADA (Americans with Disabilities Act), so no one was legally obligated to pay me. And let's just say the budget for interpreters wasn't exactly a line item. The deaf woman couldn't afford it, and the minister, bless his heart, would hand me a few bucks from the collection plate after the service. Not much, but it provided some gas for the Pinto. Gas was very cheap in 1976!

For me, it was wonderful. For her, it was life-changing. She knew ASL but, like so many people in her shoes, had no one to talk to. Her family hadn't bothered to learn sign language, which left her marooned in the quiet expanse of a small Georgia town. That first Sunday, after the service, she hugged me like I was a long-lost relative she didn't know she had. And let me tell you, it wasn't one of those polite, pat-you-on-the-back hugs. This was full-on, "You're stuck with me now," and I could feel her gratitude in my bones.

It was bittersweet. I was happy to be helping, but it came with a price. No more trips home on weekends. Instead, I was stuck in a dorm where tumbleweeds might as well have been rolling down the halls. Everyone else, including Ev, hightailed it out of there. So there I was, left with my laundromat Saturdays and a week that felt like an endless loop of solitude. My one bright spot was that hour on Sunday mornings.

And then, just when I thought I couldn't take another second of being surrounded by future farmers and football coaches, the dorm phone rang.

Now, let's paint this picture properly. It was the '70s, which meant one communal phone in the hallway. If it rang, someone, usually the guy nearest to it, had to pick up and shout your name like a town crier. Suppose you were there, great. If not? Too bad.

It was a communication system that only worked when the stars aligned, but hey, it was what it was.

That weekend, I was alone in the dorm, probably sulking to show tunes when the phone rang. It had to be Mom or Dad because, really, who else would call?

It was Mom, but the news wasn't what I expected. "Bill, Janet Bailey called. She says she needs you to call her back right away."

Janet Bailey? What? Why? I didn't even have time to theorize. I ran back to my room, fetched her number, ran to the phone, dialed her number, and got her answering machine. Damn. I left the dorm's number and returned to my dorm room vigil, staring at the phone from my door like it was a crystal ball about to reveal my future.

When it finally rang, I practically yanked it out of the wall. "Hello?"

"Bill? It's Janet."

"Oh, hi, Janet! What a nice surprise!" (Surprise? Of course she was calling back, I told her to.)

"Bill, I need you to fly back to DC. I just signed a contract for us to perform Free to Be… up the Eastern coast. We've got shows lined up in DC, Philly, and two in Boston. You have to come!"

This was it. My third out-of-body experience. It felt like a prison warden telling me my sentence had been commuted. I was so excited that I didn't even notice the complete lack of people around me with whom to share the moment.

"Hang on," I told Janet, sprinting to my room again to grab a pen and paper to jot down the details.

When we hung up, I sank back down onto the stair, letting it all wash over me. I needed to tell the church. I needed to tell the school. I needed to tell Mom and Dad. But one thing was crystal clear… no matter what anyone said, I was going.

It was surprisingly easy to get the green light from everyone. No debates, no guilt trips, just a collective "go ahead." Maybe they sensed how much I needed this. With permission granted, I dove headfirst into travel plans. Somehow, word spread around school, small towns are nothing if not efficient gossip hubs, and soon, the local Americus Times-Recorder was calling me. They wanted to write a story about me leaving college to perform in a play. A play! The article ran not only in Americus but also back home in Eastman, and suddenly, I went from "that weird Theatre Arts major" (all two of us) to a local celebrity.

This Theatre Arts major was flying to Washington, DC, to do theatre! It all felt so right!

Fast forward to the Atlanta airport, where I was waiting for my connecting flight, people-watching and mentally rehearsing my lines. That's when I spotted an older gentleman who looked oddly familiar. It took me a moment, but then it clicked, Dr. Phillips! One of the deans from Gallaudet, whose office was right across from mine in HMB. I couldn't help myself. I jumped up and ran over like I'd just seen a long-lost friend.

Of course, the moment I started signing, I froze. Suddenly, I was 18, self-conscious, and acutely aware that my recent signing experience consisted of interpreting Bible verses once a week with the Deaf woman at church. And now, here I was, signing for a PhD from Gallaudet, someone who had seen me at my peak. The pressure!

Dr. Phillips, to his immense credit, put me at ease immediately. "Signing is like riding a bike," he said. "You might feel rusty, but it'll come back." And just like that, the tension melted away. I told him about the Free to Be tour, and his face lit up. He said the Faculty Office hadn't been the same without me, that my energy and youth had made the place more fun, and that faculty and staff genuinely missed interacting with me. Then he said, "Gallaudet will be happy to see you!"

That did it. My nerves evaporated, replaced by a flood of nostalgia. I realized just how much I missed Gallaudet.

The show in DC was everything I'd hoped for and more. In fact, the entire tour, D.C., Philly, Boston, was a smash hit. We only needed one rehearsal before the magic kicked back in as if we'd never stopped performing. Seeing Mary Anne and everyone else at Gallaudet felt like coming home, even though I'd only been gone a few months. It felt like a lifetime.

After six or seven performances, the tour wrapped up, and it was time to say goodbye to my happiness, again. OK, that sounded dramatic, but in the moment, it felt true. I didn't want to return to my dreary school life with its endless monotony. Long, lonely weeks broken only by occasional laundry trips home. Oh, and seeing my parents, of course. But off I went, back to the grind.

Winter break loomed, and with it came the dreaded dorm clean-out. The school had a policy to pack up your things because there's no guarantee you'll get the same room in January. Honestly, I didn't mind. As I packed, I couldn't shake the feeling in my gut, this was it. I wasn't coming back, not to this dorm, not to this school, not to this life.

When I got home, I knew it was time. Time to sit Mom and Dad down, time to have the talk. Merry Christmas!

Welby and Mary Anne were home for Christmas, and their timing couldn't have been better. It's always good to have backup when you're about to shake up the family dynamic. Sitting Mom and Dad down, I launched into my well-prepared case for why I was deeply, soul-crushingly unhappy in Americus. I explained that most people my age go to college to find their calling, explore their passions, and fine-tune what they're good at. I already knew. My calling had RSVP'd a year ago, and I was ready to get back to it.

Dad was calm, classic Dad, and Mom… Well, Mom went full Mom. Tears, trembling voice, the whole nine yards. "All my kids have gone to college. You have to go, too!"

I took a deep breath. "Mom, am I going to college for you or for me? I know what I want to do. I worked hard for a year, and I want to keep working. College is to prepare us for work, and I'm already prepared."

Cue Mary Anne, chiming in like the voice of reason. She pointed out how lucky I was to have found my path so early and how good I was at what I did. Then Welby, always the cerebral one, who was working on his Master's or doctorate at the time, delivered the knockout punch.

"Bill... sometimes a diploma is just a receipt showing how much money you've spent on school."

Dad laughed. Mom cried harder. That's the dynamic in a nutshell, Mom is deeply invested in appearances, and Dad is the ultimate pragmatist.

I pressed on. "I'm not happy. If I go back, I'll just be wasting time, time I need to become the interpreter I want to be."

Finally, Dad stepped in. "I don't want you to do anything that makes you unhappy. If work is your path, then go back to work."

Looking back, I suspect he was also delighted not to foot the bill for another round of college tuition. But hey, a win's a win. Mom, however, wasn't thrilled. Her tears didn't exactly dry up overnight, but with Dad and my siblings on my side, she eventually relented.

I had no idea what I was going to do once I got back to Gallaudet. No job lined up, no invitation to return, no safety net whatsoever. But at the ripe old age of 18, I wasn't worried. I just knew it was the right move, and I figured, "Things will happen." And they did.

Before leaving Georgia, I called a few friends at Gallaudet to see if anyone had a couch, or preferably something slightly more permanent, where I could crash until I got back on my feet. Gina and Steve had moved out of the big Victorian, so that wasn't an option. Mary Anne graciously offered her sofa again, but I wasn't keen on reprising my role as "long-term houseguest." Then Hank, my friend from Free to Be, swooped in to save the day.

Hank, a dorm counselor, had extra space in his on-campus apartment. On campus! This was perfect. I could live, breathe, and hopefully work at Gallaudet without ever having to leave the bubble. Packing was easy. Some clothes, my record player, and my precious vinyl collection. And just like that, I moved in with Hank.

This chapter of my life was electric. It was a true leap of faith. I had no job, no money, no real plan, but I did have determination, faith, and a gut feeling that I was exactly where I needed to be. And sometimes, that's enough.

Word got around fast that I was back on campus, and opportunities began sprouting up everywhere. Hank came home one evening and mentioned that the Student Center needed an interpreter for night phone calls. A night job! This was perfect. I could leave my days wide open for job hunting, and honestly, I was so thrilled to be back, I barely needed sleep anyway.

The job itself was… unique. Picture a tiny room with a desk, a phone, a chair for the student, and me, the interpreter, perched between worlds. A student would come in, plop down, hand me a phone number, and I'd make the call. It felt oddly confessional like I was their priest or therapist.

The calls were as varied as the students themselves: begging parents for money, booking doctor's appointments, or calling a hearing boyfriend or girlfriend. Let me tell you, it was a trip saying things like, "I love you... I miss you... I miss your kisses," while maintaining professional neutrality. But the job was rewarding, not to mention a crash course in receptive skills. The diversity of signing styles, from every state and multiple countries, really sharpened my ASL.

By day, I searched for a more permanent position. It was January 1977, and Gallaudet was already in full swing. Every job had been filled months earlier, and I was starting to worry. Hank, ever the generous friend, hadn't yet kicked me off his sofa, but his place was small, and he had his hands full juggling dorm counselor duties. Between his student meetings and my unpredictable sleep schedule, privacy was non-existent. But even as I balanced naps around Hank's calendar, I never regretted coming back to Gallaudet. I was surrounded by sign language at every turn, and it was amazing.

Then Cynthia announced auditions for a new Good Vibrations show. The rule was simple. Everyone, even returning performers, had to audition. No coasting on past glory, this was a clean slate. I loved the idea. It pushed me to think about how I could showcase my "stage presence," my dance moves, and my passion for signing.

Inspired by my earlier success with "Bridge Over Troubled Water," I stuck to a similar vibe. If it worked once, why not again? But as I prepared, I realized everyone else would be leaning into current hits from 1977. I needed to stand out. So, I turned back the clock to 1975 and chose Frankie Valli and the Four Seasons

"December 1963 (Oh, What a Night)." It was retro with a beat you couldn't help but dance to.

I choreographed snazzy dance moves, weaving the signs seamlessly into the rhythm. When audition day came, it was an open room, no private performances here. Every hopeful sat and watched as others auditioned. This could have been nerve-wracking, but I love an audience. I didn't see competition; I saw a crowd.

When it was my turn, I stepped into the space and looked at everyone like they were there to enjoy the show. And they did! I was having so much fun performing, I didn't want the song to end. The room loved it. Cynthia loved it. I was back on board for the next round of Good Vibrations!

But that's not all. Something serendipitous happened during that audition. After my performance, someone approached me with a lead on a job. A position had just opened up working with Roslyn "Roz" Rosen, a legendary figure at Gallaudet.

Roz was the real deal. She earned her B.A. in Art from Gallaudet in 1962, her Master's in Education of Deaf Students in 1964, and later her doctorate in Educational Administration in 1980. She was respected, admired, and, frankly, a little intimidating. But the chance to work with her was a once-in-a-lifetime opportunity, and I couldn't wait to see where it might lead.

In 1977, Roz was appointed Coordinator of Public Law 94-142, and she needed a personal interpreter for her new role. Naturally, I leaped at the chance. When Roz and I met, we clicked immediately. She hired me despite my youth, limited experience, and the fact that my male voice would be used for her phone calls, a reality we both understood. Maybe she hired me because I was cheap labor, but I didn't care. I knew this role would be a challenge, and I was ready to dive headfirst into the deep end.

The job involved accompanying Roz to her many public appearances around D.C., Maryland, and Virginia. She'd give speeches, and I'd be her voice. There were meetings with Gallaudet's President, Edward C. Merrill Jr., and high-ranking educational officials who clearly expected me to know what I was doing. I didn't always. Still, my official title, Secretary and Interpreter for the Coordinator of Public Law 94-142, sounded so important. Too bad it couldn't fit on a business card.

Working with Roz was an absolute joy. She was whip-smart, warm, and had a laugh that could lighten the heaviest of days. I learned so much in her presence, not just about interpreting but about professionalism, grace, and the power of humor. She treated me like one of her kids, which was a blessing considering how many mistakes I made voicing for her. Roz never lost her cool. She gave me not just second chances but third and fourth ones, and I will forever be grateful for her kindness and patience.

Now, here's where it gets interesting. I'm not entirely sure if it was because of my work with Roz, but someone recommended that I interpret at Jimmy Carter's inauguration on January 20, 1977. I couldn't believe it! I was honored. Or at least I was until I realized the reality of the situation.

At first, I thought I'd be on stage, maybe a few feet away from Jimmy himself, basking in the glow of history. Nope. Turns out I was one of several interpreters stationed along Pennsylvania Avenue for the crowds on the street. OK, fine. Still an honor. Except it was zero degrees that day, with wind that felt like it had been shipped straight from the Arctic.

I thought I was clever, wearing white tuxedo gloves to keep my hands warm. Fun fact: tuxedo gloves are about as warm as tissue paper. I looked less like a professional interpreter and more like a frozen mime. My hands froze solid. Fingerspelling? Forget it. I was basically signing with two blocks of ice.

The crowd around me seemed utterly unfazed, cheering away as I silently cursed their enthusiasm. "Why aren't you watching this on TV?" I wanted to yell. "With blankets and cocoa?" Instead, I stood there, stiff as a popsicle, probably signing gibberish. I couldn't hear the speakers over the gusting wind and the sound of my chattering teeth, so I may or may not have improvised Jimmy Carter's inaugural address. To the deaf folks in my section of Pennsylvania Avenue, I'm truly sorry.

It's funny, though. I had a connection to Jimmy Carter long before that freezing day. Back when I was stuck in Americus during one of those endless weekends, I decided to drive my Pinto to Plains, Georgia, just to see what all the fuss was about. Jimmy was still campaigning at the time, and Plains was as quiet and sleepy as you'd expect from a small Georgia town.

I wandered into a little shop with a giant "JIMMY CARTER" banner above the door. Inside, a group of people stood around, laughing, and at the center of it all was an older woman holding court. It was Lillian Carter, Miss Lillian, Jimmy's mother.

I introduced myself, told her I was a student at Georgia Southwestern, and mentioned that I was a classmate of Kim Carter, her granddaughter. Kim was Billy and Sybil Carter's daughter, and Billy… Well, Billy was a character. He was famous (or infamous) for his antics, his quotes, and, of course, Billy Beer. He lived life on his own terms, and while he raised more than a few eyebrows, he didn't seem to hurt his brother's campaign one bit.

Miss Lillian was every bit as charming and sharp as you'd expect the matriarch of the Carter clan to be. She made me feel welcome, like I'd just wandered into the family living room instead of a campaign hub. It's no wonder Jimmy Carter came across as so genuine, he was raised by a woman who embodied the word.

After I introduced myself to Miss Lillian, she looked me up and down and said, "Honey, I know your hair doesn't grow that way naturally." She was, of course, referring to my perm. I laughed and replied, "No… you're right. I had some chemical help for this." She chuckled, and I knew right then I was in the presence of a force of nature.

Miss Lillian was truly one of a kind. She had her own share of fame, thanks to her wit and outspokenness. As my dad used to say in his later years, "With this amount of white hair, you can get away with anything!" Miss Lillian embodied that philosophy.

Our paths crossed again in 1979 when Evelyn was asked to sing at Kim Carter's wedding. By sheer coincidence, Welby and

I were both home for the summer. Kim mentioned to Ev that she needed someone to play the organ for the ceremony, and Ev didn't hesitate to volunteer Welby.

Welby, for context, started plunking out tunes on the family piano as a 1-year-old. By age 4, he was taking formal lessons, and by 6, he was playing classical music that would make Beethoven proud. A bona fide child prodigy, he later went on to study at Indiana University's School of Music under the legendary Sidney Foster and eventually earned advanced degrees in music. When he wasn't performing, he was teaching at universities across the country, from Idaho to New Jersey.

Welby agreed to play at the wedding, but a rehearsal was needed first. I wasn't invited to the wedding itself (a small detail I didn't take personally), but Ev brought me along to the rehearsal. The only place in Plains with an available piano was Miss Lillian's Pond House, and we were granted unsupervised access. Unsupervised!

There was a lone Secret Service agent stationed outside, presumably because Miss Lillian wasn't home. He had our names on a list and let us in. Once inside, the three of us were left entirely to our own devices.

Welby and Ev eventually started rehearsing, but not before we did some good, old-fashioned snooping. We began with Miss Lillian's refrigerator, alas, no Billy Beer, before moving on to the other rooms. Upstairs, we discovered a treasure trove. A room filled with gifts she'd received from dignitaries around the globe. It was like stepping into a miniature museum. There were African masks, Egyptian artifacts, ornate jewelry, and exotic trinkets that seemed too fragile for our clumsy hands. Knowing me, I'd break something priceless, so we wisely retreated back downstairs.

We ended up in Miss Lillian's bedroom, where the pièce de résistance awaited. A bright red phone with no dial or buttons perched next to her bed. Kim later informed us it was a direct line to the White House. Naturally, we toyed with the idea of picking it up and ordering a pizza, but common sense prevailed. We realized that whoever answered would immediately know the call was coming from the Pond House, and within seconds, we'd probably be surrounded by federal agents. Still, the thought made us laugh.

That day was an adventure for the books. We left the rehearsal knowing we'd just had a quintessential Miss Lillian experience, even if she wasn't physically there.

I'm not sure if it was my connection to Kim, my brief encounters with Miss Lillian, or the fact that Billy Carter and I shared the same name, but I somehow ended up with two tickets to one of Jimmy Carter's inaugural balls. Maybe all the interpreters were given invitations, but I liked to think it was because I was "in" with the family. After all, Miss Lillian loved my hair.

There were multiple inaugural balls scheduled that evening, scattered across the D.C. metro area. My invitation was for the D.C. Armory, not exactly the Mayflower Hotel, where the celebrities and dignitaries would be. Still, beggars can't be choosers. These balls, officially planned and sanctioned by the Presidential Inaugural Committee, were invitation-only, with pre-paid tickets issued to guests. Just being part of the evening felt special, even if I wasn't mingling with Hollywood royalty.

I invited Anne Wilson to be my date to the ball, and honestly, we had more fun getting ready for the evening than we did at the event itself. My perm was nearly grown out by this point, so if I bumped into Miss Lillian, she might not have recognized me. ("Honey, did you change your hair?")

The DC Armory was absolute chaos. The place was packed, and I couldn't help but wonder, who were all these people? How did they get an invitation? Anne and I elbowed our way to the front, where I spotted Sybil and Billy on stage. I managed to snag a quick chat with Sybil and casually asked where the President and Rosalynn were. "Oh, they just left," she said, "on their way to the Mayflower."

Damn. I knew it! The Mayflower was the place to be. But was I about to let that stop me? Of course not. I was 18, invincible, fearless, and perhaps a little too confident. (Youth, right?)

"Let's get out of here and crash the Mayflower party," I whispered to Anne. She didn't even hesitate. Moments later, we were weaving through the crowds at the Mayflower Hotel, blending in like pros. I flashed our Armory tickets, and we were in. Security? Who needs it?

The ballroom was stunning, ornate and bustling with glamorous people, the kind you see in magazines and wonder how their lives always seem perfectly polished. Sadly, we learned that Jimmy and Rosalynn had already danced their inaugural dance and moved on to another ball. Arrrrgh! Oh well. We weren't about to push our luck by chasing them around the city.

Instead, Anne and I made the most of it. We had a drink, danced a couple of times, and soaked in the magic of the Mayflower. From freezing my fingers stiff at the inauguration to gliding across the ballroom floor, it had been another unforgettable day.

Soon after the inauguration, excitement died down, and life picked up speed. Good Vibrations was in full rehearsal mode for new shows, Roz kept me busier than ever, and then Janet dropped her big news.

Janet had been working in the TV studio on campus, captioning in-house movies and TV shows recorded at Gallaudet. This was long before closed captioning became mainstream. In fact, the only organization doing anything similar at the time was WGBH in Boston, which captioned a handful of PBS programs.

Janet's job involved making these materials accessible for students, who could watch them in the library's many VCR machines or check them out to watch in their dorms, assuming they had their own VCRs, of course. (Ah, the 1970s, when home entertainment was a luxury and rewinding a tape was an art form.)

She worked alongside Sandy White in a cozy little space known as the Crow's Nest. The studio was perched in the Crow's Nest of Chapel Hall, up a creaky, narrow staircase that seemed like it belonged in a haunted house rather than a university building.

To this day, I have no idea how they hauled all that equipment up those stairs. Walking up them was hard enough without balancing, say, a giant TV monitor. Chapel Hall itself was a masterpiece of history. Built in 1870, it served as a chapel, auditorium, exhibit center, and dining hall. It was so old and stately that it was added to the National Register of Historic Places.

The National Park Service described it as "one of the finest examples of post-Civil War collegiate architecture in the U.S." Designed by Frederick C. Withers of Vaux, Withers & Co., Chapel Hall embodied the High Victorian Gothic style. The NPS even called it a "picturesque, brownstone" masterpiece with "a restraint and fine handling of materials" that created "subdued coloristic harmony." (Translation: fancy and old.)

For me, it was equal parts beautiful and creepy. Every creak of the floorboards suggested a ghost might be lurking. Still, the Crow's Nest was a hive of creativity, and whenever I visited Janet there, the energy was contagious.

I'd always loved anything related to entertainment, so Janet's job was endlessly fascinating to me. Her days were spent listening to dialogue from movies and TV shows, working a foot pedal to control a machine that stopped and started the audio so she could type everything out. Every sound effect went in parentheses, door slams, dog barks, ominous music intensifies, and all the dialogue was carefully transcribed onto long cards.

If the project was a full-length movie, it would be divided up between Janet and Sandy, her colleague. Once they finished, the next step was watching the show or movie in the studio to match captions to the characters. The cards were marked up with arrows, notes, and frantic scribbles. Then, the whole process started again, this time on special rolls of paper that would eventually be fed into a machine to finalize the captions.

By today's standards, it was ancient technology. Back then, it was revolutionary. Captioning on this scale didn't exist outside of Gallaudet and a few programs at WGBH in Boston.

And then came Janet's big news. She had been offered a new role with On the Green, Gallaudet's campus publication. It came with more responsibility, more exposure, and a chance to flex her editorial chops. Janet, one of the brightest people I know, didn't hesitate to say yes.

Janet taught me an invaluable lesson. Say "yes" to opportunities, even if they scare you. Especially if they scare you, it's advice I've passed on to newbie interpreters ever since. Don't turn something down just because it feels daunting. Say yes and find out what you're capable of. Every time I said yes, I discovered something new about myself, about life, about what I could achieve. At 18, I was all-in on this philosophy, saying yes to everything unless I knew it would hurt me.

Janet thrived in her new role. Later, not only did she start Sign Language Associates, but she also became the President of RID (Registry of Interpreters for the Deaf), the national organization that certifies interpreters. When did this woman ever sleep?

Her departure left an opening in the TV studio, and I jumped at the chance. Janet put in a good word for me with the new director, Eric Kulberg. Eric called my extension in Roz's office and asked if I could come by the Crow's Nest for a meeting. I practically sprinted to Chapel Hall, up the creaky, narrow staircase, and into Eric's office.

Eric was, in a word, a hippie. Low-rise, frayed jeans that seemed glued to his legs. A faded, funky T-shirt. A thinning ponytail and an easy smile that felt like a welcome mat. He offered me a seat, and we got to talking.

He told me he respected Janet immensely and felt I'd be perfect for the role, fast typist, fluent in ASL, and a lover of entertainment. Eric, just starting to learn sign language, admitted he could use my help with meetings involving Deaf faculty and staff. "Sandy can sign," he said, "but she's not an interpreter. Also, I think I'd like a male voice for these." (I wasn't about to overanalyze that one.)

Eric outlined the job, which would include captioning, helping with the new campus news program (News Review), voicing for the show's Deaf anchor, and interpreting for various on-air guests. My head was spinning with excitement. Then came the cherry on top. The salary was $11,300. A full $4,000 more than my Faculty Secretary position.

Roz, as always, was gracious when I broke the news to her. She knew how much I loved entertainment and agreed that the Crow's Nest was a better fit for me. With her blessing, I started the new job the following week.

Eric and Sandy wasted no time testing my mettle. My first project? Captioning Roots. Roots was the groundbreaking television event of 1977. No pressure.

Eric hired another captioner, Larry, to help. Sandy, meanwhile, became the lifeline for two rookies navigating the sprawling epic. The project was massive, but I loved every minute of it. My typing skills got a workout, and being part of a TV studio with evolving responsibilities made me happier than I'd been in ages.

To top it off, Mary Anne worked in Chapel Hall, too, at least until her office in Ole Jim was renovated. It felt like a full-circle moment, being in the same building with her again.

When we finally finished captioning "Roots," I felt like I deserved a month-long vacation to get the feeling back in my overworked fingers! That was the biggest and longest project tackled by the TV studio, and I was so happy to be a part of it. I figured if I could do "Roots," I could do anything! I spoke with Sandy and Eric and asked if they could give me a comedy because "Roots" was so heavy. They obliged and gave me "What's Up, Doc?" – a 1972 American screwball comedy film directed by Peter Bogdanovich and starring Barbra Streisand and Ryan O'Neal. It was intended to pay homage to comedy films of the 1920s, '30s, and '40s, especially "Bringing Up Baby" and Warner Bros. Bugs Bunny cartoons.

I would sit at my desk wearing my headset and cry with laughter. Listening to the movie was hilarious, and I would have to stop all the time because of the tears streaming down my face.

People would walk into the room and see me convulsed with laughter and wonder what in the world I was listening to. It must have been quite a sight. I couldn't wait to get to work every morning so that I could continue typing this movie. When it was time to add the captions to the film, I still couldn't stop laughing. To this day, it's one of my top five movies.

NEWS REVIEW started production, and once again, I felt I was in my element. I worked closely with John, the director, on the copy for the show anchor, Galinda Goss. Galinda was a student at Gallaudet, and she had the most beautiful signing style. She was probably chosen to be the anchor because of her signing and because she was really bright and on top of all the news stories that were happening. I loved working with her and felt honored to be her voice for the show.

In addition to captioning, I was often called into John's office to go over the upcoming News Review segment, help decide which stories to use, and practice voicing the copy. There was never a dull moment, and it always gave me more exposure to signing and interpreting. I had only been interpreting for a year, and by the time I turned 19 in May of 1977, I was presented with an offer that humbled and excited me. Eric announced to the office that Elizabeth Taylor was coming to campus, and he wanted me to be her interpreter for the interview that would happen in the studio. I almost suggested he find someone with more experience, but then I stopped myself. Elizabeth Taylor? Hell yeah, I'll do it!

In December of 1976, Elizabeth Taylor married Senator John Warner of Virginia. This marriage made headlines because a. Elizabeth was getting married again, and b. She was marrying a politician. This was not a Hollywood romance, and it left many people scratching their heads. So, when they arrived on campus in 1977, they were still newlyweds!

In preparation for the big day when they would be on campus, I went out and splurged on a new suit. It was brown corduroy with a bunch of pockets all over the place. The pants, of course, were bell bottoms, and the jacket had enormous lapels. I picked a white shirt – also with enormous lapels – and wore it without a tie. The top three buttons were unbuttoned, and all I needed was a huge gold chain to complete the outfit. I looked like something right out of "Saturday Night Fever," complete with brown platform shoes that matched the suit and made me about three inches taller. I was looking and feeling very groovy.

The day arrived, and I woke up with a sore throat and a slight fever. NO!!! Not today!!! I'm meeting Elizabeth Taylor!! I almost called in sick but decided I had to go. I remembered my "say yes to everything" motto, got dressed, and drove to Gallaudet. In my brown suit, shoes, and brown Pinto, I was a study in monochromatic fashion.

I was actually quite calm standing in the office until a phone call came in, and Eric announced, "She's here." We all scrambled down the stairs from the offices on the top floor down to the studio. My first thought was, "Poor Liz having to climb up these rickety stairs." It certainly wasn't glamorous, but she and Senator Warner were good sports.

After introductions, it was time for the interview. Elizabeth and Senator Warner sat on the couch, and I was sandwiched right in the middle. Across from us, the interviewer and Gallaudet student, Tom Holcomb, prepared for his big moment. You'd think I'd have asked to see the questions ahead of time to prepare myself, but nope. Between my excitement over sitting next to a Hollywood icon and the fog of cold medicine, that very practical idea completely escaped me.

The sofa was… well, let's call it "historically significant." It was old, soft, and saggy in all the wrong places. I asked Elizabeth if her back was comfortable, knowing she'd undergone several surgeries over the years. She admitted it wasn't great, so I immediately asked for a pillow. She smiled warmly and thanked me, touching my knee in a friendly, convivial way.

At that moment, I decided we were best friends.

We chatted casually while waiting for the cameras to roll. She laughed easily, her charm undeniable. Meanwhile, the Senator, seated on my left, was completely ignored. I wasn't rude; I just had priorities. My attention was entirely on Elizabeth.

Sitting so close, I had an up-close-and-personal view of her famously photographed face. Then curiosity got the better of me. "Hey… your eyes aren't violet."

She turned to me, amused. "Anytime a story is written about you, they always mention your violet eyes," I explained.

"They're blue," she said matter-of-factly. "I have very dark eyebrows and lashes, so under the lights, I think they just look violet."

There I was, sitting shoulder-to-shoulder with one of the most glamorous women in the world, casually chatting about her legendary eyes. Again, just another day at the office!

When the cameras started rolling, the vibe shifted to awkward. Tom, visibly nervous, was perspiring and fidgeting, and I quickly realized that not previewing the questions had been a rookie mistake. As I voiced his questions, Elizabeth kept turning to look at me instead of Tom, which made perfect sense as she was hearing my voice, not his. I tried nodding in Tom's direction to redirect her focus, but no luck. She kept looking at me like I was the one asking the questions.

Anytime Tom asked something she found amusing, Elizabeth would laugh, touch my knee again, and flash me a smile. Awkward doesn't even begin to cover it.

Watching the interview now is a masterclass in how not to interpret. I cringe every time. I was such a newbie that I broke practically every rule in the book. I chimed in with my own thoughts, gave Tom unsolicited advice, and basically behaved like I was a guest at their private cocktail party.

Still, I learned two things that day:

Elizabeth came to Gallaudet because she was asked. I later read that she was bored living on a farm in Virginia, so any excuse to get out and do anything was welcome.

Don't call her "Liz." Senator Warner made that painfully clear. The media might have called her Liz, but her friends and family never did. Her name was Elizabeth, and she expected to be addressed as such.

After the interview wrapped, there were group photos (Elizabeth instinctively knew how to find which camera was snapping at that moment, of course), and then she and the Senator were whisked off to their next stop on campus.

Janet took over as Elizabeth's personal interpreter for the rest of the day, including a massive celebration in the campus gym. The place was packed to the rafters with students, faculty, and staff, all cheering so loudly it felt like the roof might fly off.

The highlight of the event was Rita Corey. Rita was the true star of Good Vibrations, performing her signature song "Cabaret." She brought the house down (again), delivering a performance so electrifying that I'm convinced even Elizabeth Taylor was impressed.

It was such a fun day and an incredible experience that I completely forgot how sick I felt!

I had made friends on campus with a woman named Linda Melnick. She was an absolute hoot, bubbly, hilarious, and always quick with a compliment about my Good Vibrations performances. Linda mentioned she was a singer and performer herself but never felt comfortable auditioning for Good Vibrations. She was part of a theatrical company outside Gallaudet, where she got her creative fix.

At the time, I was so immersed in all things Gallaudet, sign language, interpreting, performing, that I'd almost forgotten my own early years of singing and dancing as a kid. Linda, as it turned out, was just the reminder I needed. She told me auditions were coming up for the next musical at the District Heights Theatre of the Arts in Maryland and insisted I audition. Following my trusty "say yes" philosophy, I decided to go for it.

The show was Little Mary Sunshine, and I chose "Look for a Sky of Blue" as my audition song. Standing in front of the producers without signing felt... odd, like I was missing an arm. But just singing again felt incredible, like reconnecting with an old friend. I was cast in the role of Slim. It wasn't a lead by any stretch, it was more of a background part, but Slim had a lot of songs, and honestly, it was just plain fun being part of a production with Linda.

Theatre folks are a particular breed of wonderful people, and everyone at DHTA had known each other for years. They were my kind of people, true-blue theatre geeks. I quickly clicked with three of them. Richard Blair, Mary Ruth Alred, and Marilyn Meyers. The four of us became inseparable, a little theatrical pack who did everything together.

We rehearsed Little Mary Sunshine during evenings and weekends while my days were still devoted to signing and interpreting. It was a busy, glorious time. Outside of the show, the four of us were always hanging out, going on trips, hosting dinners, and seeing movies. One of our favorite haunts was The Old Stein in Dupont Circle, a sing-along restaurant where Verner, the piano player, entertained a roomful of beer-drinking patrons with requests.

Let me tell you, we were known at The Old Stein. If they didn't know us when we walked in, they definitely knew us by the time we left. Richard had this deep, velvety baritone, I was a tenor, Mary Ruth had a smooth and soulful alto, and Marilyn was in a league of her own. She could go from a crystal-clear soprano to a powerhouse belt that would give Broadway divas a run for their money.

Marilyn was a star in every sense of the word. She played the title role in Mame, Dolly Levi in Hello, Dolly!, and Miss Hannigan in Annie. Her voice could knock the wind out of you, and she knew it.

One night at The Old Stein, I requested "Climb Every Mountain" from The Sound of Music because I knew Marilyn would absolutely slay it. And oh, did she ever. From the first note, she had the room hooked. Her voice soared, growing richer and louder with every line until she hit that final note like her life depended on it. The whole restaurant erupted into cheers.

It was so spectacular. I remember they comped our beers that night. No one else wanted to sing after Marilyn was done. She'd raised the bar too high.

Those nights at The Old Stein were pure magic. We laughed, we sang, and we made memories that felt larger than life. I don't know what was better, the camaraderie, the music, or the fact that I'd found my people.

The folks at DHTA told me I'd impressed them with my Little Mary Sunshine audition, and after that, I joined their Christmas show, where I got a couple of solos. Things were going well. Then, at one of their producer meetings, they decided their next production would be Peter Pan, and they wanted me to play the lead.

Naturally, I said "yes."

I was flattered, of course. Playing a lead role in a musical felt like a big leap forward. But the moment I said yes, I started thinking about what it meant to play Peter Pan. I'd only ever seen Mary Martin and Sandy Duncan in the role, and I quickly discovered why it was performed by women.

Here's the thing…

On Broadway, you couldn't weigh more than 125 pounds to fly with the famous Flying by Foy rig.

Peter had to sing a coloratura opera piece for "Mysterious Lady," which required a voice that could practically shatter glass.

The harness. Let's just say it wasn't exactly designed with male anatomy in mind.

But I wasn't going to let a few technicalities get in the way. Sure, I wasn't Flying by Foy, but I was around the weight limit, and I had an incredible falsetto that could pass for coloratura (or so I convinced myself). As for the harness… Well, I figured I'd just grin and bear it.

The theatre still had the flying system from a previous production of Peter Pan. They assured me it would work, even though it looked a bit like it had been installed by someone who'd just read a manual called Rigging for Dummies.

Here's how a professional Peter Pan works. Peter and the three Darling (that's their last name) children fly across the stage in precise, magical directions, onto the bed, to the window, and down to the floor. It's all perfectly choreographed by the Flying by Foy system, which uses trained professionals to handle the cables.

Now, here's how our production worked.

I was hooked up to the system, either Stage Left or Stage Right, and two men, volunteers, I assume, who hadn't been warned about their imminent hernias, pulled on a rope to hoist me into the air. The flying wasn't so much "graceful" as it was "mechanical." I'd creak my way diagonally up to the center of the stage, then jerk back down on the other side in what can only be described as an upside-down V. Peter Pan wasn't flying so much as he was… inching.

And the creaking was so loud that it sounded like I was piloting the Titanic through an iceberg field. Still, we were optimistic that the sound of the piano, bass, drums, and maybe my warbling falsetto, would drown it out.

Then there was the harness. Let's just say it added some unexpected compression that made hitting those coloratura high notes a breeze.

For reasons that now escape me, we decided to hold off on testing the flying system until the dress rehearsals. Priorities, I suppose. Casting pirates and Indians, sewing costumes, and transposing the music all came first. Speaking of transposing, the entire score had been written for Mary Martin, and Mary Martin and I don't exactly share the same key.

When I mentioned this to Mom and Dad during a phone call, they told me to talk to Welby, who happened to be visiting. Welby offered to transpose all of Peter's music for me. He was between teaching jobs and had the time. What a gift! Every one of Peter's many songs was adjusted to fit my voice.

The cast came together beautifully. Richard was a pirate, Mary Ruth played an Indian, and Marilyn, ever the diva, was the producer, staying offstage this time. I wasn't just playing Peter; I was also choreographing the entire show. It was a lot, but it was all going smoothly. Rehearsals were a joy; the music sounded great in my key, the flyers were made, and tickets were nearly sold out. I was over the moon. What could go wrong?

The first dress rehearsal went surprisingly well. The flying system was nerve-wracking, and yes, the creaks were there, but we figured we could drown them out. Or maybe the audience would be too dazzled by my grand entrance to care. I mean, how often do you get to see Peter Pan inching through the air like he's riding a very squeaky and very slow zip line?

I couldn't wait for the next rehearsal. I was ready to soar. Or, you know, creak dramatically.

The night of the final dress rehearsal had arrived. This was it, the last chance to iron out the kinks before opening night. Nerves were high, and not just among the cast. The crew, particularly the two guys responsible for hoisting me into the air, looked as if they'd just been told they were piloting a rocket launch.

The show had some quick set changes that needed to flow perfectly. We had to flip from the Darling children's bedroom to Neverland, then to the captain's boat, and finally to the inside of the tree where, depending on the scene, either the pirates or the Indians were hiding. It was a logistical ballet, and one wrong step could send everything tumbling, literally, as it turned out.

It was time for Peter Pan's grand entrance. I took my place at the window, ready to fly. The two burly rope-pullers gave me a thumbs-up, and I gave them one back. Up, up, up I went, soaring not-so-gracefully to the full height of the stage.

And that's when I felt it, a slight tug, just enough to make my stomach notice.

I looked up just in time to see the cable snap.

It's funny how flying up felt like it took an eternity, but the trip back down took about two seconds.

The sequence of events immediately after the fall is still a bit of a blur. In my mind, I felt the tug, then hit the floor, then heard the music stop. I remember slowly opening my eyes, surrounded by children dressed as pirates and Indians creeping closer to me. For a split second, I thought this was part of the play. When did we add this scene?

Someone yelled, "Don't touch him!" and I realized, oh… this wasn't a dream, and it definitely wasn't in the script.

The thing about flying as Peter Pan is you're supposed to do it with one leg bent beneath you and one arm extended, like you're reaching for the stars. That's exactly the position I was in when I hit the stage. Thank goodness for that because my extended arm saved my head from hitting the floor. Unfortunately, the rest of me wasn't so lucky. The weight of my entire body coming down from 20 feet was absorbed by my right foot, which took the brunt of the impact.

By the time I fully grasped what had happened, every stage-hand, actor, musician, and director had gathered around me. Their faces were a mix of horror and disbelief. I can't imagine how bad it must've been to watch me plummet from the rafters.

"What happened?" I asked weakly.

"You fell." Duh.

They helped me to my feet, or tried to. I couldn't put any weight on my right foot. The rest of me seemed relatively okay, but the foot? Not so much. Someone decided I needed to go to the hospital immediately. Good idea. Mary Ruth volunteered to drive me while Richard carried me to the car like a gallant pirate-turned-paramedic.

At the hospital, the verdict was in. I'd sprained and bruised every part of my right foot. The doctor told me, "It would've been better if you'd just broken it." Apparently, a clean break heals faster and with less pain. Great news! (Said no one ever.) He wasn't kidding about the pain, though, it was excruciating.

The beauty of community theatre is it gives everyday people the chance to perform in professional-style productions, scaled down but still ambitious. You get to sing, dance, learn your craft, and maybe one day take the leap to a professional stage.

The downside is there are no understudies. Productions typically run for just a few weekends, so it's a roll of the dice that no one will sprain, strain, or, in my case, crash-land during rehearsals.

There was a woman in the DHTA family who was officially named my understudy, but let's be real, there wasn't a snowball's chance in hell she'd actually go on. The title was more of a formality than a reality. Sure, she could stand in for blocking rehearsals if I couldn't make it, but she couldn't dance, and carrying a tune wasn't exactly in her wheelhouse. The gesture was sweet, though.

While I was recuperating at Mary Ruth's, the DHTA Board huddled to discuss the future of Peter Pan. Canceling the show wasn't an option, all the tickets were sold, and everyone had poured too much time and effort into the production to let it fizzle. They decided to delay the opening until I was back on my feet, or, rather, foot. No pressure, right?

My job at Gallaudet was incredibly understanding. They gave me time off, even though I didn't technically need my foot to caption or interpret. What I did need it for, however, was driving my Pinto to work. Their kindness was greatly appreciated. Meanwhile, Mary Ruth was an angel, cooking my meals and helping me shove a coat hanger down my cast whenever the itching became unbearable. That's friendship on a whole other level.

We finally opened Peter Pan two weeks after my fall. I was in a soft cast and still in considerable pain, but hey, the show must go on! My cast was painted green to match the costume, and I wielded a brown cane that doubled as Peter's sword. We even attached leaves to the cane to make it look less... medical.

Despite the doctor's orders not to put pressure on my foot, I danced like nothing had happened. As the choreographer, I'd come up with some fantastic moves for Peter, and there was no way I was going to let a little thing like a crushed foot stop me. Unless someone sawed it off, I was dancing.

We scrapped the cursed flying rig once and for all. Good riddance! Instead, I and the Darling children simply pretended to fly through the window. Was it a letdown? Sure. Singing "I'm Flying" while firmly rooted to the ground felt a little ironic, but that's showbiz. We reworked the choreography to compensate, and I relished the challenge of having to think on my feet.

Welby traveled up from Georgia to see the show he'd helped make possible by transposing all of Peter's songs. He brought Mom and Dad with him, and Evelyn joined, too, making it a full family affair. I'm sure Dad was silently questioning his decision to support my move back to D.C., especially as he watched his 19-year-old son prance around in green tights with a cane-turned-sword. But they could all see how happy I was, and that made all the difference.

Mary Anne came to one of the performances as well, though I can't remember if I'd arranged for an interpreter. The DHTA Board wouldn't have batted an eye at the expense. Let's face it, they were probably relieved I didn't sue after falling from the sky. (My 1978 brain didn't even consider it.) I was just thrilled to have the lead role in a musical that brought the house down. Accidents happen, but they really should've retired that creaky, medieval flying contraption years ago.

The show ran for five evening performances and five matinees, and I turned 20 right in the middle of it all, on May 12. Talk about a memorable birthday.

Meanwhile, back at Gallaudet, exciting changes were underway. The university was building a state-of-the-art library, complete with a brand-new TV studio.

The Crow's Nest had always been charming, in that "let's put on a show in the barn" kind of way. But it was tiny, cramped, and limited what we could do. The new studio was a game-changer. Two enormous soundstages, the latest audio and camera equipment, and shiny new soundproof offices. (Soundproof? We worked with deaf people. I still don't get it, but nobody asked for my opinion.)

I loved my new office. I shared it with Larry, a fellow captioner, and we spent most of our time laughing. Larry was from North Carolina and had the perfect Southern drawl paired with a wicked sense of humor. Our office quickly became the go-to hangout spot. Supervisors were stationed elsewhere, so we were like kids left unsupervised in a candy store.

This was also the era of "smoking everywhere," and Larry was a chain smoker. Our office was small, windowless, and constantly clouded in cigarette smoke. Somehow, no one seemed to mind. It was the '70s; secondhand smoke wasn't the villain yet.

It was in this new space that I finally learned to drink coffee. Up until then, I was always the oddball who said, "No, thanks," when offered a cup. Everyone was shocked. I'd explain that while I loved the smell of coffee brewing, thanks to my parents, who drank black coffee religiously, I couldn't stand the taste. But peer pressure (and the allure of adult sophistication) eventually won me over.

Every morning at work, someone would bring in a box of donuts, and the coffee pot would fill the air with that intoxicating aroma I'd loved since childhood. Larry or Sandy, probably in cahoots, took it upon themselves to "teach" me how to drink coffee. "Just because your parents drink their coffee black doesn't mean you have to," they said, practically rolling their eyes at my rookie hesitation.

So, they handed me a cup of coffee doctored up with cream and sugar, paired with a donut. And let me tell you, they were right. The coffee-donut combination was nothing short of divine. That was my first cup of coffee, and I haven't looked back since. I blame Gallaudet for my lifelong coffee addiction.

As time went on, my responsibilities at work grew. I was still captioning, but now with shiny new equipment and deadlines. Deadlines! Suddenly, the pace picked up, and the stress levels weren't far behind. Our little team of five captioners was expected to churn out completed shows like a finely tuned machine.

On top of captioning, I was still voicing for News Review, interpreting meetings, and occasionally stepping in as on-air talent for various projects. It was exhilarating but exhausting. I began to wonder if I'd have the energy for another Good Vibrations show if Cynthia decided to organize one, and I opted to take a break from District Heights Theatre of the Arts. The next musical they had planned didn't thrill me, and frankly, I didn't see a part for myself in it. It felt like the right time to shift focus entirely to work.

By 1979, the workload was relentless. The pressure to meet deadlines started to weigh on everyone. Mistakes felt inevitable, and I worried about how those errors might impact the quality of our work. My coworkers were feeling it, too, there was an unspoken understanding that we were all doing our best to keep the wheels from flying off.

And then came the announcement that two representatives from a new organization called the National Captioning Institute (NCI) would be visiting campus to administer a captioning test.

NCI, based in Bailey's Crossroads, Virginia, was a nonprofit dedicated to delivering high-quality captioning services. Other than WGBH in Boston, Gallaudet was the only other major employer of captioners at the time. We were essentially pioneers in the field, and NCI wanted to pick our brains, and test our skills in English grammar, typing, idioms, and editing.

About a week after taking the test, I got a call from NCI inviting me to their offices for a meeting. I assumed it was to give feedback on the test and maybe suggest ways to improve it or make it more relevant.

When I arrived at their sleek new offices, I was greeted by Sharon Earley and her business partner, Deborah Popkin. After declining a glass of water (rookie mistake), I sat down, ready to talk shop.

"Thank you for participating in our guinea pig group of test takers," Sharon began. "You made the highest score. We'd like to offer you a job."

I blinked. "I'll take that glass of water now."

Deborah smiled and explained their vision. They'd already hired a team of caption editors for their East Coast office. Now, they were looking to build a team for their West Coast office, in Hollywood, California.

Hollywood? California? Movie stars? Swimming pools? My brain could barely process the words.

As I sat there, stunned, Deborah leaned forward. "We understand you have a job at Gallaudet, and you weren't looking for a change. But tell us what we'd need to do to get you there. You'd be the only editor fluent in ASL. We need you."

This was surreal. I'd never even thought about leaving Gallaudet, let alone moving across the country. I loved my work, my friends, and my sister. Everything in my life felt rooted in D.C.

How many out-of-body experiences can one person have in a lifetime? I asked for a second glass of water and sat there, completely at a loss for words.

I gave my two weeks' notice at Gallaudet and began the process of untangling myself from a life I'd worked so hard to build. All my projects were divided up between Larry, Carol, Gwen, and Sandy to ensure a smooth transition, or at least minimize the chaos. Then I started calling everyone I knew with the news.

Naturally, Mom and Dad had questions. "Are you sure this is the right decision?" Mom asked, her voice heavy with worry. "What about Mary Anne? And Gallaudet? And everything you've built?" Dad chimed in with his own practical concerns, but I reassured them the best I could. Honestly, I was scared too. I had made a name for myself on campus, had a community that loved me, and was now leaping into the great unknown. But wasn't that the whole point? To say "yes" and see where it led?

It was now the early fall of 1979, and I had been living back in Fairlington Villages, where it all started. This time, the unit had been completely renovated because all the apartments were becoming luxury condos to purchase. Richard, our friend Mickie Ballotta, and I shared one of those condos. When you walked out the front door, there was an unobstructed view of the Washington Monument. The three of us were perfect roommates and had so much fun living together. Richard worked for the National Park Service, and Mickie and I both worked at Gallaudet.

Richard and Mickie, bless them, threw me a farewell party at our place, and it was the kind of send-off you'd see in the final act of a feel-good movie. Everyone came. Janet, Mary Anne, the casts of Good Vibrations and Free to Be, and all the wonderful folks from DHTA. My colleagues from the TV studio joined in, too, and at some point, Janet and I ended up performing an impromptu medley of our greatest song-signing "hits." (Of course, we did.)

Later, I found myself outside with Mary Ruth, Marilyn, and Richard, the four of us huddled together in the cool night air, crying like we were starring in the series finale of our own little sitcom. It was one of those bittersweet moments where you know you're loved, but the weight of what you're leaving behind feels almost unbearable.

Before leaving D.C., Janet and I had the bright idea to videotape our performances for posterity. Since I worked at the TV studio, my coworkers were more than happy to lend us the space, equipment, and a small crew to make it happen. We lit up the soundstage, turned on the cameras, and captured every song.

Years later, I transferred those old VHS tapes to DVDs and sat down to watch. The entire time, I had a grin plastered across my face. Were we really that good? Were we really that flexible? Were we really that thin? The answers, obviously, were yes, yes, and unfortunately, not anymore.

Life at Gallaudet really was going very well, even though I was busier than ever. I thought I would be there for the rest of my life. I was happy with my home life, and I even decided the old Pinto had to go. Dad bought the Pinto for me for my 16th birthday from my favorite teacher in Junior High, Nannie Rose Hargrove. Her daughter, Nancy, taught me how to play the drums, and we became great friends in Eastman. The Pinto was Nancy's car, and I loved it. The gear shift was on the floor, and the backseat folded down, and it had an 8-track player! I couldn't believe it was really mine! I outgrew it, though, and felt I needed a new and dependable car. A car I didn't have to worry about blowing up if hit from behind.

So, I purchased my first car and felt so adult. I bought a 1979 Hondamatic. This was a little Honda that you had to shift from first to second gear but without a clutch. I don't think it caught on in popularity, but I loved it. I picked brown, the same color as my Pinto, and really felt like a grown-up because I now had heat and air conditioning!

When my plane descended into Los Angeles, I stared out the window in disbelief. The city sprawled out endlessly in every direction, stretching all the way to the Pacific Ocean. It was unlike anything I'd ever seen. New York was big, sure, but it was crammed together, vertical, self-contained. L.A. looked like a city someone spilled across a map.

Thankfully, I had two connections waiting for me on the West Coast. Well, "connections" might be a stretch. Mary Ruth had introduced me to Patrick, who lived in Hollywood, and I'd met a guy named Steven at a party in D.C. a few months earlier. Both had given me their numbers, so technically, I "knew" people.

As the moving van pulled out of Fairlington Villages, carrying my boxes, clothes, and my new trusty Hondamatic, I called Steven to let him know I was on my way. Unfortunately, Steven informed me he'd be in Europe when I arrived. Timing, as they say, is everything.

So, I called Patrick. "Hi, Patrick. Remember me? The guy moving to a city of nearly four million people where you're the only person I know?" No pressure, right?

I hung up and stared at my now-empty bedroom. I was leaving behind four and a half years of incredible friendships, a job that I loved, a nurturing interpreting community, and, most heartbreakingly, my sister. Mary Anne had always been my anchor. She truly wanted the best for me, and as her "baby brudder," I knew she was worried.

Yeah. Me, too.

The plane touched down, and I stepped into the chaotic, smog-filled embrace of LAX. It was October 1979, and I stood there for a moment, bags in hand, trying to process what was happening. Just hours earlier, I'd left Reagan National Airport in the middle of a snowstorm. Now, I was surrounded by palm trees swaying in the sunshine.

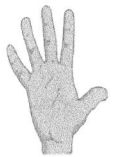

Cultural Collision

Culture shock

I took a deep breath. "Oh boy," I muttered to myself. "Here we go."

I hopped into a taxi, and the driver turned to ask where I was headed. Excellent question. All I had was Patrick's address. I had no clue how sprawling L.A. actually was.

"Where?" the driver asked, furrowing his brow. "That street could be anywhere."

Could it, though?

Apparently, yes. The Greater Los Angeles area wasn't just one city; it was a massive patchwork of towns and neighborhoods like Inglewood, Santa Monica, Hollywood, and the ever-mysterious San Fernando Valley, to name a few.

Thankfully, my cab driver was patient and resourceful. He pulled out a Thomas Guide, which I quickly learned was the Holy Grail for navigating this city. This wasn't just a map; it was a book, a thick, cumbersome tome with every street and neighborhood painstakingly cataloged. Later, as a freelance interpreter, my Thomas Guide would become a permanent fixture in my lap. A coffee-stained, dog-eared mess that never left my side.

After what felt like a road trip across state lines, we finally found the correct Clinton Street in Hollywood. Pro tip is to never underestimate the number of Clinton Streets in Los Angeles.

When we arrived, the meter read $20. My jaw nearly hit the floor. Twenty dollars! In 1979, that was practically a month's rent, or at least, it felt that way. Today, the same ride would cost well over $100, but at the time, it was enough to make me break out in a cold sweat.

Patrick greeted me warmly and showed me to my temporary accommodations which was a futon on his living room floor. It wasn't glamorous, but it was a roof over my head, and for that, I was grateful. As luck would have it, his apartment was close to Vine Street and the ABC studios where I'd be training with NCI.

With my moving van still en route, I didn't have a car, which made me feel like an alien in a city so car-dependent it might as well be part of the L.A. municipal code. I relied on the bus to get to Vine Street, which, combined with sleeping on a futon, quickly wore thin. I knew I needed to find a place of my own, and fast. I'm sure Patrick felt the same.

Still, he was a great sport. Despite taking in a near stranger, he made me feel welcome. We became friends through the experience, bonded by proximity and mutual good humor. On my first night in Hollywood, he casually mentioned that he had tickets to see Peter Allen at the Huntington Hartford Theatre (now the Ricardo Montalbán Theatre) on Vine Street.

Peter Allen! My first night in L.A., and I was already seeing a celebrity. Talk about a Hollywood welcome.

The theatre was tucked just south of Hollywood Boulevard, and standing on the corner of Hollywood and Vine felt like one of those surreal "pinch me" moments. At least, it did for about thirty seconds. Then reality hit. It was just two ordinary streets. No glamorous movie stars strolling by, no red carpets materializing underfoot. I tried to keep the excitement alive, but the grimy sidewalks and the lingering smell of hot dogs made Hollywood feel less like "Walk of Fame" and more like "Walk with Caution."

"This is Hollywood," Patrick said, matter-of-factly, with a shrug. He launched into an explanation about how it was an industry town, studios were the factories, post-production houses were the assembly lines, and apparently, glamour didn't make the cut.

Still, I was thrilled to be there, feeding off the buzz in the air like it was my own personal espresso. During intermission, we wandered outside, and there she was, Stephanie Powers, in the flesh, signing autographs. Stephanie Powers was starring in "Hart to Hart" with Robert Wagner, and right then and there, I decided my new normal would be casually brushing shoulders with celebrities. Well, it wasn't. But it wasn't a bad start to my L.A. adventure.

Work began while I was still crashing at Patrick's place. The office had an instant camaraderie. Everyone was young, eager, and ready to dive into this pioneering work of creating captions for Deaf and Hard-of-Hearing audiences. There were only eight of us doing this, four editors on each coast, making us feel like captioning superheroes.

Our training took place at ABC's Vine Street studio, a working hub alive with the hustle and bustle of live productions. One day, Barry Manilow himself strolled down the hallway, rehearsing for a special. I practically levitated. Seeing celebrities became a regular occurrence, like spotting pigeons in New York, but I never stopped getting giddy. Hey, they go shopping just like the rest of us, I learned.

After work, I cruised around Hollywood in my trusty (read: damaged) Hondamatic, searching for an apartment. The moving company had left my car with a giant dent, a "welcome to L.A." gift, and the company didn't feel obligated to take responsibility. Sharon, ever the problem-solver, handed me cash to fix it, but I decided the dent gave the car character. Besides, Hollywood traffic was sure to do it again. Why fight fate?

I eventually found a place on Whitley Avenue, right at the top of the hill. The view was great, Hollywood Boulevard stretched below, with Frederick's of Hollywood lingerie store adding its neon charm to the scenery. My apartment was snug, tucked into the hillside, and perfect for this new chapter of my life. It wasn't glamorous, but it was mine.

I have no idea why I didn't venture beyond my little bubble when apartment hunting. Surely, there were plenty of other neighborhoods, probably ones where you didn't share a zip code with Frederick's of Hollywood, but no one pointed me in any direction, so I stayed put. Hollywood felt familiar in its odd, grimy way.

Back then, my rent with Richard and Mickie was a very reasonable $200 per month. I was earning a little more than $11,000 a year at Gallaudet, but now, drumroll, please, I was pulling in a whopping $16,000 at NCI. A small fortune! That raise gave me permission to splurge on an apartment for no more than $325 a month. Oprah rich? Not quite. But still,…rich for me!

When I saw the sign for a one-bedroom apartment on Whitley, I buzzed the manager and asked, "How much?" He answered, "$325." I thought, "Well, isn't this destiny calling?" Moments later, I signed the lease.

The apartment was massive. A sprawling one-bedroom palace where the dining room opened onto the pool. Me, by the pool in December, pretending to be one of those glamorous Hollywood stars that I knew I'd see every day. Life was good. Well, good-ish. I was still sleeping on a used mattress (yes, ew), but I made up for it with a sofa and chair that had been repurposed from a play Patrick worked on. Very bohemian chic. My dining area boasted a single card table with a folding chair, and on the walls hung my prized art collection: two theatre posters from D.C. Clearly, I was ready for a spread in Architectural Digest.

Patrick and I didn't see much of each other. He was more of a friend of a friend, which is code for "nice guy but not my vibe." Instead, I spent most of my time with Steven, my one true L.A. friend. Steven was fascinating. He spoke a ridiculous number of languages and was studying Turkish and Japanese. Our shared love of language bonded us instantly. He also knew a little ASL, so he'd practice with me whenever we went out, to the bemusement of strangers who probably had no idea what we were doing.

Training at NCI was going well, but I couldn't shake the homesickness. Los Angeles was enormous, confusing, and coated in a thick layer of smog. The roads felt like an unsolvable puzzle, and the traffic made me question if anyone in this city actually worked. I missed D.C., its people, its rhythm, its lack of traffic jams on the way to the grocery store. I missed it so much that I asked for a transfer to NCI's Virginia office. Surely, I thought, this would be the best of both worlds. A new job and my old life.

Sharon and Deborah weren't thrilled with my request. They told me a transfer wasn't possible until a spot opened up in Virginia. Until then, I was advised to stick with the training and "try to like" Los Angeles. A pep talk for the ages.

Eventually, I started exploring the city more, which helped. Plus, there was the promise of a new office location. We'd soon be moving from ABC's Vine Street studios to Sunset-Gower Studios, a name that sounded impossibly glamorous. My excitement grew when I learned what was being filmed there. The Facts of Life, Benson, SOAP, and General Hospital. These were shows I actually watched! It wasn't quite brushing elbows with Barry Manilow again, but knowing I'd be working mere steps from Mrs. Garrett and Dr. Monica Quartermaine? That was enough to keep me going.

When I learned that some of the past shows filmed at Sunset Gower Studios included I Dream of Jeannie, Bewitched, The Flying Nun, and The Partridge Family, I knew I had to hold out until we made the move. Working in a place infused with the magic of Samantha's nose wiggles, Sister Bertrille's aerodynamic habits, and the groovy, polyester aura of the Partridges felt like an incredible opportunity. This was history, people. It felt like fate was giving me a nudge, whispering, "Hang in there, your sitcom dreams are just around the corner."

I reminded myself that this chapter of my life was being served to me on a silver platter. I had to be grateful for the opportunity. Besides, going back to D.C. would feel like hitting rewind on a tape deck. I wouldn't be returning to Gallaudet, and I certainly didn't want to go backward in my career. Forward was the direction, even if that meant occasionally inhaling smog and navigating L.A.'s freeways.

It was during one of these internal pep talks that I spotted a sidewalk Santa. Not your typical jolly, red-suited Kris Kringle. No, this Santa was sporting red shorts trimmed with white fur that stopped at his knees. A West Coast twist on North Pole couture. I laughed out loud, and at that moment, something clicked. L.A. was weird, it was kooky, and it was absolutely perfect for me. I withdrew my transfer request. This quirky city had won me over.

The move to Sunset Gower Studios finally happened, and it was worth every minute of the wait. Our new offices were brand new, sleek, and ridiculously modern. But the real thrill was walking past the sound stages every morning, Hondamatic keys jangling in hand, as I soaked in the hum of a working studio. I'd always dreamed of being part of the entertainment industry, and here I was, smack in the middle of it all. Sure, I wasn't writing scripts or starring in movies, but I was in the heart of Hollywood, and that was good enough for me.

Training wrapped up, and I was officially a working caption editor, back on the grind of chasing deadlines. The captioning process at NCI was light-years ahead of Gallaudet's methods. Here, we worked with enormous computers that added captions as we typed, futuristic technology that made me feel like I was in some sort of Star Trek episode. But with great technology came great responsibility, or, in our case, a giant book of captioning rules.

And oh, those rules. There were two in particular that made me question the sanity of whoever had devised them. Rule one: captions had to be edited down to just a few words because someone had done the math to determine how many words the average deaf person could read per second. Rule two: captions couldn't linger on the screen during an edit. If a character spoke a line, the caption had to disappear the moment the next character popped onto the screen. This gave us editors mere seconds to distill dialogue like, "Well, what do you want me to do about it?"

into a handful of digestible words. Come on, what words could possibly convey that sentence in half a second?

As if that wasn't enough of a challenge, there was the matter of shifts. Both coasts worked around the clock to ensure captions were ready for network deadlines, which meant a rotation of day shifts and, gulp, graveyard shifts. Let me be clear. I am not a night owl. Never have been, never will be. My body clock is set to farmer mode, up with the sunrise, down with the sunset. The thought of staying awake through the night was pure torture.

This was especially tough because my pre-L.A. life had included stints in theatre at DHTA in Maryland and dinner theatre in D.C. While I adored performing, those late nights drained me. My brain functioned during daylight hours, and no amount of stage makeup or applause could change that. Even in the glow of Hollywood's promise, I had to admit that I just got tired.

Working the graveyard shift at NCI was an endurance test I was doomed to fail. I tried everything to stay awake, coffee strong enough to dissolve a spoon, jumping jacks in the breakroom, even power naps that weren't so much "power" as they were desperate collapses. None of it worked. And if my assigned show to caption that week was Hour of Power, a religious program featuring the unrelentingly serene Pastor Robert Schuller, I was toast. The man had the soothing presence of a bedtime story and the pacing to match. By the time he got to his third scripture, I felt like I'd been hypnotized. Alone in the studio, with no coworkers to commiserate with, it was pure torture. Just me, the clock, and a gentle-voiced pastor slowly winning a battle against my eyelids.

When my shift ended, I stumbled out into the blinding Hollywood sunshine. I might as well have been a vampire emerging from a crypt. Squinting, hissing, shielding my face like I was auditioning for Nosferatu: The Musical. All I wanted was to lay horizontal, but unlike a vampire, I couldn't sleep during the day. Torture upon torture.

I begged Deborah to keep me on the day shift permanently. Surely, my overtures of misery and melodrama had moved her? Nope. "Fair is fair," she said, the corporate equivalent of "Suck it up, buttercup." But then came a small miracle. John, one of the other editors, preferred working nights. Fantastic! Problem solved! Or so I thought. Poor John wasn't exactly what you'd call... deadline-friendly. He was soon let go for underperforming, which meant I was back on the dreaded rotation, facing my nocturnal nemesis once again.

By June 1980, I had been with NCI for eight months. Things were going fine at work, fine in the way oatmeal is fine. It's nourishing; it gets the job done, but it's not thrilling. I missed interpreting. NCI had hired a deaf woman named Leslie, who was brilliant and a phenomenal editor, but she was oral and didn't use ASL. That opened the door to a new kind of interpreting for me: oral interpreting. During staff meetings, I'd focus on making my lips clear and precise, using my hands only for emphasis or occasional signs. It was a whole new skill set, and I quickly became good at it. Leslie eventually became a supervisor, and working with her was an invaluable experience. Years later, when oral interpreting became a more prominent part of my career, I look back on those early days with gratitude. Leslie taught me so much without ever realizing it.

Meanwhile, my personal life took a turn when Steven told me his friend Allen desperately needed a roommate to avoid moving out of his apartment. Cue my next adventure: breaking my lease and moving into an old Hollywood four-plex. The place was massive, glass doors, a fireplace, and a view of the Hollywood sign from the bathroom! Yes, I could live with that. Allen's apartment came furnished, but he kindly carved out a corner of the living room for my sofa and chair. With the money I'd saved, I finally treated myself to a new bed. A new chapter had begun, and this one came with a proper mattress.

Around the same time, I started taking dance classes at Joe Tremaine's studio in the Valley. It was there I met Joseph Tulloch, a fellow dance enthusiast and someone who truly appreciated the art form. One day, Joseph mentioned that his friend, a professional dancer, was coming to town. Her name was Debbie Quinn, and he invited me to join them at the beach in Santa Monica when she arrived. I had no idea at the time, but meeting Debbie Quinn would change the course of my life. Funny how the most significant moments often start with something as casual as "You wanna come to the beach?"

When Debbie told me she was a dancer who worked on The Love Boat, I had a minor starstruck moment. "You work on the TV show, The Love Boat?" I asked, envisioning her shimmying past Captain Stubing and Isaac, the bartender. She laughed. "No, not the TV show. I work for Princess Cruises. I'm usually on the Pacific Princess, the ship they sometimes use for location shoots."

"Oh, I see," I said, my mental picture adjusting from glamorous sitcom hijinks to real-life cruise entertainment. I was impressed. "Wow. I've never met anyone who's even been on a cruise, let alone worked on one. That must be so much fun!"

A few minutes later, Debbie's face lit up with an idea. She remembered that one of the Assistant Cruise Directors had just left, and Princess was looking for a replacement. "You have to be at least 21, good with people, and able to sing and dance," she explained. She immediately asked, "Should I set up an audition for you? It'd be in the Princess Cruises offices in Century City with the President of Entertainment."

The only catch? The audition had to be during the week, smack in the middle of my workday. Century City was no quick jaunt from Hollywood, and the timing was going to be tight. But I figured it was easier to beg forgiveness than to ask for permission from Deborah and Sharon. They liked me, after all, and what's a little tardiness when you're chasing the possibility of a high-seas adventure?

With butterflies the size of seagulls in my stomach, I hopped into my little Hondamatic and sped toward Century City as fast as my car could sputter. Parking, however, was an ordeal that practically devoured my lunch hour. By the time I finally found a spot, I was equally stressed and determined. No way was I backing out now. I was still in my say yes to things era, after all.

Princess Cruises' offices occupied the 30th and 31st floors of one of the sleek Century Towers. The elevators were swift, and before I knew it, I was being met by Brian Carter in the hallway. Brian, a Brit who radiated the confident ease of someone who'd hosted more than a few cocktail parties, ushered me into a room to meet the musical director, Robert Sigler. Bob was perched at a piano, sheet music at the ready.

He asked me to sing a piece he'd prepared. With a deep breath and an internal prayer to the cruise gods, I sang my heart out. They followed up with a request for a time step, which, thankfully, was well within my repertoire. Then, as if this audition wasn't already veering into A Chorus Line territory, they asked me to perform a little bit of choreography. I dove into the Crapshooter's Ballet from Guys and Dolls, a routine I'd performed during a dinner theatre stint in D.C. Miraculously, I remembered it. While dancing in Century City, I noticed the clock ticked dangerously past the end of my "lunch hour."

Afterward, Brian led me into his office for a sit-down interview. He began explaining the job and its responsibilities. I would be entertaining passengers with daytime activities like Bingo, trapshooting (good thing I had a BB gun as a kid), and, wait, horse racing? On a ship? He mentioned attending the Captain's Cocktail Parties (yes, please!) and performing in production shows at night. "Two shows a night," he added casually.

"And then you'd introduce the midnight cabaret," he said, as though midnight wasn't an unholy hour for someone like me who preferred early sunsets and early beds. Midnight? I'd have to rethink my vampire-adjacent sleep schedule.

While he talked, Brian showed me glossy brochures of the Princess fleet: the Sun Princess, Island Princess, and Pacific Princess. The ports of call looked straight out of a travel fantasy, exotic, exciting, and brimming with adventure. The food photos alone were enough to make me gain a few pounds just sitting there.

But as dazzling as the brochures were, I couldn't stop glancing at my watch. The clock was ticking, and I was going to be very, very late getting back to work.

When I looked up at Brian, his next words hit me like a rogue wave. "Can you be in Alaska in a week?"

Wait, what? Alaska? A week? My mind sputtered as I blurted, "No, I have a job in Hollywood, and I would need to give them two weeks' notice!"

Brian, unbothered by my momentary panic, nodded as if this was all part of some grand cosmic negotiation. "Okay, can you be in Alaska in two weeks?"

"Yes," I said, without hesitation, as though I'd always dreamed of swapping smoggy L.A. for icy fjords.

He handed me a stack of glossy Princess Cruises brochures to "help soften the blow" when I returned to my current job and announced my resignation. As I left Century City and pointed my little Hondamatic back toward Hollywood, my mind spun faster than my tires. There was so much to figure out. Moving my belongings, what to do with my car, saying goodbye to my apartment, not to mention the six weeks of training NCI had poured into me and the plane ticket they'd paid to bring me to L.A. None of this was going to make for an easy conversation. By the time I pulled into the gates of Sunset-Gower, a deep sense of dread had settled in my stomach.

Still, I walked into the office, plastered on a smile, and shouted, "I'm back. Sorry!" before bolting to my cubicle to type up my letter of resignation. The conversation with Brian was still swirling in my head as I clacked away on the typewriter. So many details! I'd need a passport pronto, plus an entirely new wardrobe, a blue blazer, white pants, white shirts, white shoes, and blue and white shorts (though I wouldn't exactly need those in Alaska). And then there was the small matter of uprooting my entire life.

Once the letter was typed and ripped out of the machine with the dramatic flourish it deserved, I marched into Deborah's office, armed with my resignation and a big, glossy brochure. I handed her the letter first and watched as her face registered the gravity of the moment. Before she could say a word, I placed the brochure on her desk as though presenting an olive branch, or, in this case, an iceberg-carved peace offering.

She flipped through the pages slowly, her expression unreadable. The ships, the exotic ports of call, the endless buffets, she examined it all with the quiet intensity of someone genuinely considering booking a trip. Finally, she closed the last page, set the brochure down, and looked up at me.

"Do you realize how much money we invested in your hire?"

"Yes," I said, bracing myself.

"If you handed me your letter of resignation for any other job, I think I would've killed you. This…" She tapped the brochure. "This is a chance of a lifetime, and you'd be a fool not to take it."

For a moment, I was stunned. Then I think I ran around her desk and hugged her like she'd just handed me the keys to a ship instead of permission to leave. "Can you believe the food? The buffets? The ice sculptures?" I asked, babbling in my relief.

"I can't," Deborah said with a smile. "I'm jealous."

And just like that, the hardest part was over. She promised to break the news to Sharon, who was working in the Virginia office. "She'll take it the same way I did," Deborah assured me.

I was 21, standing on the brink of something extraordinary, and the people who mattered most at NCI understood why I had to say yes. Even they could see it. This was my chance of a lifetime.

Life turned into a whirlwind after my meeting with Deborah. Just as I was trying to juggle my rapidly expanding To-Do list, Richard called out of the blue with an announcement that left me slack-jawed. He was moving to L.A.! My D.C. partner-in-crime was trading the capital for the City of Angels. He was leaving behind family, friends, and everything familiar to try his luck in the entertainment industry.

"Wait, you're seriously moving across the country?" I asked, stunned.

"Yep," he said, cool as a cucumber. "It's time."

"Well, I've got news, too," I replied. "I just accepted a job on a cruise ship, but hey, you can take my place in the apartment!"

It was the perfect solution. Allen wouldn't lose a roommate, Richard would inherit a ready-made social network, and he'd even have a car to drive. Mine. Because why not? I was about to live in a floating hotel, I wouldn't need it.

Things were falling into place, but my To-Do list wasn't getting any shorter. NCI, to their credit, was incredibly supportive. They gave me longer lunch breaks, promised no more graveyard shifts (bless them), and cheered me on as I prepared for this once-in-a-lifetime adventure.

I called my parents to share the big news. I rattled off details about my soon-to-be life at sea including the bars, the dancers, the shows, the food. It was all so shiny and exciting.

Dad, ever the wisecracker, replied, "Well, Bill, your Navy sure sounds different than mine."

They gave me their blessing, and I could hear the mix of pride and amusement in their voices.

When Richard finally flew to L.A., I introduced him to Allen, his new roommate, along with Joseph, Patrick, and Steven. It felt like I was passing the baton of my life. Handing off my apartment, my car, and my circle of friends was strangely bittersweet. I had just started to feel comfortable in Los Angeles, but now I was packing it all up and moving on. I felt a pang of guilt leaving Richard just days after he'd made the big leap to L.A. It was like we were trading places, I was jumping ship (literally), and he was setting down roots.

The guilt didn't stop there. I felt bad about everything, the short eight months I'd spent in L.A., the money NCI had spent hiring and training me, and the fact that I was now throwing myself into a world completely foreign to everything I'd known. Sign language, interpreting, and the Deaf community had defined my life. And now? I was going to be an Assistant Cruise Director. What did I know about being an Assistant Cruise Director? Absolutely nothing.

But there was no time to second-guess myself. I was too busy trying to check every box on my list and prepare for this new chapter. All I knew about Princess Cruises was that it was an American company operating under the British flag of P&O Cruises. Everything else? I figured I'd learn on the job. Sink or swim, quite literally.

The Sun Princess, I learned, was the smallest ship in the Princess fleet. I'd secretly been hoping to work on the Island Princess or the Pacific Princess, the two largest and most glamorous ships. They were twins, state-of-the-art for 1980, and practically palatial compared to the Sun. Of course, by today's standards, all three ships would probably look like glorified lifeboats. But back then they were the pinnacle of luxury.

The closest I'd come to a cruise experience before this was the Lurline, the ship that brought us back from Hawaii (my birthplace) when I was two. Needless to say, I didn't remember much about that trip. This time, though, I'd be stepping onboard as part of the crew. It was daunting and exhilarating all at once.

My parents had never vacationed at sea. Mom would've loved the idea of sipping cocktails on the Lido Deck, but Dad? Not so much. After 30 years in the Navy, the mere thought of boarding a ship that didn't involve rank and salutes was a hard no. "Why would I pay to go on a ship?" he'd say. "They used to pay me to be on one!" That was that. Dad made the decisions, and Mom, reluctantly, stayed on dry land.

As for me, I'd never met anyone who had been on a cruise, let alone worked on one. The whole idea of life at sea felt thrillingly foreign, like stepping into a movie where I didn't yet know my lines.

My new gig would begin aboard the Sun Princess, with the promise of a future transfer to one of the larger ships in the fleet. All Assistant Cruise Directors rotated four months on, two months off, which meant I'd be scoring a four-month paid vacation every year. Not too shabby! The pay was modest $1,000 a month, which was $4,000 less annually than I'd made at NCI, but Brian had reassured me, "You won't be spending much after the first few cruises. Plus, food, lodging, and laundry are covered." Financially, it was a wash. But honestly? I wasn't chasing a paycheck. I wanted to sing, dance, and see the world, all while someone else footed the bill.

The day to leave finally arrived. I said my goodbyes to everyone. Deborah, Richard, Allen, Steven, Joseph, my trusty bed, and my equally trusty car. I handed my car keys to Richard and packed my life into two suitcases, which were now bursting with an all-blue-and-white wardrobe. As the taxi pulled up, I couldn't help but think about my very first ride in L.A., the one where the driver had squinted at my handwritten address for Clinton Street like it was some kind of treasure map. Now, here I was again, climbing into a cab, heading back to LAX, but this time en route to a life filled with question marks instead of smog.

The descent into Vancouver was nothing short of magical. The city looked like a postcard, all dramatic mountains rising up from the sea and boats bobbing in the harbor as if they were waving hello. It was cloudy and cool, a sharp contrast to L.A.'s sun-drenched June. As the plane touched down, I felt a swirl of excitement and nerves. I had just turned 22, and while the world felt full of possibilities, my head was full of questions. What happens next? Where do I go? Will I look like an idiot?

Customs was my first hurdle, and it showed. I had never gone through Customs before, so I had no clue what to expect or how to act. My excitement must've been palpable because the officer barely looked at my stiff, brand-new passport before sizing me up. "Work or vacation?" he asked, his tone all business. "Work!" I said proudly, like I'd just aced the question on a pop quiz. His brow furrowed. "You're here to work in Canada?" Wait. Was that wrong? Panic set in. "Uh… no," I stammered, realizing I'd just contradicted myself. "You just told me to work." Oh no. Full eye contact. He was watching me unravel in real time. "Well, yes. I mean, I'm here to work, but not in Canada. Um. I'm here to work… in Alaska. On a cruise ship. The Sun Princess. It's in Vancouver now, but I'll just be working in Alaska. You know, which is part of the U.S.!" By now, I was sweating so much I could've watered his ficus. "Is this your first cruise?" he asked dryly, clearly enjoying himself. "How can you tell?" I replied, attempting to salvage my dignity. He stamped my passport, handed it back, and said with a hint of amusement, "Have a nice day."

Outside the Customs area, I spotted a Princess Cruises representative holding a sign with my name on it, BILL PUGIN, bold and official. Relief washed over me. Finally, someone to shepherd me through this new adventure, or at least get me to the Holiday Inn without incident. I had one night in Vancouver before embarking on the Sun Princess the next day.

The following morning, it was pouring rain, because of course it was. A car picked me up and whisked me to the pier, where several ships loomed like glittering giants. It was all very dramatic. My bags were whisked away to the lobby, and I was instructed to board the ship and report to the Cruise Director's cabin. Easy enough, right?

Not so much. As I stepped aboard the Sun Princess, I felt like Maria walking into the Von Trapp mansion for the first time, completely lost and mildly terrified. The ship was a hive of activity, buzzing with worker-bees darting in every direction to prepare for the sail to Alaska. I asked a handful of people how to get to the Cruise Director's cabin, but either no one heard me or no one cared. Not exactly the warm welcome I'd imagined.

The thing is, Brian Carter had conveniently forgotten to mention a critical detail during my interview. The Assistant

Cruise Director I was replacing was British. Actually, everyone on the Cruise Staff was British. And, as it turns out, the idea of an American stepping into that role wasn't welcomed with open arms. By the time I set foot on the gangway, word had already spread like wildfire. I wasn't just the new hire, I was the American, and I was despised before I even had the chance to call my first Bingo game.

To make matters even more surreal, I learned that I wasn't just some singing, dancing member of the Entertainment Staff. Oh no. I was an Assistant Cruise Director, which came with two stripes on my uniform. Two! In Her Majesty's Navy, no less! I was essentially an officer in the British Navy. An American. This was clearly not something anyone had prepared for, least of all me. I thought I'd signed up for talent shows and shuffleboard tournaments, not navigating international relations.

After a series of frustrating wrong turns, I finally found the Cruise Director's cabin and knocked. The door opened, and I met John Mercer, the man tasked with explaining my new reality.

He wasted no time laying it all out. "The passengers will be old, the weather will be cold and raining, and you need to be in your blues and whites for Cruise Staff introductions later tonight." Lovely. Before I could ask how many pairs of white pants I'd actually need to survive Alaska, he added, "The real fun starts tomorrow morning. You'll meet the musical director, and you'll need to learn the shows as quickly as possible."

Learn the shows? All of them?

Apparently, yes. We'd be at sea all day, and I'd spend it rehearsing in the International Lounge while passengers wandered in and out, probably pausing to judge my progress between shuffleboard games. There were six production shows to learn, complete with choreography, entrances, exits, and the ever-important microphone cord wrangling.

Daunting didn't even begin to describe it. Thankfully, I've always been a quick study, a skill that would later serve me well when memorizing lines for television. But that first day? That was a mountain to climb. It was trial by fire, or in this case, trial by two-stripe uniform and a mic cord.

This was before the ships had cordless microphones, which meant I had to master the delicate art of mic choreography. Every microphone cord was a potential death trap for all of us on stage, and it fell to me to make sure no one's pirouette ended in a lawsuit. Honestly, the mic tech alone could've taken weeks to learn. But I didn't have weeks, I had two days. Two days to learn the mic technique and my parts in the shows. What exactly had I said "yes" to?

John introduced me to two members of the Cruise Staff, Anzia and Jim, who, thankfully, seemed to take pity on me. They were British (of course), and they saw how the officers and other Brits onboard were treating me - somewhere between "polite indifference" and "active disdain."

I decided to channel the tactic Evelyn and I had perfected when we were kids starting at a new school. Make them love me! I was determined. But my first hurdle? The accents. This was not

Julie Andrews in Mary Poppins. This was a full-on linguistic assault. I couldn't understand a word Jim said. Every time he gave me instructions, I'd glance over at Anzia for a translation. This amused them both to no end.

It wasn't just the accents, it was the expressions, too. They spoke at lightning speed and tossed in phrases like "tickety-boo" as if that meant anything. I'd nod along, pretending to understand, much like I had done when I was first learning sign language. Pretending to understand is never a good plan. When I'd ask them to repeat themselves, they'd get annoyed, as if my confusion was an intentional affront. And if I dared gripe about not understanding, the officers would shoot back with, "Well, we invented the language, and you Americans just bastardized it." Right. Sure. Let's not bring "aluminium" into this, folks.

Still, I was determined to make this a positive experience. I threw myself into the job with all the enthusiasm of someone who hadn't quite processed what they'd gotten into. I learned the shows, mic cues and all, while simultaneously mastering the British way of calling Bingo (it involves rhymes, jingles, and random phrases like "two little ducks, quack quack" for I-22, because why not?). I ran Horse Racing, which involved a track on the floor, wooden horses, and passengers betting as though they were at the Kentucky Derby. I learned how to load and fire a .22 shotgun for trapshooting, which felt both empowering and mildly concerning, especially when the wind caught the clay pigeon and carried it over the pool with the sharpshooting passenger following it with the gun.

I polished my ability to have short, meaningless cocktail conversations with passengers, "Yes, the food is incredible, isn't it?", and gained the confidence to talk to a thousand strangers on a microphone like it was no big deal. But perhaps the greatest skill I developed during those first few weeks? The ability to nap anywhere, anytime. Between activities, I learned how to fall asleep in seconds flat, a skill so ingrained that even now, I can nod off before the end of a sentence. (I'm not kidding. It's my superpower.)

After a while, life at sea started to blur. Passengers came and went, a parade of the same questions, the same smiles, the same white-and-blue hair. The rain and trees of Alaska began to lose their charm, even for a wide-eyed 22-year-old. I found myself counting down the days until summer ended and we could trade cold, wet Alaska for the warm, sunny ports of Mexico and the Caribbean.

The Purser's Office had a book entitled Stupid American Passenger Questions. At first glance, I thought, here we go, another way for the Brits to look down their noses at us colonials. But after flipping through its pages, and later experiencing many of the "highlights" firsthand, I realized the book wasn't just cruel British humor. It was a necessary document of survival.

At first, I thought the entries were fictional, little jabs at American tourists that had gotten out of hand. But no. These were actual questions, asked in all earnestness by actual passengers. Some of my personal favorites: What time is the midnight buffet? Do these stairs go up? Does the crew sleep onboard? Are the eagles we see real, or are they provided by Princess? The list went on. Hundreds of questions, each one more baffling than the last. On tough days, I'd swing by the Purser's desk, flip through the latest additions, and find solace in the fact that no matter how overwhelmed I felt, at least I hadn't asked if stairs only worked one way. A good laugh always makes me feel better.

I quickly learned that many passengers left their brains at home when they packed for a cruise. It wasn't their fault, exactly. Something about the endless buffets and the gentle rocking of the ship seemed to lull them into a kind of food-and-sun-induced fog. Sometimes, when addressing a room of 500 passengers on the microphone, I'd blurt out, "It frightens me that you people vote in my country!" It usually got a laugh. They knew I had a point.

And let me tell you, cruises are really about one thing. Food. Passengers made it their personal mission to never miss a meal. Afternoon tea? Check. Midnight buffet (which, in case you were wondering, did start at midnight)? Double-check. By the time the Italian waiters started strolling the decks with trays of 12:30 a.m. pizza, people were practically in a carb coma, but they kept eating.

The sheer amount of food consumed onboard led to an unfortunate phenomenon I liked to call Formal Night Fails. On a seven-day cruise, there were two Formal Nights, and many first-time female passengers only packed one gown. By the second Formal night, thanks to five days of continuous eating, these women would find their zippers stubbornly refusing to go all the way up their backs. The seasoned cruisers, meanwhile, had it all figured out. They packed a second gown in a slightly larger size. Pro tip.

Finally, the Alaska season ended, and with it, the endless rain, pine trees, and totem poles. The Sun Princess was repositioned to the Mexican Riviera and Caribbean itineraries. I couldn't have been more thrilled. No more gray skies or damp jackets. Just sun, sand, and warm breezes. The Sun Princess was finally living up to its name.

There's something else about the Alaska season, though. It occasionally came with onboard deaths. The crowd skewed very senior, and sometimes 95-year-old Grandpa just didn't make it to the end of the cruise. The first time it happened, I was horrified. The Cruise Director, however, was unfazed. "It's a death for them, but it's a berth for us," he quipped, delivering the line with a shrug so casual it could've been rehearsed. We used to say that the average age of an Alaskan passenger was deceased. Gallows humor, for sure.

One of the rare crew members who actually liked me was Jackie Madison, another American. Jackie was hired as the Children's Counselor when the ship left Alaska and traded its dreary, cold itineraries for warm, tropical cruises. Let's just say she had very little to do during the Alaska season. There weren't exactly hordes of kids running around the totem poles.

But when the ship transitioned to the sunny family-friendly cruises, the kids came pouring in, and it was Jackie's job to wrangle them. By day, she was a kindergarten teacher in Oceanside near San Diego, but she'd take time off to do the occasional cruise, which seemed like the perfect gig for someone who loved kids and loved getting paid to hang out in the Caribbean.

Jackie and I clicked immediately. We were stupid-silly together in a way that baffled the Brits onboard. They didn't understand our humor, and honestly, we didn't understand theirs either. Every time we did something we thought was hilarious, we'd get these bemused, vaguely judgmental looks from the officers and crew, which, naturally, made us laugh even harder. It was a feedback loop of absurdity, and I loved every minute of it. Jackie was my partner in crime. We made a great team.

Jackie would often tell me about her best friend back in San Diego, Brian Tash. According to her, he shared our exact sense of humor and was someone I absolutely had to meet. Brian was also a teacher, and when I was on leave, we arranged a meeting. He and I spoke on the phone a few times beforehand, and Jackie was right, he had the same sense of humor, and always laughed at my jokes. Let's be honest, someone who laughs at my jokes is immediately a keeper. I love a good audience.

We planned for me to take the train down to San Diego one weekend, and Brian promised to show me around town. But, I had no idea what Brian looked like. When I asked him to describe himself, he said, "I'm 5'7", average weight, gray hair." "Gray hair?" I asked, puzzled. "Yeah," he replied, completely unfazed. "It turned gray in my twenties." So, he was an early-gray 32, and I asked what he'd be wearing to make it easier to spot him. "A turquoise polo shirt and white shorts," he said. My twisted brain immediately thought, wouldn't it be hilarious if I got off the train wearing the exact same thing? Of course, I couldn't resist. I went out and bought a turquoise polo shirt. White shorts were already in my wardrobe rotation, and set the plan in motion.

When the train pulled into the station, there he was, standing in front of his 1978 Fiat Spyder. As soon as I stepped off the train, dressed like his doppelgänger, he doubled over in laughter. Right then and there, we became best friends.

Brian has been there for me through thick and thin ever since. Whenever I needed someone, I could count on him. He's the kind of friend who shows up when it matters most, the one you know you can trust with anything, even your BMW. Once, I needed him to keep my car in his garage. The only catch? I told him he couldn't drive it. Ah, selfish youth. But Brian, ever the good friend, didn't even complain.

There's one cruise I'll never forget. I had recently transferred from the Sun Princess to the Island Princess when Cruise Director Jim Everett called me into his office. The way he looked at me, I thought I was in trouble. Instead, he hit me with a curveball. "We've got eight deaf passengers embarking on this week's two-week cruise from L.A. to San Juan through the Panama Canal. Can you help?"

Could I help? Of course! I practically leapt out of my chair with excitement. It wasn't just that I'd get to work closely with the group, interpreting their games, the captain's cocktail parties, events, and tours, it was the opportunity to reconnect with a skill I had been missing dearly.

One of the four couples was Benny and Sarah Jason, and they were delightful. Little did I know that seven years later, I'd meet their son, Jack Jason, and we'd become good friends and colleagues. To this day, Jack and I are still friends, and his 101-year-old father, Benny, vividly recalled that cruise. Sadly, Benny passed away just as I was finishing this book. I was hoping he would've had the chance to read this! If Jack's name rings a bell, it's because he's the personal interpreter and business partner of Marlee Matlin. Small world, huh?

Interpreting for the group didn't just fill my heart, it earned me major points with the officers and crew. I'd mentioned in passing that I was an interpreter before my cruise ship days, but now they were seeing me in action. It was like they suddenly realized I had the ability to do something no one else could. The group had an incredible time, and at the end of the cruise, they thanked me for being their interpreter. I, in turn, thanked them for showing up. They reminded me just how much I loved interpreting and how much I missed it.

When my four months at sea were finally up, I disembarked for my two-month leave. And that's when it hit me. I was a man without a plan. No apartment. No car. Just me and a duffel bag of clothes that smelled faintly of seawater and Italian food.

Meanwhile, Richard had been making moves of his own. While I was busy dodging totem poles and trapshooting at sea, he had landed a job as a tour guide at Universal Studios. It was the perfect gig for him. He loved people, had a killer sense of humor, and could probably convince anyone that Jaws lurking in the lagoon was a real shark. Guests at Universal didn't know how lucky they were to have him.

Richard had also befriended another guide, Bobbi Stevenson, and the two of them decided to get an apartment together in Studio City. Bobbi didn't feel safe living alone, and Richard wasn't thrilled with the commute from Allen's Hollywood apartment to Universal, so they teamed up and found a great two-bedroom, two-bath unit just a stone's throw from the studio.

Bobbi was a professional dancer who spent her off-days auditioning when she wasn't guiding wide-eyed tourists through the magic of movie-making. She and Richard graciously offered to let me crash on their sofa until I figured out my next steps. It wasn't ideal, but it gave me some breathing room. I knew I wanted to visit my parents in Georgia, but first, I needed a bit of time to recalibrate.

Bobbi was fantastic. She had the same quick wit and fun-loving spirit that Richard and I had, and we hit it off immediately. Even though I was sleeping on her sofa and essentially living out of a suitcase, we got along great. The three of us became fast friends, the kind you know are for keeps. And sure enough, all these years later, we're still in each other's lives.

Bobbi eventually became a successful realtor, and when I bought a house in Las Vegas in 2020, guess who I called? Bobbi was my agent. Talk about full circle. From the Universal Studios tour circuit to the Vegas housing market, Bobbi's still got it.

Toward the end of my first week crashing on Bobbi's couch, she came home with thrilling news: she'd been cast in the Las Vegas production of A Chorus Line! Naturally, I was excited for her, what a fantastic opportunity! But I was also a little excited for myself because her big break meant one thing. I got to move off the couch and into her room. Timing, as always, was on my side.

With Bobbi off to Vegas, Richard and I slipped seamlessly back into our old routine, picking up right where we'd left off as roommates in D.C. He was still driving my trusty Hondamatic, and we came up with the perfect arrangement for when I was back at sea. Richard had a friend who needed a place to stay temporarily, so he would take over my share of the rent whenever I was on the ship. Problem solved. It was the kind of arrangement that felt impossibly adult and responsible for two guys in their 20s.

When I returned to the Island Princess, the Mexican Riviera and Caribbean cruises were my new stomping grounds. This was so much better than Alaska! Don't get me wrong, Alaska is stunning, a once-in-a-lifetime destination, and everyone should experience it before the glaciers melt. But when you're in your 20s, "stunning" isn't as appealing as fun in the sun. Sure, I probably should've been slathering on SPF instead of soaking up rays on deck, but who thinks about their future dermatologist bills when they're young and golden-brown? (Today, my dermatologist is thrilled with the choices I made back then. Thrilled and very wealthy. You're welcome, doctor.)

That year with Princess Cruises flew by in a whirlwind of ports, passengers, and performances. I'd spent time on all three ships in the fleet and sailed to incredible destinations: Alaska, Mexico, the Panama Canal, the Caribbean, including San Juan, Puerto Rico; St. Thomas in the Virgin Islands; Colombia; Venezuela; and countless other exotic stops. I'd learned how to hold the attention of a thousand people, how to call Bingo like a pro, and how to seamlessly combine singing, dancing, and navigating mic cords. Most importantly, I'd learned a lot about myself.

I had achieved exactly what I'd set out to do, see the world, perform, and get paid for it, but by the end of the year, I was restless again. I missed interpreting and found myself wondering if I could build a career on land. It wasn't easy to walk away from a job like that, but something in me knew it was time to move on. One year felt right. I resigned.

I had no plan. Absolutely not. But I've never liked safety nets, and opportunities had a way of finding me when I needed them. Why should that change now?

Back in Studio City, Richard was thrilled to have me back as his full-time roommate. I had saved a bit of money during my time at sea, so paying rent for a while wasn't a problem. Richard and I agreed to split the insurance on the Hondamatic, which we'd now officially share. It was a solid plan, and for a brief moment, life felt comfortably simple.

I told myself I'd take some time to relax before diving into the job hunt. Going back to NCI crossed my mind, but I quickly dismissed the idea. Returning to my old job felt like moving backward, and I had a firm policy against that. Besides, they'd hired someone to replace me the moment I'd left for the Sun Princess. "Something will come up," I assured myself.

And, of course, something did.

I received a call from Sacramento from a woman working for a brand-new program at AT&T, the Telephone Company. Her voice had that businesslike tone that made me sit up straighter, even over the phone. She explained that the state of California was about to launch a groundbreaking initiative by providing free TDDs (Telecommunication Devices for the Deaf) to qualified Deaf and Hard of Hearing residents. They were compiling a list of interpreters to interview and test for the program, and apparently, I had come highly recommended.

Who recommended me? No clue. To this day, I'm grateful to the mystery person who put my name in the mix.

Interpreters from all over California were being considered, and ultimately, four would be chosen. The job would be based in downtown Los Angeles, where four interpreters would work alongside four hearing phone reps. Our role would be interpreting for people coming into the center to get their TDDs. There were three different models to choose from, and it would be our job to interpret the reps' descriptions of each one.

Here's the kicker. This was a full-time position paying $600 a week. Six. Hundred. Dollars. At Princess, I'd been pulling in $1,000 a month, so this was practically a windfall. Plus, I'd be living at home and doing what I loved, interpreting. It felt too good to be true.

The interview process was as rigorous as it was fascinating. First up: scenarios. The woman in charge of the program, herself an interpreter, asked very specific questions designed to see how we'd handle the diverse range of Deaf clients in California. Language levels varied widely in the community, so clarity and adaptability were key. For example, if the AT&T rep described the keyboard of the TDD and mentioned the "O" for the operator on the telephone, we couldn't assume that the client automatically knew what an operator was or what they did.

Hearing people grew up using the phone, but many Deaf individuals hadn't had that experience. This was the pre-cellphone, pre-texting, pre-email era, when TDDs were a literal lifeline for communication. Never assume anything. Every detail had to be clear.

The process unfolded in stages. First, a written test and interview. If you made it through that, there was a phone interview. If you passed that, you earned an in-person interview, a kind of final audition.

The in-person interview was where I was most comfortable. It felt like a performance, and as anyone who knows me could guess, I love performing. I walked in confident, quick on my feet (and hands), ready to take on whatever they threw at me.

They wanted to see if I could adapt, change my approach, my signs, my facial expressions, when the client didn't understand. One of the interviewers would pretend to be a confused client, and I had to figure out how to get the message across. Could I reframe the concept? Use a different sign? Add a visual cue? It was a high-stakes game, and I loved every second of it.

It was a challenge, but I was up for it!

It was a long week of waiting for an answer, but when it finally came, it was worth every agonizing minute. I got the job! Out of many interpreters interviewed, they'd narrowed it down to four: Francine, Kayelle, Jeanne, and me. The first three were CODAs, Children of Deaf Adults, and I was the lone SODA, Sibling of Deaf Adults. I made it!

The job was incredible, and I woke up every morning genuinely excited to head downtown. The interpreting world is small, so I already knew Francine and Kayelle, and meeting Jeanne was an absolute pleasure. The four of us clicked instantly, forming a dream team of interpreters. Even the commute was enjoyable. Since we all lived in the San Fernando Valley, Francine, Kayelle, and I would often carpool to work. On the days we didn't, I actually enjoyed taking the bus. It felt responsible, one less car clogging L.A. freeways, and it left Richard free to use the Hondamatic. Everyone wins.

There were so many reasons to be happy. My year at sea had been thrilling, full of new faces, exotic destinations, and experiences I'd never forget, but now I was doing something entirely different, interpreting every day in a program that had never existed before. It was exciting to be a part of something groundbreaking. That said, I did miss performing. I missed the shows, the rehearsals, and the creative process of building something from scratch. The applause was great, sure, but I'd always loved the behind-the-scenes work even more, testing things out, tweaking routines, and practicing dance moves with a partner until everything clicked into place. There was nothing like that sense of creative flow.

Luckily, our apartment was within walking distance of Joe Tremaine's Dance Studio, so I made a point to take classes whenever I could. It felt good to reconnect with my dance roots. Joe's studio had already been the launching pad for so much, after all, it's where I met Joseph, who introduced me to Debbie, who led me to Princess Cruises. Dancers are a tight-knit group, always swapping tips about jobs, auditions, and people who know people. One day, someone mentioned a small agency looking for actors, so I thought, Why not? I scheduled a meeting with the William Felber Agency and, just like that, I had an agent!

I was officially part of the Hollywood audition circuit. Great, right? Well… not exactly. The agency sent me out on a handful of auditions, but the whole process turned out to be more frustrating than glamorous. The auditions always seemed to conflict with my job, and I never quite fit the mold of what producers wanted. I was short, reasonably cute (weren't we all at that age?), but I didn't have "model looks." Sure, I could sing and dance, but so could half the population of Los Angeles. "Hey, I played Peter in Peter Pan!" Yeah, big deal. This wasn't District Heights, Maryland. This was the Big League, and I was just one more grain of sand on L.A.'s endless beach.

Richard and I, along with every other aspiring actor in town, clung to our copies of Drama-logue like lifelines. This weekly publication was the actor's bible, packed with listings for everything from low-budget films and student projects to Equity, non-Equity, Dinner Theatre, and Community Theatre auditions. We scoured each issue, highlighters in hand, searching for the next big break, or, let's be honest, the next small break.

Richard and I both managed to snag parts in student films, which were mostly an excuse to have "actor" on our resumes. But Richard took it one step further, he booked a small role in a low-budget film where he played an Indian. (We're talking 1980s casting here. Sensitivity wasn't exactly top priority.)

I auditioned for that same film, but when it came time to take off our shirts, the casting director "thanked me" and sent me on my way. Richard, with his 6'3" frame, dark features, and dimpled chin, booked the part, of course. Did I mention I'm short?

One day, while flipping through Drama-logue, our weekly ritual, we both spotted a listing from the Burbank Theatre Guild. They were casting for Grease. We exchanged that classic "I'll-do-it-if-you-do-it" look and decided to audition. Neither of us had ever done the show, but we loved it, and with the rights newly available for non-professional productions, this was one of the first theaters to mount it. We had no idea what roles we'd be right for, but we figured, why not?

Joseph, my friend and talented pianist, offered to coach me for the audition. He suggested a cool idea. I'd stand on stage, croon a falsetto doo-wop a cappella intro, look dramatically at the pianist, say, "Hit it!" and launch into "Goodnight, Sweetheart." (Yes, the same falsetto I'd used in Peter Pan. Who knew it had staying power?) I don't remember what Richard sang, but we both booked the show!

I was cast as Sonny, the Italian greaser (thank you, community theater casting logic), and Richard was cast as Vince Fontaine, the sleazy radio DJ. The rehearsal process and performances turned out to be the best stage experience of my life. To this day, it's still one of my fondest memories.

The cast was a mix of professional actors and enthusiastic talent, and the show was a perfect showcase for everyone involved. Casting directors and agents packed the seats, and the energy was electric. Edgar Wood, the director, even asked if I'd help choreograph the show, and I jumped at the chance. Staging the second act opener, "Hand Jive," was a blast, I felt like I was back at sea directing the entertainment. The show was a huge hit, earning glowing reviews and leaving the cast with bonds that lasted for decades.

Even my parents came out to see it, which meant so much to me. And the friendships I made? Lifelong. Ross, Garry, Kathy, Bill, Debra, Sharonlee, every one of them amazing and talented. I still cherish the connections I made during that show.

At the time, life felt like a balancing act, but in the best way. I was interpreting for AT&T, earning great money, performing in Grease, dancing at Joe Tremaine's studio, auditioning for projects, and just… living. Sure, there were moments when I missed life at sea, the camaraderie, the adventure, but I was determined to make things work in L.A., and for the most part, I was succeeding.

About a year into my job at the TDD Center, I got a surprise call from Mick Nutter, one of my closest friends from my cruise ship days. Mick was a waiter on the Sun Princess, and we'd become fast friends thanks to our shared, gloriously warped sense of humor. Mick had the kind of laugh that was contagious, once he started, everyone around him would inevitably join in.

We'd been thick as thieves onboard, so when I had to switch ships, it was a sad day. But we'd promised to keep in touch, and true to his word, Mick was calling all the way from Bournemouth, England. Hearing his voice instantly brought back the laughter and warmth of those days at sea, and I couldn't wait to hear what he had to say.

So, Mick called with what he thought was a brilliant idea. "Fly to London," he said. "I'll pick you up, take you to Bournemouth, and then we'll hit some European countries." He made it sound so casual, like we'd just pop over to Paris for lunch. But how could I say no? I'd never been to Europe, and what better way to see it than with a local as my tour guide?

First things first, I had to clear it with Charlotte, my supervisor at the TDD Center. I hadn't taken a single vacation in a year, and when I floated the idea, she didn't hesitate. "Ask the others if they can handle the workload," she said. So, I did. Francine, Kayelle, and Jeanne all insisted I go. Two weeks, they said. Take the time. Have fun. I didn't need to be told twice.

I booked my ticket and landed at Gatwick Airport, where Mick and his flatmate George were waiting to greet me. Mick had never learned to drive, so George had been roped into chauffeur duty. Mick sat in the backseat, giving me the prime spot to soak up the English countryside during the three-hour drive to Bournemouth. I was sitting where the driver should sit, and we were driving on the wrong side of the road. This was all new to me!

The jetlag of my first transatlantic flight hit me like a ton of bricks, and instead of marveling at the quaint villages and rolling hills, I promptly passed out in the front seat. So much for the scenic route.

Once I recovered, though, I had the time of my life. We explored London, flew to Spain, took the train to Paris, Amsterdam, Italy, and back to England, all in six weeks! Ahem. Six weeks. Somewhere around week three, I stopped thinking about my two-week timeline entirely. I was having too much fun, and calling the office to check in felt... optional.

To top it all off, I made a detour on my way back to L.A., stopping in Washington, D.C., for a celebration at Gallaudet. They asked Janet and me to perform some of our songs for the crowd, which was an absolute thrill. Mom and Dad were there, too, and seeing them in the audience made the experience even more special.

Looking back, I suppose you could call me "young and a bit irresponsible." But in my defense, it was an exciting time. Europe had been a whirlwind of adventure, and capping it off at Gallaudet felt like the cherry on top. I just assumed everyone back at the TDD Center would be just as thrilled about my extended trip as I was.

While I was in D.C., I had all my rolls of film developed. This was the 80s, after all, and I couldn't wait to share the photos with everyone back at work. In my mind, I pictured myself holding court in the break room, passing around pictures of the Eiffel Tower and Buckingham Palace, while my co-workers ooh'd and aah'd over my tales of European escapades.

When the day finally came, I packed my lunch, my photos, and my excitement and hopped on the bus downtown. As I walked in through the back door of the office, one of the reps looked up, clearly startled.

"What are you doing here?" she asked.

Huh? "What do you mean, what am I doing here? I'm back!" I replied, confused but still chipper.

I strolled into the main office where the TDDs were displayed, grinning ear to ear, and announced, "I'm back! I have photos!"

Silence. You could've heard a pin drop. It was so quiet, one of the deaf clients could've heard a pin drop.

Uh-oh. Something was off. Where were the streamers? The balloons? The giant "WELCOME BACK BILL" banner I had vividly imagined?

"Hi, Bill," Charolotte said, her voice polite but cautious. "I have to say... I wasn't expecting to see you."

"Oh?" I replied, still holding out hope for some kind of warm welcome.

"Well," she continued, "we assumed you quit. You were gone so long, and, well, without a word, we just carried on with three interpreters instead of four… and we were fine."

Ouch.

I thought about asking if anyone wanted to see my photos, the Palace! The Eiffel Tower! The six weeks of spontaneous joy!, but even I could sense that this wasn't the moment. After a few awkward hugs, I turned around, lunch and photos still in hand, and slunk back out the same back door I had waltzed through moments earlier, my tail firmly between my legs.

The bus ride back to Studio City was brutal. Every bump in the road felt like a personal reminder of my foolishness. I didn't know what to do next. I couldn't believe how foolish I had been. It wasn't like I could keep blaming "youth" forever. I was in my 20s, I should've known better. But I didn't. I genuinely thought everyone would be happy to see me, eager to hear about my adventures, ready to gather around for a slideshow of my European antics. I hadn't stopped to think about how my absence might have impacted them. Selfish. That's the word. Selfish and ashamed.

By the time I walked past Joe Tremaine's Dance Studio, my usual sanctuary, I had no desire to step inside. Dancing felt impossible. The only thing I felt was fear, this gnawing, growing fear about what would come next.

When I got home, I dropped my lunch on the kitchen counter and tossed the unseen photos onto the table, their glossy stories of Paris and Amsterdam now just paperweights for my guilt. Richard was at work, and the apartment was eerily quiet. It was the kind of silence that made you confront yourself, which I wasn't exactly in the mood for.

After a few minutes of wallowing, I noticed the blinking red light on the answering machine. Remember those? Back then, there was nothing quite like the thrill of walking in and seeing that little beacon of hope. Someone had called. Maybe it was good news. Maybe life wasn't over.

There was one message. I pressed play.

"Hi Bill. This is Colleen at Princess. Can you please call me as soon as you can?"

Colleen Baldwin! Now there was a name that could bring a smile to any cruise staffer's face. She was Brian Carter's assistant and the unofficial problem-solver for anything and everything. If you needed to change a flight, get a message to Brian, or smooth over a crisis, Colleen was your girl. And unlike Brian, Colleen was always in a good mood, or at least she faked it masterfully.

I picked up the phone and called her back.

"Bill! Hi!" she said, cheerful as ever. "Thank you for calling back. We need you. There was a shake-up recently with the cruise staff, and we could really use your help. Would you consider coming back to work? We'll put you in the Pasadena studio ASAP to learn the new show, then fly you to San Juan to join the ship."

"Yes," I said, without hesitation.

She didn't need to sell me on it. I was ready. Colleen promised to follow up with the details once everything was finalized, but at that moment, I didn't care about logistics. I had a job again!

The timing couldn't have been more perfect. It felt like a lifeline had been tossed my way, and I wasn't about to let it slip through my fingers. I was employed.

I was back in my blue and whites, ready to embrace the high seas once more. This time, though, I had a new philosophy. Enjoy the ride. The first time I worked at sea, I spent half my energy plotting my escape, convinced I needed to "get serious" about my career. But this time, I had a revelation. What if I just had fun? Learn, grow, meet new people, and, most importantly, stop trying to outrun my own good luck.

One thing about life at sea, you've got a captive audience. It's basically networking on a floating hotel, where nobody can ghost you because they physically cannot leave. This method had worked wonders for me before, so why mess with a winning formula?

Then came the news. A brand-new ship was joining the Princess fleet. Not just any ship, the industry's newest, biggest, most technologically advanced wonder to ever grace the waves. And, as if the universe was winking at me, I was handpicked for its elite cruise staff.

Promotion time! I was stepping up from Assistant Cruise Director to the illustrious title of Deputy Cruise Director. This meant more responsibility, more money, and one step closer to becoming a Cruise Director. The chain of command would be Jim Everett as Cruise Director, me as Deputy, and Paul O'Laughlin as Assistant Cruise Director. Rounding out our entertainment team were four dancers: Susan, Lisa, Cindy, and Mary Ann. We were a dream team, or at least we would be once the ship actually existed.

Back in Studio City, life had its own kind of rhythm. Richard was still driving the Hondamatic, which we continued to share when I was in town. If there was an award for longest-running custody battle over a car, we would have been contenders.

During a break from the ship, I found myself in Ojai, visiting one of my favorite dancers, Heidi, at her father's house. We were both on leave, and since work friendships on a ship are forged in the fire of shared performances and just how odd it is to live at sea, our bond was strong. Years later, I would even sing at her wedding reception, a full-circle moment that, at the time, I never saw coming.

Heidi's sister had a 1978 BMW 320i for sale, and I was in love. With the car, that is. Sleek, classic, and just the right kind of impractical. It had everything I wanted. Style, speed, and a manual sunroof!

The only problem? The price tag was $7,000. My savings account laughed in my face. But where there's a will, there's a slightly awkward request for financial assistance. I marched into Brian Carter's office at Princess, full of purpose and just enough delusion to be convincing. "I want to buy a BMW," I announced. Brian leaned back in his chair, unimpressed. "Okay... good for you. What does that have to do with me?" "Well," I said, as if this was the most logical thing in the world, "I don't have all the money yet, and I was hoping you'd give me an advance on my pay for the next few months." Brian smirked. "It's good working at sea, isn't it? You deserve to be driving a BMW!" Just like that, the deal was sealed. The car was mine.

And what a car it was. Gray exterior, camel-colored leather interior, everything manual, from the roll-down windows to the sunroof that slid back with the kind of mechanical precision that made me feel like I was operating something far more sophisticated than just another '70s relic. But most importantly, I didn't have to share the Hondamatic anymore. Freedom smelled like gasoline and slightly worn leather.

While I was busy zipping around in my new (to me) Bavarian dream machine, my time onboard had taken a decidedly Italian turn. When I first started working on ships, the Brits treated me with indifference. The Italians, on the other hand, took me in as one of their own.

I became obsessed. Their style, their culture, their food, their cars, everything about them exuded effortless cool. They could wear a simple t-shirt and jeans and look like they were about to be photographed for the cover of L'Uomo Vogue. Meanwhile, I'd put on the same thing and look like I was about to ask if you wanted fries with that.

Determined to crack the code, I started studying Italian, hanging out with them every chance I could. After the shows and cabarets, I'd find myself in their quarters, drinking Spumante and practicing my language skills. And let me tell you, after a couple of glasses of wine, I was fluent. Or at least, I thought I was.

The truth is, I may never have looked Italian, but I sure felt it. And sometimes, that's all that matters.

The new ship was under construction in Helsinki, Finland, and it was set to be a game-changer. The Royal Princess. Even the name had a regal flair, like a floating Buckingham Palace.

We were getting more and more excited as the details trickled in. This ship was going to be the greatest thing afloat, a gleaming masterpiece complete with an actual professional theater. And when I say professional, I mean dressing rooms. Real, actual dressing rooms. Up until then, costume changes had been an exercise in speed and spatial awareness. The makeshift dressing areas on the older ships were small sections we had to cordon off with curtains, which meant eight people crammed together, frantically swapping outfits like some sort of manic, nautical Project Runway challenge. If you've never experienced the scent of gin and tonic seeping through sweaty pores in close quarters, I assure you, it is not a fragrance anyone should bottle.

The Sun, Island, and Pacific Princess? They suddenly felt like rinky-dink bath toys compared to the soon-to-be-launched Royal Princess.

Back in LA on leave, Richard told me he was ready for a change from Universal. He wanted something new, something different. Richard had the kind of personality that could charm just about anyone, exactly the kind of person you wanted around passengers who might be on their fifth piña colada before lunch. I introduced him to Brian Carter, hoping there might be a spot for him on the cruise staff.

Brian said he didn't need anyone new on the Entertainment Staff. But then he took one look at Richard and had a lightbulb moment. The new ship would need a Fitness Director, and Richard was in great shape. Just like that, Richard was hired. We were going to be shipmates. Again. It was almost too good to be true.

We had been friends, then roommates in DC, then roommates in LA. We had shared apartments, cars, and more than a few absurd adventures. And now we were about to sail the world together.

The flight to Helsinki was long, but excitement kept me going. That, and possibly a few of those little bottles. I landed in Finland, ready to start this grand new chapter, except my luggage had other plans.

My blues and whites? Gone. My tuxedo? Missing. My show shoes? Who knows. I was standing in the Helsinki airport with nothing but the clothes on my back and a rapidly dawning realization that I was going to have to get creative.

Enter my fellow crew members, who, in a true show of shipboard camaraderie, started loaning me their clothes. At some point, I think I even ended up wearing a few things from the dancers. I had never felt more flexible!

Thankfully, I had the foresight to carry my coat with me, because Helsinki in November is not for the underdressed. Each day was a relentless parade of gray, cold, and wet, a perfect setting for a Scandinavian crime drama, but slightly less ideal for a cruise rehearsal. And as if the weather wasn't dreary enough, we had two weeks of relentless construction noise as the ship took shape around us. The soundtrack of my life was now an endless chorus of hammering, drilling, and the occasional shouted order in Finnish.

Every morning, I made a hopeful pilgrimage to the Purser's desk.

"Has my luggage arrived?"

"Not yet."

By the second week, I was starting to accept my fate as a sartorial scavenger. And then, miracle of miracles, my bags finally arrived. I had never been so happy to wear my own underwear.

England, here we come!

Now, I don't know about you, but when I board a ship, I like to assume it's been, you know, in the water before. A test run, a practice lap, just a little something to confirm that it floats. But the Royal Princess? She was brand new, freshly built, and about to take her maiden voyage. Everyone was a little on edge, but I figured the builders had done this before. Finland seemed like the kind of place that knew how to construct things that wouldn't sink. So, I put my faith in Scandinavian engineering and hoped for the best.

That said, the ship was a disaster zone. The inside was still under construction when we set sail for England, meaning we were basically rehearsing our performances in an active worksite. Imagine trying to execute a perfect jazz routine while dodging power drills and navigating around stacks of drywall. To make matters worse, Finnish announcements blared over the loudspeakers at random intervals, which I could only assume were messages like, "Please do not trip over the extension cords. Management is not responsible for injuries sustained during a high kick."

Rehearsing for the shows was a challenge, not only because of the construction chaos, but also because we suddenly had a much bigger stage to work with. Princess Cruises had pulled out all the stops, and the performance space was spectacular. This meant reworking everything, which is where our choreographers, Gretchen Goertz and Kathy Orme, came in.

Gretchen and Kathy were brilliant. Former dance partners turned powerhouse directors, they ran a tight ship (pun very much intended). They knew how to whip a cast into shape and make every show feel like Broadway-on-the-high-seas. They also became lifelong friends of mine, though at the time, I was mostly focused on staying in their good graces and not being responsible for a badly timed lift that sent a dancer flying into the orchestra pit.

The entertainment on Princess Cruises had a reputation for being the best at sea, and Gretchen and Kathy were the reason why. They had impossibly high standards, and we loved them for it.

By the time we arrived in Southampton, the entire ship was a frenzy of last-minute preparations. We had two weeks before the big event, our christening. This was the moment the ship would officially be welcomed into service, and it had to be perfect. More importantly, it had to be ready for our first batch of British passengers, who would board for the maiden voyage from Southampton to Miami.

And speaking of excitement, there was another reason why this christening was a big deal. It wasn't just any ship launching, it was The Royal Princess. And when you name a ship The Royal Princess, you need a royal princess to christen it.

Diana, Princess of Wales.

The whole ship was buzzing. Diana was the epitome of grace, style, and global stardom, and she was going to be there, standing on our deck, holding our champagne bottle, making our ship feel like it had truly arrived. It was almost too much to process.

So while the final screws were being tightened and the last coats of paint were drying, we were all giddy with anticipation. The Royal Princess was about to make its grand debut, and we were about to witness history.

I had been chosen to be part of the organizing staff, which meant I was now in daily meetings with the Captain, Deputy Captain, top-ranking officers, and an assortment of other VIPs who were responsible for making sure this event went off perfectly. I had also been tapped as the Entertainment Staff representative in the Receiving Line. In other words, I was about to shake hands with actual royalty. No pressure.

The planning meetings were relentless. Every second of the day had to be accounted for, from HRH's (Her Royal Highness, apparently, this was the only acceptable way to refer to her in all official documents) arrival to her final departure. She would be sharing the day with the President of Finland, a nod to the country that had built our magnificent new ship.

Meanwhile, frogmen were diving around the hull, security was in a constant state of high alert, and we were all being drilled on royal protocol as if failing to execute a proper greeting would result in immediate exile. It was a lot.

The instructions were repeated so many times I could recite them in my sleep. Do not touch a member of the Royal Family unless they extend a hand. If she does, bow your head slightly and say, "Your Royal Highness, it's a pleasure to meet you." If she's being introduced to a woman, that woman must curtsy. (I did not practice my curtsy. I had heard she had a sense of humor, but I figured that might be pushing it.)

At one point, I found myself thinking, she's not my princess. Not in an anti-monarchy kind of way, just a simple reminder that she was a human being, like me, and there was no reason to be nervous. I mean, really. I had worked with demanding cruise passengers. I had danced in tight spaces next to sweaty gin-and-tonic-soaked colleagues. I had been thrown onto a brand-new, still-under-construction ship and somehow survived. What was one polite exchange with Princess Diana?

And yet, as I studied the meticulously scheduled itinerary (for the hundredth time), I noticed an additional duty assigned to me.

After our official handshake in the Receiving Line, she would proceed to lunch with the Captain, President Koivisto, and other dignitaries. My job? To fetch Her Highness when lunch concluded.

Let's break this down: Meet her in the Receiving Line. Watch her head off to an elegant lunch while I, presumably, ate something less elegant elsewhere. Retrieve her post-lunch and escort her up the stairs, where her Lady-in-Waiting would then guide her to the restroom. I could handle that.

The big day arrived, and, despite my previous bravado, I was a wee bit nervous. And by wee bit, I mean my palms had basically turned into small swimming pools. The entire ship was in full royal-visit mode. Helicopters hovered overhead, frogmen lurked below, and every crew member was decked out in their crispest uniforms.

Then, as if scripted by the BBC for maximum cinematic effect, the royal train carrying Princess Diana and her entourage pulled into view.

Outside the ship, the streets were lined with British schoolchildren, all enthusiastically waving their little Union Jack flags like they'd been training for this moment their whole lives. A band played next to the podium where Princess Diana would later deliver her remarks before smashing a bottle of champagne against the ship's hull.

The excitement was palpable. The Royal Princess was about to be christened by the Royal Princess. And I was about to be part of a moment that would be replayed on television screens across the world.

No pressure at all.

I had never been to a ship's christening before, so I wasn't exactly sure how the whole thing worked. Did she just march up to the ship, bottle in hand, and chuck it at the hull like a contestant in some sort of aristocratic strongman competition? Because that ship was far from the dock, and while Diana seemed capable of many things, I wasn't convinced she had the arm strength of a seasoned cricket player.

Would she lob it? Would it be undignified? What if she missed? What if it just bounced off the side of the ship like an awkward champagne-soaked tennis ball? Would there be backup bottles, or was this a one-shot deal? And if the bottle did break, was there an official protocol for how many seconds of polite applause were required?

I was already nervous, and now my brain had decided to spiral into a full-on overthinking event.

The entire ship was lined with crew members, all craning their necks to catch a glimpse of HRH as she made her way from the train to the podium. Cameras were locked and loaded, ready to capture a royal moment worthy of a souvenir plate (of which I have!).

And then, there she was.

Tall. Stately. Effortlessly elegant. Waving at the sea of school-children and all of us perched on the decks like overly enthusiastic seagulls. She was dressed entirely in red, right down to a stylish red and white sailor-style hat. Not an actual sailor's hat, mind you. Hers was the kind of hat that I'm sure cost more than my car and was one-of-a-kind.

I snapped a few photos, then forced myself to stop and just watch. Take it in. And this is where my brain, true to form, fixated on something completely unnecessary. Her feet.

Her feet looked enormous. This had to be an optical illusion, some combination of her tall frame and the way she walked with her feet in "first position," like a dancer. And of course, she was a dancer, so it made sense. But still, my mind latched onto it, deciding that of all the details to analyze about Princess Diana, her foot placement was the most pressing. I'll get a closer look when I meet her, I thought. Because obviously, that's what one does when in the presence of royalty, conduct a mental investigation into their feet.

This was a monumental day for Diana as well. It was her first public appearance without Prince Charles, and with little Prince Harry having just been born, all eyes were on her. The royal family was undoubtedly watching closely, ready to assess her performance with the same level of scrutiny usually reserved for Westminster dog shows.

She approached the podium, looking poised and polished, and in that unmistakable, perfectly clipped Royal Family accent, she declared, "I christen thee Royal Princess. God bless her and all who sail in her." And that was it. Short, sweet, and straight to the point. Then came the moment I had been waiting for, the bottle. Instead of hurling it like a medieval knight storming a castle, she simply pulled a lever. The bottle, attached to a rope (because of course, there was a rope), swung gracefully through the air and smashed against the ship's hull. It broke. Success! That was it. No dramatics. No close calls. Just a dignified swing, a satisfying smash, and one very well-christened ship. Captain John Young, my favorite captain, by far, then escorted her aboard for a grand tour, which would culminate in the lounge, where we were all lined up, waiting for our moment. If she extended a hand, I would be ready. And, perhaps, I'd finally get to solve the mystery of those feet.

The lineup was a carefully curated cross-section of ship life, featuring representatives from every department. There was a bedroom steward, a wine steward, a bartender, a laundry worker, you get the idea. The whole Royal Navy of hospitality.

I was second to last in line, which meant I had plenty of time to marinate in my own nerves. While everyone else was focused on standing perfectly still and exuding an air of dignified calm, I was busy sweating through my uniform and experiencing an existential crisis in real-time.

All of us in the lineup had our necks craned to the left, watching as Princess Diana made her way down the line, meeting our fellow shipmates one by one. It was a fascinating process, like watching a conveyor belt of politeness.

Captain Young was her human GPS, gently guiding her without actually touching her (touching was a no-no, remember). His role was to announce each person, at which point Diana would extend her hand, the person would curtsy or nod, deliver their pre-rehearsed line, and she might say a word or two before moving on. Efficiency at its finest.

She was getting closer. My inner monologue was not helping. Okay, Bill, keep it together. She's just a person. She's not your princess. She's not your boss. You don't even live here. This is fine. This is totally fine. Oh wow, she really is beautiful. She is always smiling. She's going to be queen one day. I'm about to meet the future Queen of England. Ohhhhh Myyyyy Goddddd. And then, before I could formulate another panicked thought, she was in front of me. "Your Royal Highness, this is Bill Pugin representing the Entertainment Staff." Time slowed. My training kicked in. I knew exactly what I was supposed to do. She raised her hand ever so gracefully, expecting me to gently take just her fingertips in mine. A delicate, refined exchange of civility. A mere whisper of a handshake. That was the plan. That is not what happened.

Instead, I grabbed her entire hand with both of mine and pumped her arm up and down like a farmer trying to coax water from a very reluctant well.

"Oh my god, it is such an honor to meet you!" I blurted out, my voice suddenly a full octave higher, words firing out of my mouth in an uncontrollable staccato rhythm.

There was no nod. No composed, well-rehearsed line. Just…
me, aggressively shaking the future Queen of England's hand like
I was trying to resuscitate it.

Diana, to her credit, did not recoil in horror. Instead, she
looked momentarily surprised before breaking into a dazzling
smile. "Oh! An American!" she exclaimed.

Out-of-body experience, party of one.

I was floating above myself now, watching this unfold like a spec-
tator at my own personal disaster. Well, Bill, it's been a good run.
You had a career. You had a promising future. Hope you enjoy
your new life as a guy who used to work on ships before being
immediately deported for improper royal etiquette.

I turned to Captain Young for reassurance. There was none.
He was frozen. Mouth open. Expressionless. As if his brain had
short-circuited and he was actively rebooting. This is it, I thought.
I'm going to be fired before lunchtime. And then, miraculously,
the best thing happened. The princess kept talking to me.

I knew she loved actors and entertainers, that she was often
spotted in the West End seeing shows. She had been a kindergarten teacher, a "regular gal," a non-royal who had suddenly become one. Maybe, just maybe, she wasn't horrified by my over-
enthusiastic handshake.

"Yes, I'm American," I said, regaining some composure. "How
could you tell?" She laughed, an actual, full-on laugh. "How did
you find yourself on a British ship then?" she asked. I shrugged.

"Well, I auditioned. They liked me, and here I am!" And just like that, I had survived my royal encounter. Barely.

While we were deep in conversation, me, a humble cruise ship entertainer, and her, the most famous woman on the planet, I became acutely aware that the entire lineup had now subtly (or not-so-subtly) shifted their gaze to the right. Everyone was watching.

Meanwhile, poor Captain Young, ever the professional, was doing his best to send me silent but very loud body language cues. A slight lean forward. A subtle shift in stance. A desperate flick of the eyes toward the clock. All translating to: For the love of God, Bill, wrap it up. We have a schedule.

But when Diana kept chatting, he gave up. And here's the real kicker, I completely forgot to look at her feet. All that buildup, all that curiosity, and now? Nothing. I was too busy staring at her face.

I mean, it was the face. The most photographed face in the world. And up close? Absolutely flawless. A soft glow, like she had her own built-in lighting team. And that thin line of blue eyeliner under her eyes made her already impossibly blue eyes even bluer.

Then, as if she had all the time in the world, she kept going.

"What kind of shows do you do onboard?" she asked.

Oh, we're still talking! I haven't been dismissed yet!

"We do mini production shows of popular Broadway and West End musicals," I said, regaining my professional composure. "Shows like Fiddler on the Roof, for example. We also have a fantastic team of writers and choreographers who produce original shows. You'd like them. You should book a cruise and see us!"

She laughed out loud again. Okay, now this is getting surreal. Was I actually charming the future Queen of England? Was I about to invite her to an open mic night in the crew bar? For a moment, I had the ridiculous urge to say, "Go on, Diana, kick off your shoes, let's grab a Guinness and talk shop." "So, you keep long hours, do you?" she asked, still engaged. "Yes, indeed," I replied, trying to sound casual, as if my brain wasn't currently doing cartwheels. "You must drink a lot of coffee, I presume." "I do," I said. "Except here, I drink a lot of tea!" Oh God. What was that?

It was the verbal equivalent of tripping over my own feet. But miraculously, miraculously, she laughed again. Honestly, at this point, I felt like we were best friends, and she was about to ask for my number so we could continue this conversation over brunch.

And then, like a perfectly timed party pooper, Captain Young stepped in. This time, he nearly brushed her shoulder, a very bold move in the "don't touch the royal" rulebook, and said, "Your Highness, we must be moving on. The dining room is waiting to serve you an incredible lunch." Oh, come on, Captain. Talk about putting a crimp in my schmoozing style. Diana turned back to me, smiling. "Very nice to meet you, Bill." And just like that, she moved on. She reached the last person in line, said nothing, and was gone. And there I was, left standing with a lingering warmth in the air where she had just been, completely sure of one thing:

Princess Diana and I were obviously best friends now. What happened next reminded me of the grand finale of every Miss America pageant, the moment when all the contestants abandon their carefully poised disappointment and swarm the winner in an explosion of hugs, tears, and hairspray. Only, in this case, I was the winner, and my sash read "Accidentally Charmed the Future Queen of England." The entire lineup, everyone, rushed me. The Pakistani painter, the Chinese laundry worker who didn't speak a word of English, the bartender, the bedroom steward. Suddenly, I was the most interesting person on the ship. "What did she say?" "What were you talking about?" "Why was she laughing?" "Why did the captain look like he was about to keelhaul you?" It was a blur. One minute, I was just another crew member in line, and the next, I was apparently the ship's official Royal Correspondent. But there was no time to bask in my newfound status. I had a job to do. I was assigned to wait outside the dining room and escort Diana up the staircase after lunch. Simple enough, right? I just had to stand there, look presentable, and not do anything to land myself in maritime history as The Guy Who Messed Up a Royal Escort. She emerged, flanked by Finland's President, Mauno Koivisto, his wife, the captain, and a member of her personal entourage. A perfectly rehearsed diplomatic procession. And then, Diana turned to me.

She reached out, slid her hand into the crook of my arm (definitely not in the protocol manual, but who was I to argue?), and said, "Hello, Bill. Nice to see you again."

I could've fainted. Right there, dramatically and with gusto. But unfortunately, this was not the moment to collapse into a heap of royal-induced euphoria. I had one very specific task. Walk her up the stairs without incident. So I focused.

There were two sweeping staircases that curved up to the upper level, with elevators in the middle. The entire area was blocked off for photographers, who had positioned themselves like paparazzi vultures, ready to capture every second of this VIP procession.

Click. Click. Click. The sound of cameras snapping was relentless. Well, I thought, if they're going to take photos, I might as well give them something to work with.

I walked slowly. Elegantly. I was now, officially, a part of history. Princess Diana, arm in arm with me, the President of Finland just a few steps behind. If ever there was a time to practice good posture, this was it.

At the top of the staircase, I passed her off to her Lady in Waiting. Mission accomplished. I stepped aside, standing by the glass doors to open them for her as she left. She turned back to me, smiled, and said, "Thanks, Bill."

And then, just like that, she was gone, off to finish the rest of her scheduled visit. I stood there for a moment, watching her walk away, knowing that no matter what else happened in my life, I would always have this moment.

Princess Diana knew my name. And for one afternoon, I had been part of the story.

Years later, I met a man who worked for the royal family at Buckingham Palace. Naturally, I seized the opportunity to tell him my now-legendary Day with Diana story, complete with dramatic reenactments (the handshake! the laughter! the stairway procession!). Then, I asked him the million-dollar question.

"Any chance I could get copies of the official photos? You know, the ones where it's just me and Diana, best friends forever, strolling arm in arm like we were about to grab a pint at the pub?"

He sighed, the way people do when they have to be the bearer of bad news. "Every photo taken by photographers other than paparazzi must be approved by the palace," he explained. "If there were any with you in them, they probably weren't even developed."

Not even developed. It was as if my very existence had been politely erased from royal history. He must have felt bad for me, though, because later that year, I received a Christmas card from The Royal Household.

Just a card with a handwritten note saying it was nice to have met me. It was the same card, apparently, that the Queen sent out to everyone on her list. I considered it a consolation prize worthy of framing.

The day of the christening had come to an end, and collectively, we all exhaled. The bottle had broken, nobody had slipped, and everyone remained upright and unscathed. Success! I was finally ready to settle down, maybe even relax for a second.

Then, I was summoned to the captain's office.

Captain John Young was a legend. A first-rate captain, a natural leader, and a man who could command a ship while delivering the driest, most wicked one-liners you'd ever hear.

He once announced at a cocktail party, "This ship is being run by the British, and you will be fed by the Italians. Aren't you glad it isn't the other way 'round?" Iconic.

He and I had even performed a skit together on the Pacific Princess a couple of times, where I had to jump up and down on one leg (with my other leg tied behind my back - wearing a raincoat so it looked like I had only one leg) while he delivered a dramatic soliloquy. I know that sounds completely bizarre, and frankly, it was. But it was a crowd favorite.

Captain Young was always amazed at how long I could jump on one leg, deliver my lines, and remain in character. "I don't do this skit often," he once told me, "because I've never found anyone who could jump that long without toppling over."

Ah yes, that and keeping a basket on my head. Just two of my many talents. Anyway, I loved this guy. But as I walked into his office, I had no idea if the feeling was mutual. He looked up from his desk, his face unreadable. "You broke all protocol." I swallowed. "I know. And I'm truly sorry, but," "And she loved it." Wait. What? "She was happy," he continued. "And that was the most important thing. Had it been the Queen, we'd be having a very different conversation." Then he leaned back in his chair and smiled. "This is why you were hired. And one of the reasons you were picked for this ship. Job well done." Did I mention how much I loved that guy?

The ship was still a work in progress when the passengers arrived for the inaugural cruise. Crew members scurried around, adding last-minute plants and hanging art, trying to make it look like we hadn't just finished assembling the place with an Allen wrench and sheer optimism.

Meanwhile, the rest of us were still figuring out how to navigate the ship ourselves, which made it especially entertaining that we were also expected to lead tours for the new guests.

I voiced my concerns to Jim, our Cruise Director, in the most diplomatic way possible.

"This is insane." There were hundreds of passengers and only a handful of us. The logistics made zero sense. Half the guests would get bored and wander off halfway through, which would inevitably lead to an impromptu game of Where's Margaret? as we tried to track down rogue retirees lost somewhere between the casino and the buffet.

To make matters worse, we kept bumping into each other's groups, then racing back to the lobby to pick up the next batch of unsuspecting passengers. Classic Jim.

Jim was an idea machine. And when I say "idea machine," I mean constant, unstoppable, caffeine-fueled inspiration with absolutely no off switch.

One time, at 2 a.m., he woke me up because he had a brilliant idea. "We should put balloons in the public bathrooms!" "Why?" "… I don't know yet."

Things often didn't make sense with Jim. He never slept. He'd just stand around, coming up with things we should do, and then expect us to execute them as if he were some kind of benevolent (and slightly unhinged) cruise ship deity.

Occasionally, I'd remind him of one of his more out-there ideas, and he'd have absolutely no recollection of ever saying it. Poor Jim. I suggested he switch to decaf.

Trials at Sea & Homecoming

The Cruise from Hell

The trip to Miami was a disaster. A violent storm hit, and it didn't just last for a few choppy hours, it went on for days. The sea was so rough that fish were literally found flopping around on the balconies of the upper decks. UPPER. DECKS. How? Did they leap up there out of sheer terror? Were they trying to warn us? The waves were that high. Since this was the ship's maiden voyage, we had no real idea how she'd handle under pressure, and it wasn't long before people started tossing around the T word. (Titanic.) Not great. The shows had to be canceled because it was far too dangerous to attempt anything resembling choreography. You don't truly appreciate gravity until you try to pirouette on a stage that's actively attempting to hurl you into the audience. We were lucky that our 700 passengers were British, because if they had been American, there would have been full-scale panic, lawyers on speed dial, and threats of lawsuits before we even reached the halfway point. In all my years at sea, I had never suffered from seasickness. Not once. My only affliction was the occasional dull headache, and this headache lasted the entire trip. To make matters worse, the storm delayed our arrival in Miami by two or three days. We were running out of food. At one point, in what I thought was a very practical suggestion, I proposed cooking the fish we had found on the balconies. Nobody laughed. They thought I was joking. I wasn't.

Here's an article describing the whole event:

November 19, 1984

"The record-setting cruise ship Royal Princess embarked on her maiden voyage, departing from Southampton, England, for Miami, Florida, with approximately 700 passengers on board. The transatlantic trip began only four days after the British-registered vessel, which had been built for Princess Cruises by the Finnish corporation Wärtsilä at its Helsinki shipyard, was christened at Southampton by Diana, Princess of Wales.

Hundreds of invited children were in attendance to watch Diana crack a bottle of Krug champagne against the ship. Other dignitaries at the ceremony included Mauno Koivisto, President of Finland. "Diana, wearing a bright red suit and hat, was launching her first ship," reported the Canadian Press news agency. "She pulled a white lever to release the specially doctored bottle which broke successfully against the white hull."

The Royal Princess, at a cost of $165 million, was the most expensive passenger ship built up to that time. It also had the distinction of being the first cruise ship to have only outside passenger cabins (oceanview rooms lining the edges of the vessel) rather than any inside passenger cabins (rooms built in the middle of a deck and without windows or other outlets for outdoor views)

The ship left Southampton for her maiden voyage shortly after 1:00 p.m. on November 19, and the rough conditions that she soon encountered invited comparisons with an ill-fated ship from more than seven decades earlier. A Knight-Ridder Newspapers article reported, "The Titanic ran into ice. The Royal Princess ran into 60-knot [111.1-kilometers-per-hour] winds with the blow of a hurricane. Both were on their maiden trans-Atlantic voyages from Southampton, England, to America. Both were being called the most luxurious, expensive ships ever built. Both ran into a little bad luck their first time out."

As the Knight-Ridder account so helpfully confirmed, the Royal Princess, unlike the Titanic, remained afloat.

This was, in large part, thanks to Captain John Young, who expertly maneuvered the ship out of harm's way, steering her south past the Azores before finally turning west toward Miami. A perfectly executed "let's not go down in maritime history for all the wrong reasons" strategy.

Of course, this little emergency detour meant we arrived in Miami two days late. The British passengers, true to form, handled it all with stoic grace, at least, until they stepped onto dry land. Then, they stumbled off the gangway like disoriented newborn deer, wobbling and squinting into the Florida sun, no doubt questioning every life choice that had led them onto that ship.

As soon as we were released from duty, I bolted. First stop was the ground. I kissed it. We had been through things. Second stop was a payphone. (Remember those?) I called Mom and Dad, ready to deliver my survival report. "I'm alive! Oh, and also, I hung out with Princess Diana."

If the British Inaugural Cruise had been a saga of storm-induced trauma, the American Inaugural Cruise was shaping up to be something completely different.

Not only were we embarking American passengers (God help us all), but we were also bringing aboard the entire cast and crew of The Love Boat.

Even though we were sailing on the Royal Princess, for the purposes of television magic, it would still be called the Pacific Princess. No one wanted to confuse the audience at home. ("Wait, there's more than one boat?! Inconceivable!")

This was, without a doubt, one of the most exciting cruises I had ever experienced. For starters, let's talk about the guest list. Lana Turner. Stewart Granger. Hayley Mills. Linda Purl. Anne Baxter. Menudo.

Yes, Menudo.

And among them? A 12-year-old Ricky Martin. Just a tiny, adorable, not-yet-shaking-his-bon-bon Ricky, the youngest member of the group. (We had no idea at the time that we were witnessing the early days of a future international superstar. We just thought, "Wow, that kid can sing.")

The stakes were high. New shows. New stage. New theatre. And now, a celebrity-filled audience. We had to be on. Thankfully, filming went off without a hitch. So did the weather. And the voyage through the Panama Canal. By the time we reached Los Angeles, the whole thing had been chef's kiss perfection. But the real show was our grand arrival.

As we sailed into LA Harbor in San Pedro, we were escorted by multiple fireboats, shooting water high into the air in dramatic fountains. Helicopters buzzed overhead. The docks were packed with press, cameras flashing, reporters eager to capture the moment.

The newest, biggest, most modern ship afloat had arrived, filled with celebrities, The Love Boat cast, and one very exhausted but thrilled entertainment team. It was a Hollywood-level spectacle. And it was great fun to be a part of it.

Another adventure from my time at sea took place in the Caribbean.

We were docked in St. Thomas, and I had a few hours to kill before I was needed back onboard. With no particular plans, I wandered into Cardow Jewelers to visit my friend Chuck Smith, the store manager.

"I'm bored," I announced, plopping down like an overgrown child who had just finished all his chores and was now demanding entertainment.

Chuck, being a man of solutions, had an idea. "I'll drive you up to The Castle," he said. When someone casually offers to take you to a castle, you say yes.

The Castle was a real castle, perched at the top of a mountain, overlooking all of St. Thomas, the harbor, and the endless stretch of sea beyond. It was owned by the same person who owned Cardow Jewelers, because apparently, when you sell a lot of diamonds, you reward yourself with medieval-style real estate. The estate was used for VIP events and had played host to dignitaries, celebrities, and now, me, a guy who just happened to be bored on a Friday.

Chuck mentioned that his friend Bob and Bob's wife, Mary, were staying at The Castle and assured me they wouldn't mind if I hung out for a bit. So up the mountain we went.

The Castle was stunning. The kind of place where you half-expect someone to hand you a goblet of wine and declare you the heir to a long-lost throne. Chuck made the introductions, made sure I was settled, and then, just like that, drove away, leaving me with Bob and Mary, two people I had never met in my life.

Luckily, they couldn't have been nicer. Bob immediately offered me a scotch and soda, which, considering it was still morning, felt like an interesting choice. Naturally, I accepted. (When in Rome, or in this case, a mountaintop Caribbean castle...)

We settled in, drinks in hand, and Bob began peppering me with questions. He wanted to know everything, what life was like at sea, how I got into entertainment, how I got into sign language interpreting. He was genuinely curious, which made for easy conversation.

There was something warm and engaging about him. The kind of person you instantly like. At one point, I joked, "Are you a professional interviewer?" He laughed. "No, just a curious person. It helps in my work." "Oh? What do you do?" "I'm a writer. I write books." I took a sip of my scotch, nodding as if I were making polite conversation at a PTA meeting. "Books? Anything I might have read?" Bob smirked. "Do you travel a lot in airports?" "Uh... yeah?" "Then you've probably seen my books there." A few beats of silence. And that's how I found out I had just spent the afternoon drinking scotch with Robert Ludlum. Robert Ludlum. The man who had written 27 best-selling thrillers, translated into 33 languages, sold in over 40 countries. The mastermind behind The Bourne Identity and countless other books that millions of people devoured worldwide. I had never heard of him. And I think he loved that. I didn't gush. I didn't ask him to sign anything. I wasn't a fanboy. I was just some guy drinking scotch in his borrowed castle, treating him like a regular person. A few weeks later, while flying out of San Juan, I spotted The Bourne Identity at the airport bookstore. I bought it. And then I read all the Bourne books. And then I watched all the movies.

And just like that, I had another story to add to my ever-growing collection of "Oh, that? Just another casual brush with greatness in my young, absurdly charmed life."

I had moved again.

This time, I was living with Brian in his adorable townhouse in Encinitas, a laid-back beach town in North County San Diego. It was the kind of place where people surfed at sunrise, rode their bikes to taco stands, and generally looked like they had figured out the meaning of life. I, on the other hand, did not surf, did not skateboard, and was growing increasingly restless.

Brian, lovely as he was, probably wouldn't mind having his small space to himself again. My BMW was still parked in his garage (did I ever let him drive it?), but it was time to move on.

So, naturally, I packed up and moved in with a friend in Van Nuys.

Yes, back in the Valley.

I felt like I should be in Los Angeles, where all the action was happening. And by "action," I mean traffic, smog, and questionable life decisions.

My friend Lowell Steiger was thrilled to have a roommate, mostly because it meant someone else would be around to help take care of his dachshund, Spiker. (Priorities, people.)

The move also meant I could start up classes again at Joe Tremaine's and be ready to rejoin the ship when the time came.

Speaking of Being Restless…

I had met George Goodstein a few years earlier when he and his mother took an Alaskan cruise. He was a physician from

Portland, Oregon, and when he invited me up for a visit during Oktoberfest, I thought, Why not?

I had never been to Portland. I had time. It sounded fun.

So off I went, and what I found was a city bathed in shockingly perfect weather, blue skies, crisp October air, and none of the endless gray, drizzly hipster gloom I had always associated with the Pacific Northwest.

George introduced me to his friend Barb, and the three of us spent the weekend drinking wine, exploring the city, and laughing more than I had in ages.

At some point between pints of beer at Oktoberfest, and deep discussions about life choices, I casually mentioned that I was living in Van Nuys, constantly battling traffic and smog. One of the things I loved about being at sea was the fresh air, the wide-open space, and the glorious absence of cars honking at each other for no reason.

Since Princess would fly me wherever I needed to join the ship, I wasn't tied down to LA. This is when George and Barb had their lightbulb moment. "Why not live in Portland?" "It's fun," they said. "It's smaller than LA," they assured me. "It has great coffee," Barb added, as if that was the ultimate selling point.

Then Barb threw in the kicker, she was restless too. She had a great dog named Willa, a house full of furniture (I, despite my many moves, still only owned bedroom furniture), and a brilliant idea. "Let's find a place together! It'll be so much fun!"

I flew back to LA, walked into the apartment, and casually informed Lowell that "I'm moving to Portland!" Lowell was, shall we say, less than thrilled. But it all worked out. He survived. Spiker survived. We're still great friends to this day.

And so, with a U-Haul attached to the BMW, I made my way north, ready for my fresh start in the Pacific Northwest. Then I arrived. And, um… What happened to the blue sky? I never saw it again.

Barb had managed to find us a house in Northeast Portland. Not just any house, a beautiful house, one that had even been featured in Sunset Magazine. It was charming, it was picturesque, it was everything a person moving to Portland could possibly want. So, I moved in.

Well, technically, my bedroom furniture moved in, because that's all I owned. I set it up, sat on the bed, looked around at my very empty but magazine-worthy surroundings, and waited for the weekend.

Barb was scheduled to arrive on Saturday with the moving van, her furniture, and her dog, Willa. In the meantime, I had the house to myself, just me, my bed, and the occasional Sunset Magazine-induced delusion that my life was about to become a sophisticated Pacific Northwest dream.

Reality Check

It never stopped raining.

Portland, it turned out, had exactly one sunny day per year, and I had already used mine up on my Oktoberfest visit. The sky was a permanent shade of gray, the air was damp, and my car, my beautiful BMW, was pelted with eggs twice for the crime of having California plates.

Apparently, Portlanders were not thrilled about Californians moving in and "California-izing" their city. (I was not a real estate developer! I was not opening a juice bar! I was just trying to exist!)

To make matters worse, I called George, one of the two people I knew in Portland, to let him know I had arrived. "Oh, hey!" he said. "Yeah, so, I just accepted a job at a hospital in Philadelphia." ...Excuse me?

I now officially knew one person in Portland. And she hadn't even arrived yet. Saturday arrives. I spent all morning watching the window, waiting for the moving van, for Barb, for Willa. Finally, Barb pulled up. No van. No Willa. Instead, she walked up the front path carrying a bottle of wine and two glasses. Something felt... off.

I opened the door, fully prepared to say, "Hey, where's the van?" but before I could get the words out, she started crying. Sobbing.

I stood there, in my furniture-less, Sunset Magazine-featured home, unable to even offer her a seat (because again, NO FURNITURE), and just let her get it out. And then she hit me with it. She couldn't move in. Because. She. Thought. The. House. Was. Haunted. Let Me Get This Straight...

I had given up my perfectly good apartment with Lowell. I had packed a U-Haul. I had driven to Portland. I had unloaded my bedroom furniture. I had installed a landline (because this was back when people had to do that). I had found out George had moved to Philadelphia. And now, Barb wasn't moving in because she felt the house was haunted.

I lasted in Portland a total of eight days. Barb's father worked for an airline, and after hearing the sad, bizarre tale of my eight-day misadventure in Portland, he felt so bad for me that he had most of my things flown back to Los Angeles. No charge. Honestly, the man deserved a medal.

Barb, ever the optimist, suggested we just find another house. I, however, was no longer feeling particularly adventurous. For the first time in my life, saying "Yes" had completely backfired. I had taken a leap, and instead of landing gracefully, I had face-planted into a haunted, friendless, furniture-less existence in a city that egged my car. I was done.

Years later, I would end up back in Portland working on film projects with Marlee Matlin, and those would be wonderful experiences. This? Not so much. The final slap in the face came as I was literally driving out of town. I had returned my U-Haul, packed my BMW to the absolute limit with everything that wasn't being flown to LA, and hit the freeway, eager to escape. I could barely see out of my side mirrors, but I did not care. I just wanted out.

And then, because Portland simply could not let me go without one final indignity, I got pulled over. The officer strolled up to my overstuffed car, took one look at me, and handed me two tickets: Speeding. (Okay, fair. I may have been driving with a slight sense of urgency.) Apparently, a precariously balanced tower of clothes, a TV, and life regrets was considered a "visual obstruction." Goodbye, Portland.

There was no way I could go crawling back to Lowell's place after leaving him in the lurch like I had. So, once again, I called Brian.

Me: "Hi, can I come home?" Brian: Sigh. "Of course."

Basically, I was asking him to save my butt again, and because Brian is a saint among men, he agreed. And just like that, I was back in Encinitas, trying to figure out my next move. I had another four-month stint at sea coming up, so once again, Brian babysat my BMW for me.

(Have I mentioned what a phenomenal friend he is?)

By this point, I had been dealing with some serious back issues for about a year. Performing two shows a night onboard the ship was no joke. And when you factor in the constant movement of the vessel, it became something closer to Cirque du Soleil: Maritime Edition. Here's the situation…

I was 5'7", the dancers were Vegas-sized, the ship was never still. Lifting showgirls on solid ground is already a feat of strength. Lifting them on a moving ship? That was an entirely different level of insanity. I used to joke with the dancers, "Maybe skip the midnight buffet tonight? Just a thought." The truth was, they weren't the problem. It was physics.

When the ship pitched one way, the dancers were light as a feather. When it pitched the other way, mid-lift, suddenly, I was holding what felt like a grand piano. Show after show, night after night, it started to take a serious toll. And my back was letting me know that this might not be sustainable.

In addition to my nightly performances, I was also responsible for lugging incredibly heavy boxes of Bingo cards from the storage locker to the lounge. Twice a day, every day. Now, you might be thinking, How heavy can a box of Bingo cards be? Let me tell you. When you're hauling enough cards for a thousand enthusiastic Bingo players, many of whom buy in bulk like they're stocking up for an apocalypse, it adds up. And, because efficiency was apparently more important than spinal integrity, I was always told to double or triple up on the boxes to "save time." Then, there were the clay pigeons.

Yes, clay pigeons for Trapshooting. (Because nothing screams "relaxing cruise" like standing on the deck of a moving ship, firing a gun at small flying targets.) These boxes were even heavier than the Bingo cards.

And if that wasn't enough, sometimes I was also the only person available to move the heavier set pieces for our shows. I had become the unofficial Pack Mule of Princess Cruises. My poor back.

Time for a Change

I had been working at sea longer than I originally planned, and while my heart was still in it, my spine was issuing strong objections. It was time. One more cruise, and then I was done. I had loved my time onboard, but the ports were becoming a little too familiar. Another season in Alaska. Another trip to Mexico. More trans-canal voyages in Panama. Rinse and repeat.

The exception? The Mediterranean. I adored the Mediterranean. Europe had completely drawn me in, and I knew, I knew, I needed to spend more time there. And since my final four-month contract would be in the Mediterranean, I made a bold decision. When the ship reached Naples, I wouldn't be getting back on. I would stay.

Next Stop: Italy

Thanks to years of working with my Italian shipmates, my Italian had significantly improved. (A steady diet of Spumante and late-night conversations in the crew quarters will do that.) But I wanted to take it even further. So, I applied to a language school in Florence, Centro di Lingua, to really immerse myself. Before I left for my final contract, I got the news that I was accepted. And just like that, the plan was set.

I did my last few cruises, and when the Royal Princess docked in Naples, I walked off, for good. I was restless again, which usually meant something exciting was about to happen. I was also a little scared, which was another very good sign. What was next? Say yes.

Florence Bound

I took the train to Florence to meet with the school and discuss my living arrangements. They gave me three options: stay in a youth hostel (I was past my hostel years), live with a local family (I cherished my privacy too much), or move into an apartment arranged by the school.

I chose the apartment. I was officially starting my new life in Italy. My apartment was the gatehouse of an old Italian villa.

Not an apartment in a charming city center, not a flat above a café where I could lean out my window and dramatically sigh like some forlorn poet. No, I was living in the gatehouse of an old villa on Poggio Imperiale, a long, winding road that led to one of the ancient doors of Florence.

Honestly, it sounded romantic. It looked romantic. In reality, it was drafty, slightly dusty, and had just enough cobwebs to make me question whether I was sharing the space with a very sophisticated family of Italian spiders. But still, Florence!

Florence, the birthplace of the Renaissance. Florence, surrounded by the rolling hills of Tuscany, lined with elegant cypress trees, and filled with vineyards producing world-class Chianti. Florence!

Every local I met made sure to remind me that the dialect spoken there was puro Italiano, pure Italian.

I already knew from my years onboard the ships that Italian wasn't one language but an entire ecosystem of dialects. I had witnessed full-blooded Italians struggle to understand each other when someone from Naples suddenly veered into Neapolitan or when a Sicilian dropped a few words that sounded more like ancient Greek than anything you'd find in an Italian textbook.

But here I was, in the birthplace of the purest Italian. If I was going to master the language, this was the place to do it.

Before School, Some Adventures

I dropped off my suitcases, took a look around my new (new?) gatehouse, dusted off a few cobwebs, met the villa's owner, and promptly left. Because, naturally, the best way to settle into a new home is to not be there.

I had two weeks before classes started, and I wasn't about to let them go to waste. First stop was Lago di Como, to visit some friends from the ship. From there, Venice. That adventure would require another book!

Academic Adventures Abroad

An Unexpected Study Buddy

On the train to Lago di Como, I shared a compartment with a guy named Andrea. He was on his way to Milan for voice lessons (because of course he was).

At some point, he noticed my stack of Italian textbooks, and we struck up a conversation. Now, here was the fun part, he didn't speak a single word of English. So, I had no choice. If I wanted to keep up, I had to fully commit to speaking Italian. And I loved every minute of it.

By the time we arrived, we had exchanged numbers, and Andrea promised to help me with my homework once I got back to Florence. True to his word, two weeks later, I called him, and just like that, I had a study buddy. A great friend. And, most importantly, a lifeline when my Italian grammar started betraying me.

Arrivederci, Gatehouse

I ended up staying in Italy longer than I originally planned, which, let's be honest, was not a problem. I traveled. I ate ridiculous amounts of pasta. I actually started to feel fluent. I made some wonderful friends. But at some point, I hit the wall.

I had reached a limit. I was functional in the language but missed deeper conversations. I needed to talk about more than food, directions, and the weather. And I was ready to leave my drafty gatehouse. It was time.

Time to leave my life at my gatehouse of solitude and figure out what came next. After all my months in Italy, I found myself back at Brian's. I'm sure I had my own key by this time! Brian, my ever-patient, ever-reliable friend, took me in yet again. But at this point, I even felt like I was pressing my luck. I needed a plan. A real one. I missed the Deaf community. I missed interpreting. It was time to get back to it. The BMW, my beloved BMW, had been sitting idle for so long that it now needed repairs. And honestly? I just did not want to deal with it. So, I sold it. Gone was my sleek, camel-leather-interiored status symbol. In its place? A very sensible, very reliable used Toyota Tercel. Was it glamorous? No. Did it get me from Point A to Point B without passive-aggressively demanding expensive maintenance? Yes. And that was good enough. Where to Live? I knew I needed to be in Los Angeles.

The entertainment industry was here. The huge Deaf community I was already a part of was here. The energy of the city, the kind that made you feel like anything could happen, was here.

Richard, meanwhile, was still working onboard the Royal Princess and had given up our old Studio City apartment. Instead, he and two friends, a former Universal Studios co-worker and Ben, the ship's doctor, had found a duplex on Croft Avenue in West Hollywood. Splitting rent three ways made sense for Richard, since he was gone so often.

As for me? I left the Valley behind and found a tiny studio apartment on Doheny Drive, right on the border of West Hollywood and Beverly Hills.

Technically, my mailbox was in West Hollywood. Technically, my parking space was in Beverly Hills. So, naturally, I told people I lived in Beverly Hills. (Well, my car did, anyway.) Another Move? Why Not? Roberto Clema, my old friend and stage manager from the Princess fleet, had also decided to leave the ships and give Los Angeles a try rather than return to his hometown of Trieste, Italy. We had always gotten along great onboard, and one day, I had an idea. "Let's be roommates!" I suggested. And because I am nothing if not consistent, this meant, drumroll, please, moving again. The studio on Doheny was far too small for two people, so we found a massive four-plex on Alfred Street. One street over from Croft, where Richard lived. Honestly? It was perfect. I got to practice my Italian with Roberto, and I was exactly where I wanted to be.

Back in Action

Once I was settled (again), I hit the ground running. First stop was GLAD, Greater Los Angeles Council on Deafness. I went through their evaluation process, and, cue dramatic music, was placed in their highest pay category. (Well, hello, validation.) That meant I could start working freelance jobs immediately. I also started working at California State University, Northridge

(CSUN), interpreting for their deaf students. CSUN was basically "Gallaudet West", home to one of the largest Deaf Studies programs in the country, with a thriving community and the National Center on Deafness (NCOD) right on campus. I was back in the world I had missed so much. And this time, I was here to stay.

One of the things I loved about educational interpreting was the sheer variety of subjects. One day, I'd be in a psychology lecture, the next, an advanced physics lab. If I had actually retained everything I interpreted, I'd be the smartest person in the world. Sadly, that is not how it works.

Interpreting is this bizarre mental relay race where information enters your ears, gets processed at lightning speed in your brain, and then comes flying out through your hands and face. There is no time for retention. The moment a thought leaves your fingers, it vanishes into the void, never to be seen again.

Which, incidentally, is great for confidentiality. I've always thought it was funny when people asked me to sign NDAs (Non-Disclosure Agreements). Sure, I'll sign it. But the second I walk out of the room? Gone. (I am, quite literally, the safest person to tell a secret to.)

The Chemistry Class That Almost Killed Me

At CSUN, I was assigned to interpret an advanced chemistry class for a student named Cathy. The class was three hours long. It was in the warm springtime. It was scheduled right after lunch. And it was taught by a soft-spoken German professor who delivered lectures in an uninterrupted monotone that could lull even the most caffeinated person into a coma.

I tried everything to stay awake. Slapping my cheeks. Leaving the room to splash water on my face. Wiggling my foot like I was sending Morse code for SOS. Nothing helped. Every day, my head would droop until my chin hit my chest, but my arms never stopped moving. Cathy, my poor student, had to kick me in the shin every class just to keep me conscious.

So, in addition to my aching back, I now had bruised shins.

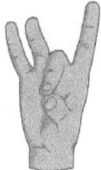

Performance & Partnerships

Please, For the Love of
All That is Holy, Give Me a Team!

Desperate, I went to Gary Sanderson, head of the interpreting department, and begged for a team.

Team interpreting is the sane way to do things, two interpreters take turns every 20 to 30 minutes, allowing each other to rest, recover, and, you know, not fall asleep in front of an entire classroom. It helps everyone, the interpreters and the deaf students, because they get a fully alert interpreter at all times.

Gary's response? No dice. There weren't enough interpreters to spare, so I had to stick it out, grin and bear it, hang in there. (I was running out of "hanging in there.")

One day, I was venting to my colleague, Lou Fant, who, in the world of interpreters, was the gold standard. The Meryl Streep of ASL, if you will. Lou just laughed and said, "Oh, I used to fall asleep all the time. And like you, my hands never stopped signing." That made me feel infinitely better. If Lou Fant could doze off mid-lecture and still be considered one of the best interpreters out there, then maybe I wasn't a total disgrace.

As much as I tried to push through, my back had other ideas. Sitting in those rock-hard wooden chairs for hours, contorting my body to interpret from the best angle, trying to find any position that didn't feel like medieval torture, nothing worked.

But Gary's words kept ringing in my ears. Stick it out. Grin and bear it. Hang in there. I did. Until I couldn't.

I saw a specialist, and, surprise!, I had two ruptured discs in my back. Well, no wonder I had been in so much pain. After all the necessary pre-op procedures, I checked into Cedars-Sinai for a double laminectomy.

These days, they do this kind of surgery laparoscopically, zap zap, you're home before your Uber even arrives.

But in 1986? Oh no. Back then, they sliced you open like a Thanksgiving turkey, did everything by hand, and sent you home with a lovely scar as a parting gift.

The doctors left just enough disc to act as a cushion between my vertebrae, and scar tissue would eventually form to stabilize everything. In the meantime, I was in the hospital for eight days, including my 28th birthday.

(Pro tip: If you're going to spend your birthday anywhere, avoid post-op in a hospital bed. The balloons all read GET WELL, and the cake is terrible.)

Princess Comes Calling

At some point during my recovery, I got a call from Colleen Baldwin at Brian Carter's office. "Hey, how are you doing?" she asked.

Which was a very polite way of saying, So, we heard your spine exploded, any chance you want to come back to work? They were putting together two new shows and really wanted me back.

I was flattered. I was tempted. But I had already started making a name for myself in the interpreting field, and I was enjoying my work at CSUN. So, I told her I'd think about it. Because I apparently could not stay put for more than five minutes, I moved again.

My friend Leslie Jon, another shipmate, had just rented a beautiful duplex directly across the street from Richard on Croft Avenue. (Croft was slowly becoming my own personal version of Melrose Place - an actual street that was just down the road.)

Leslie thought it made perfect sense for me to move in with him. He could help take care of me while I recovered. Richard was right across the street.

And if anything really went wrong, Ben, the ship's doctor, was also right across the street. (Honestly, it was almost like I had built a cruise ship support network, just without the ocean.)

Roberto didn't mind the change, so I recruited a few friends to pack me up yet again and move me from Alfred to Croft. (At this point, I should have just kept everything in boxes.)

Life with Leslie

Living with Leslie Jon was never dull. Leslie was Mr. Personality. A true star entertainer on Princess, he was loved by everyone and had a massive social network.

His friends? Oh, just Lauren Tewes, aka Julie McCoy, the Cruise Director on The Love Boat, and Linda Hart, one of Bette Midler's legendary Harlettes, who later went on to perform in Broadway musicals.

Days were filled with lunches, parties, spontaneous cocktail hours at 2 p.m., it was a social whirlwind.

The plan was for our schedules to overlap, when Leslie was at sea, I'd be home, and vice versa. But even when we were both home, we had a great rhythm. We had a fantastic friendship.

And so, one day, I told Leslie, "I think I'm going to take Princess up on their offer. Just for a while." Famous last words.

Back to the High Seas

Colleen arranged for me to fly to San Francisco and meet the Royal Princess during its repositioning cruise to LA.

I'd get to watch rehearsals for the new '50s Show and get a feel for what I'd be doing once I officially rejoined the team.

So there I was, boarding the ship with my cane, hobbling around like a dramatic film noir character, but happy to see familiar faces.

Some were new dancers and cruise staff. Others were old friends.

Richard, in particular, had finally made the switch. He had left his job as Fitness Director and was now in my old role as Assistant Cruise Director. A perfect choice. Richard loved to perform, and had always been great at it. And just like that, I was back. Sort of. For now.

Watching the rehearsal was bittersweet. I wanted, desperately, to jump up on that stage and be part of it. The music, the energy, the camaraderie. But as I watched the dancing, the lifts, the sheer physicality of it all, a sinking feeling settled in my gut. I couldn't do it.

They were expecting me to be ready to rejoin the ship in a matter of weeks, but my body had other plans. Two missing discs don't just magically regenerate. I knew it.

And so, when the Royal Princess docked in LA, I disembarked. And I never went back.

A New Stage

In late 1986, I was asked to interpret for an organization called the Media Access Office.

This group, founded in 1979, was revolutionary in the entertainment industry, pushing for real, tangible change when it came to actors with disabilities. They set out to level the playing field, ensuring:

Performers who use wheelchairs would audition in actual casting offices (not parking lots, thank you very much).

Deaf performers would have qualified sign language interpreters at auditions and on set.

Blind and low-vision performers would receive their audition sides in Braille, large print, or another accessible format.

At the time, these were radical ideas.

The Media Access Office was making real waves, and to this day, their work continues. They even produce the annual Media Access Awards, which honor producers, directors, and casting professionals who create authentic, thoughtful representations of disabled characters in TV and film.

At one of the meetings, I met Jean Kennedy Smith.

Jean was President Kennedy's sister.

Jean was deeply involved in the world of disability advocacy. In 1974, she founded Very Special Arts (VSA), an organization dedicated to providing people with disabilities opportunities for self-expression through drama, dance, music, creative writing, and visual arts.

And as it turned out, VSA was hosting an event I was about to be very involved in.

Held at The Music Center in downtown Los Angeles, The Very Special Arts Festival was a huge event. I was asked to teach a song in sign language to all the kids attending. It worked like this:

The festival was set up with multiple tents, each dedicated to a different form of artistic expression. Kids, many with Down syndrome or kids in wheelchairs, would rotate through the tents, experiencing everything from painting to music to dance. I was stationed in the Song Signing tent.

Group after group of kids came through, learned the song, and moved on. Then another group. Then another. And then something wonderful happened. Many of the kids came back to my tent, eager to sign the song again. It became their favorite part of the festival. And for me it was just wonderfully rewarding.

A Familiar Face, and a New One

The festival's hostess that year was none other than Lauren Tewes. Yep, Julie McCoy from The Love Boat.

It was great seeing her again, and throughout the day, she kept popping into my tent, checking in, saying hi. Lauren and I worked together onboard several times over the years when they came on to film the show. We also socialized quite a bit at Leslie's place.

Then, during one of her visits, she wasn't alone. She walked over with a bright, mischievous grin and said, "Bill, I brought Marlee Matlin in to see you. She said she was curious about who was teaching the song-signing. I'd like to introduce you." And just like that, everything changed. Marlee Matlin was the very special guest at that year's Very Special Arts Festival. And by special, I mean she had just won the Academy Award for Best Actress in Children of a Lesser God. And now, here she was, standing in my tent, watching me. I waved and signed, "Hi. Hold on. I'm about to start this round. Stick around and join in!" I wasn't sure what to say to an Oscar winner who was casually observing my work. That year, I was teaching "Day by Day" from Godspell.

The song was perfect for the festival because it was simple, repetitive, and easy for the kids to pick up. I always wanted them to feel successful when they left my tent.

As I led the group through the song, I glanced over and saw Marlee and Lauren signing along, smiling and swaying to the music.

Marlee was in her element. She had grown up signing songs and had even played Dorothy in a children's theatre production of The Wizard of Oz as a kid.

Lauren knew I was an interpreter, but she had never seen me in action. Now, here she was, watching me run my own mini Broadway revue for kids in wheelchairs and Down syndrome superstars.

When the kids finally filed out, Marlee came over. She admitted she had been skeptical about someone teaching kids to sign songs (which, honestly, I understood). But after watching me work, she loved what she saw. I congratulated her on the Oscar (as one does), and she and Lauren went off to fulfill their festival duties. Little did I know that day was just the beginning. Marlee and I would go on to become great friends, working together on so many projects in the years to come.

I was relentless in my pursuit of interpreting jobs (aggressive is such an ugly word, let's go with enthusiastic). But I also wanted to keep one foot (and both hands) in the entertainment industry. Francine Stern was my fellow interpreter from the phone company, and together, we started interpreting shows at the Mark Taper

Forum. That gig led me to Sheldon Altfeld, the creator of The Silent Network, a cable show filmed at KCAL-9. Sheldon and his co-producer, Dawn Jeffory-Nelson, took me under their wing, and soon, I became the show's resident interpreter. One of their biggest productions was Off Hand, a weekly talk show hosted by Herb Larson, with Lou Fant as his interpreter. Sheldon had a knack for pulling in big-name celebrities, and working on the show was an incredible experience. I had gotten a small taste of TV production back at Gallaudet on News Review, but this was the real deal. I was standing in a Los Angeles studio, combining my two greatest passions: Interpreting and entertainment. And I had a very strong feeling that things were just warming up. After a while, I became the substitute co-host/interpreter for Off Hand whenever Lou couldn't do the show. This meant I was now voicing for Herb Larson and signing for the guests. And let me tell you, I was in heaven.

This tiny cable show gave me huge exposure in both the Deaf and interpreting communities. I was already working at CSUN, freelancing all over LA, and now, with The Silent Network on my resume, I was officially in demand.

I was busy. And I loved it.

A few months after my surgery, I got a call from Bob Daniels.

Bob had seen me interpret at the Mark Taper Forum, and apparently, I had made an impression.

We met up, and he grilled me about my life, my years at Gallaudet, my dance background, my interpreting work. (He probably knew my mother's maiden name by the end of it.) Then he told me what he wanted.

He was producing a show for the 38th National Association of the Deaf (NAD) Conference in Salt Lake City, and he needed a male dancer who could sign songs. Sign. Me. Up. (I will now stop apologizing for puns. They are inevitable.)

It turned out Bob needed more than just a dancer. He needed a choreographer. That was me! The only issue? My back. I wasn't about to start throwing people in the air (my lifting days were behind me), but I could still choreograph, I just had to be strategic.

No jumping. No lifting. No sudden moves that might send me straight back to Cedars-Sinai. I could do this.

One of the performers in the show was a young woman named Terrylene.

She was adorable. Bright. Eager. Full of energy. She came from a multi-generational Deaf family, and she had the most infectious laugh, the kind of laugh that instantly made you want to be her friend.

She pulled me aside and said, "Give me difficult choreography. I'm a dancer. I love a challenge."

Well. Okay, then.

I staged the opening number with "Magic to Do" from Pippin (because what's an NAD show without a little razzle-dazzle?). Then, I choreographed "All That Jazz" from Chicago for just me and Terrylene. And let me tell you, she wasn't kidding when she said she could dance. She had technique. She had flair. She had a presence. And she could act, too. She had just guest-starred in an episode of Cagney & Lacey. After the NAD Conference, Terrylene and I became fast friends. One day, she looked me dead in the eye and said, "From now on, you're my interpreter." No question mark. No hesitation. Just a statement of fact. Terrylene was everywhere. In addition to our work together at the NAD Conference, she was also involved with Very Special Arts, where Jean Kennedy Smith had taken a personal interest in mentoring her. Soon, the three of us found ourselves as guests on The Home Show, hosted by Gary Collins.

Terrylene signed one of her original poems. I voiced for her. Then we all moved to the couch for an interview. Jean glowed as she talked about Terrylene's talents. Then, surprise!, she pivoted and started talking about me. She mentioned my work with Very Special Arts, my coast-to-coast interpreting resume, and basically gave me the best unpaid PR campaign of my life. It was a great plug for Terrylene. It was a great plug for me.

Another Move? Of course.

Since I was no longer working for Princess, my roommate arrangement with Leslie wasn't quite working anymore. He was off the ships for longer stretches and really wanted his privacy. I got it. So, naturally, I moved again! This time, I landed back on Alfred Street in a cozy one-bedroom in a 12-unit building.

Then, my new landlord Seymour offered me a deal. Manage the building (collect rent, call a plumber, water the plants), get a huge rent reduction, enjoy free utilities and cable. Well, if you insist! I was already juggling a packed work schedule, freelancing, staying busy in the industry, so I decided to add "part-time building manager" to my resume. It seemed like a reasonable opportunity to take on.

At some point, my work requests tripled. I couldn't keep up. So, I started accepting jobs, then calling other interpreters to see if they could do them. I paid them their hourly rate. I charged the client slightly more. Suddenly, I had unintentionally started a business. I hadn't planned on becoming an entrepreneur. (I could barely plan my own grocery shopping.) Suddenly, I found myself running a company.

Introducing… SCRIPT

I needed a name. Something clever. Something that captured the intersection of interpreting and entertainment. And then it hit me. SCRIPT. Southern California Registry of Interpreters for Professional Theatre. It was perfect. It had "script" in the name (a staple of theatre, TV, and film). It showcased our work in interpreting for entertainment. It made me sound much more organized than I actually was. And just like that, my little operation had a name, a purpose, and, before I knew it, a very full calendar.

When Terrylene was still in high school, she wrote a play and submitted it to Very Special Arts. That play changed everything. She won first place, which put her directly on Jean Kennedy Smith's radar. And then the play was promptly… put on a shelf. (Because apparently, even award-winning scripts have to wait their turn.)

Then, in late 1986, Ms. Smith called with big news. They wanted to produce Terrylene's play. In London. New York and London were the theatre capitals of the world, and this was an extraordinary opportunity.

The Pugin Family in 1962. I was always looking adoringly at Evelyn.

*With big sister Evelyn on my first
day of climbing the academic ladder!*

I was the only kid who could keep the basket on my head.
I was a Good Do-Bee!

Me with Janet Bailey performing
another show stopping routine at Gallaudet.

Me with Mary Anne – always my guiding light on my career path.

A night on the town for President Jimmy Carter's inaugural parties!

*Free to Be...You and Me with Hank Young. Notice my perm!
Playing a couple of babies with Barb Goettsch.*

Liz sends love ∧

That wasn't the University of Texas' "Hook 'em, Horns" sign Liz Taylor was making, but "I love you" in the sign language of the deaf. Liz was the star speaker at Washington, D.C.'s Gallaudet College, the national college for the deaf, and delighted her audience with a few signs learned in advance. And interpreter Bill Pugin? He's relaying Liz's message of love: "I think the whole world should learn it."

My People Magazine claim to fame with Elizabeth Taylor.

With roommates Richard and Mickie just before my move to L.A.

Hello Hollywood! My first professional headshot – circa 1980.

With Debbie Quinn – who introduced me to Princess Cruises!

Performing a 1940s routine onboard The Sun Princess.

Captain John Young trying to be serious while I jump on one leg...for a very long skit onboard the Pacific Princess.

With the Kit Kat Dancers in Cabaret onboard The Sun Princess.

The one and only Brian Tash. The best friend who never got to drive the BMW!

Ron Perlman and me – Beauty and the Beast.
I'm the beauty, Ron's the beast!

My apartment in Florence – the gatehouse to an old Villa. I shared it with a lot of dust and cobwebs!

With Mick Nutter on my first trip to Europe – just before I was fired from the TDD Distribution Center.

Inching toward the ceiling in Peter Pan – just before the accident.

With Terrylene performing All That Jazz at the
NAD Conference, Salt Lake City.

Jeffrey in the front yard of the Califa house with Bosco and Bianca.

With Marlee and Jeffrey. They adored each other!

As Ben Douglass on location with Reasonable Doubts – 1991.

With the other Greasers in Grease – Burbank Theatre Guild

New mom Marlee with baby Sarah – somewhere on location.

On the set of Hunter with the amazing Phyllis Frelich.

John Arce signing to my singing onboard a Caribbean cruise.
We won the Talent Show!

About to start the table read for The River Wild. Sneaking a glance at Meryl, I couldn't believe we were in the same room! Also in the pic: Curtis Hanson, director; Joey Mazzello and Stephanie Sawyer playing the children of Meryl and David Strathairn.

Meryl Streep and me...sort of.

A Christmas photo with Bosco and Bianca – 1994

Interpreting for President Ronald Reagan.
My first experience with Secret Service started at this event.

Praying that I didn't drop Barbara Walters while dancing in the Mediterranean!

THE DAMON WAYANS PROJECT
PILOT EPISODE

CAST

DAMON	DAMON WAYANS
BERNARD	DAVID ALAN GRIER
CAPTAIN CAROL CZYNENCKO	ANDREA MARTIN
CARROL LAFONTAINE	DOM IRRERA
STACY PHILLIPS	MELISSA DESOUSA
JIMMY TACINO	JULIO MECHOSO
BILLY CAVANAUGH	GREG PITTS
DR. HELEN TROY	PHYLLIS FRELICH
BOBBY	BILL PUGIN

GUEST CAST
(in order of appearance)

The Cast List for the ill-fated Damon sitcom.

Roberta (RJ) Munsey and I "not working" in Hawaii.

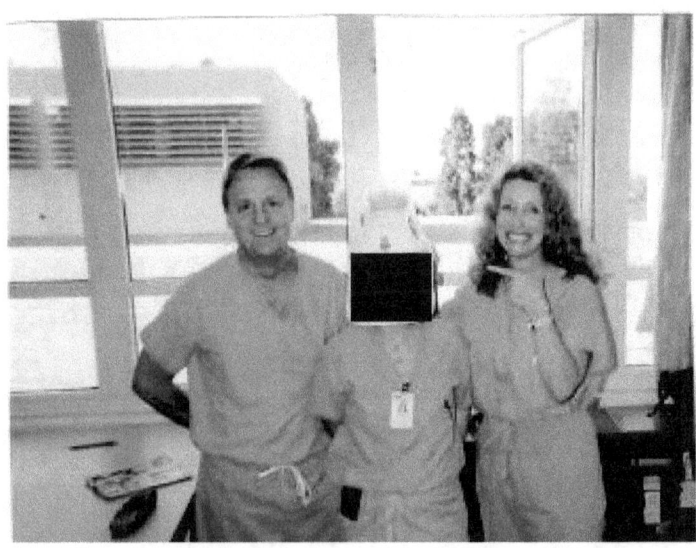

With RJ and our med student at UCLA. We did something right because the student became a doctor!

Clutching the tear in my shirt after my lion attack in Africa!

Steve Bock and I having tea in Shanghai.
It was one of the few things I was brave enough to consume.

*Trying to be brave and "save face"
while eating another mystery meal in China.*

Christmas shopping in Shanghai!

With Dad shortly after Mom passed away.
The greatest man I'll ever know.

David Copperfield working his magic on me.

Dancing with Marlee and Fabian Sanchez for
Dancing with the Stars – 2007.

Shooting Red Blooded in Atlanta with Marlee.

At home with Natalie Portman.

Hanging out with Paul McCartney in Beverly Hills.

Shooting the breeze with Anne Hathaway on set in Majorca, Spain.

Driving to some celebration with Nigel Sanches.

It's always a good time when I can spend it with Evelyn!

Translation, Tension & Triumph

Off to the UK

Terrylene asked me to be her interpreter. Jean Kennedy Smith agreed to send me along, and I quickly packed my bags before they could change their minds.

Our job was to work with The King's Head Theatre to get the play translated into English (because ASL and English are completely different languages), cast with British actors, and produced for a London audience. The translation process proved to be the biggest challenge.

Terrylene had written the play using ASL grammar and structure, which is beautiful and visual, but not exactly readable for someone expecting standard English.

And to make things even trickier, the producers wanted the script British-ized (is that a word?) to appeal to local audiences.

We were put up in a lovely B&B near King's Cross Underground Station and chauffeured to and from the theatre each day.

Now, the owners of this B&B were very polite, but I don't think they had ever seen a deaf person interacting with an interpreter before.

So, naturally, they were mystified by us.

And that was before The Great Egg Debacle.

I had already learned on my first trip to England that when it comes to breakfast, you get what the kitchen decides you should have. Doesn't matter what you order. The first time I experienced this, I had confidently requested two eggs over medium, burnt bacon (I like everything burnt, just like Mom used to cook!), wheat toast, coffee with cream. What I received was entirely different from my request. Two runny eggs (barely cooked), floppy, raw-looking bacon (tragic), white bread.

So, I already knew we were in trouble when Terrylene, every morning, ordered "Well-done eggs. Hard. No runny yolk. None." And every morning, they brought her runny eggs. She couldn't eat them. But, bless her heart, she kept trying. Until, finally, after several mornings of the same sad scene, I had an epiphany. This is the literal definition of insanity.

So, I did what had to be done. I marched into the kitchen myself and stood with the cook. I instructed him, slowly and clearly. "Crack the eggs onto the skillet." He did. "Now walk away." He froze. Absolute panic crossed his face. "No! I have to flip them!" "Not yet. Let them cook." He looked like he might have a heart attack. Finally, when the eggs were sufficiently solid, I nodded.

"Now flip them, and walk away again." "But they'll be like rubber!" he gasped. "Exactly," I said. "Just the way she likes them."

And that's how I, a man with zero culinary aspirations, became the only person in London who could successfully get a Deaf actress a proper breakfast.

We took a break from translating the play and shifted our focus to casting, production values, and all the other magic that brings a show to life.

Theatre 101: You can't put on a play if half the audience can't understand it. The King's Head Theatre brought in Elizabeth Quinn, a well-known Deaf British actress who had played the lead role in London's 1983 production of Children of a Lesser God. Having her input was invaluable, except for one tiny complication. Everyone was using BSL, British Sign Language. (BSL and ASL are about as similar as English and Mandarin.) So, here's how our interpretation relay worked. I signed ASL to Terrylene. A BSL/ASL interpreter then interpreted my interpretation into BSL.

And somewhere in the mix, the producer and director were talking in heavily British-accented English, which sometimes required interpretation of its own.

I loved this process.

I was learning BSL on the fly, bouncing between languages, and witnessing just how complicated yet beautiful multilingual communication could be.

The Translation Showdown

After a while, it became clear that we needed to hit pause. Without a fully polished English translation, there was only so much we could do.

So, the producers and theatre team stayed behind to fine-tune the translation, while Terrylene and I headed back to the U.S. A few months later, we were flown back to London for round two.

This time, they put us up in a one-bedroom flat in Fulham, which, to be clear, was not actually available. The theatre negotiated with a local woman to give up her home for a few weeks so we'd be more comfortable.

Terrylene and I felt so cosmopolitan, hopping on the red double-decker buses, commuting to our director's home like two theatre professionals in a foreign film.

We were artists and globe-trotters, but also about to drive each other crazy. Problem #1 was we had to share a bed. Fine. It was big enough, and if I snored, it wouldn't bother Terrylene. Problem #2 was that Terrylene liked to get up at 2 AM to make tea and write. Now, as someone raised in a hearing world, I am painfully aware of how much noise a kitchen makes at night. Terrylene? Not so much.

Every morning, I had to give her a lesson in How Not to Sound Like a Burglar When Making Tea at 2 AM. "You can hear all that?" she asked, genuinely baffled. "Uh... yeah. At 2 AM, it's really loud." So, I taught her the fine art of opening drawers without them slamming back shut, retrieving silverware without causing a full-scale cutlery avalanche, closing cabinet doors like a polite human being instead of a haunted house poltergeist. It was an adjustment, but eventually, the late-night tea ceremonies became slightly less like an air raid drill.

Meanwhile, the translation process was slow. The director would read a passage, ask Terrylene what it meant, and then convert it into English. But here's where things got tricky. His writing style was very sophisticated and very British. (Think Downton Abbey meets Shakespeare, with a dash of Masterpiece Theatre.) Sometimes we'd ask if he could "split the difference" between British literary drama and plain, American English.

But as the revisions piled up, so did Terrylene's frustration. She felt like her words, her intent, were getting lost. The play was starting to feel less like her own and more like a stranger's interpretation of what she had meant. And… Scene.

Finally, we hit an impasse. The decision was made that we'd go home. The director would come to California later to continue the process. Very Special Arts had poured a lot of time, money, and energy into this project. I was worried. Sure enough, when the director arrived in LA, the same frustrations picked up right where they left off. The process stalled. Then it stopped. The play was dropped.

I felt awful for Terrylene. This was her baby. And now, it was going nowhere. I held onto hope that someone, someday, would revive it. But for now, we had to move on. Soon after, Terrylene was cast in a recurring role on the CBS show Beauty and the Beast. She played Laura, a deaf woman who became part of Vincent's underground world. She booked three episodes, and I interpreted for her on set. Which was great! Except for one small thing...

The Gas Mask Situation

Vincent (the Beast) lived in underground tunnels. These tunnels were filled with "atmospheric smoke". I don't know what they used to make the smoke, some kind of toxic oil blend, apparently, but it was so bad that we had to wear gas masks whenever we were filming underground. Let me tell you something, interpreting while wearing a gas mask is not easy. I have never worked so hard in my life to make sure Terrylene could see my facial expressions under that mask. But hey, Hollywood magic, right?

The second episode featuring Terrylene was called "Sticks and Stones". This was the Deaf Gang episode. I was able to be the interpreter for both the auditions and the shoot.

Wrangling a Deaf Gang

The storyline was a deaf girl who once lived underground with Vincent falls in with a street gang, threatening to derail her first serious love affair. (Classic primetime drama with a side of social commentary.)

Since this episode required an actual gang of Deaf actors, every single deaf person in the right age range came in to audition. It was a long process, but in the end, they cast seven or eight Deaf actors to be gang members. (Thankfully, none of them had to wear gas masks this time.)

Meanwhile, I was the only interpreter on set, running around like a lunatic, making sure everyone understood everything. And while I was speed-signing my way through scene after scene, Lou Fant, hired as the technical advisor, was relaxing in his chair. At one point, I ended up near him, exhausted. Lou just grinned and said, "I'm so happy it's you doing all the work, my boy, and not me!" He was living his best life. Meanwhile, I was herding cats.

Despite the chaos, the episode turned out great. It was also a milestone, the first time open captions were used on any show so that the hearing audience could understand what the Deaf actors were signing. The producers had wanted authenticity, and it paid off. They could have taken the easy way out, hired hearing actors, had them fake their deafness, and called it a day. But they didn't. They cast actual Deaf actors, they made sure the episode was accessible, and for their efforts, they won an award at the next Media Access Awards. Finally, Hollywood doing it right.

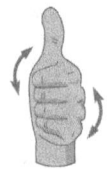

Spotlight & Solidarity

The NAD Conference: 1988

The next NAD (National Association of the Deaf) Conference was in El Paso, Texas. To this day, I still don't remember how the interpreters were chosen for the big gala, but somehow, I made the cut. And what a group it was! Gary Sanderson, Cath Richardson, Lou Fant, me, and a couple of other high-profile interpreters. This was another interpreting dream team.

Being picked was a huge honor, kind of like being asked to sit at the cool kids' table in the interpreting world.

We were all seated in the front row of the theatre, microphones in hand, ready to voice for some of the most prestigious Deaf people in the country.

And then, because he was Lou Fant, Lou did something to calm all of our nerves. He wouldn't admit it, but we knew.

He was set to voice for Herb Larson, the MC for the evening (also his co-host from "Off Hand" who he could interpret for in his sleep). Lou wrote books on interpreting. He was a legend.

So naturally, when Herb walked on stage and signed something as simple as "Good evening", Lou… missed it.

He missed it. Then he casually motioned for Herb to repeat himself. Cue the laughter from the entire front row of interpreters. Lou had intentionally messed up to remind us that even the greats aren't perfect. And just like that, our nerves were gone.

The highlight of the evening was seeing every single actress who had ever played Sarah Norman in Children of a Lesser God come out on stage. One. By. One. First, Phyllis Frelich, who originated the role on Broadway and won a Tony Award for it. Then, every other actress who had played Sarah in regional productions, touring shows, and international stagings. And finally, Marlee Matlin, who had played the role in the film.

The audience loved it. It was powerful. A moment in time that felt historic.

And as I sat there, in the front row, mic in hand, surrounded by the best of the best, I realized that this was a fantastic moment in my interpreting life.

Two things happened in El Paso that changed the entire trajectory of my interpreting career.

1. Phyllis Frelich Noticed Me.

The Tony Award-winning, Broadway legend, originated-the-role-of-Sarah-Norman Phyllis Frelich.

She saw me interpret, walked right up to me, introduced herself (as if I didn't already know who she was), and asked if I would interpret some upcoming meetings she had scheduled in

Los Angeles. I was star-struck but played it cool. "Of course," I said, as casually as one can while internally screaming.

2. I Crashed Marlee Matlin's Conversation.

One evening, Marlee was standing with a group of people, some of whom I knew. So, naturally, I walked right up and inserted myself into their conversation. (Confidence is key.)

Looking at Marlee, I grinned and said, "Need any practice signing 'Day by Day'? I'd be happy to help." She laughed. We clicked instantly. The next day, we were all on a bus heading to another venue.

Marlee got on, saw me sitting with someone else, and, without hesitation, announced, "Thanks for saving me a seat!"

Then she came back and marched right up to me and asked, "Do you know Jack?" (Jack being her interpreter.) "No, we haven't met," I said. "Make it happen," she ordered. That bus ride was the start of a beautiful relationship.

There was a young, up-and-coming writer at the conference named Chris Beakey, who was reporting on the event for Gallaudet. He was hearing, learning ASL, and eager to tell great stories. We hit it off and became very good friends. Chris has since gone on to become an accomplished thriller novelist. (If you're looking for a great new book, go read Chris Beakey's work!)

By March 1988, I was asked to interpret at the Westwood Playhouse (now the Geffen Playhouse) for a benefit performance called A Night at the Movies.

This was not just some small, local fundraiser.

This was a star-studded, who's-who event filled with Hollywood royalty. And among them was Phyllis Frelich. Now, this was a theatre crowd. And Phyllis wasn't just any actress, she was a Broadway Tony Award winner. She commanded the stage. She commanded respect. And that night, she made a huge impression on the audience and every other celebrity in the room. As for me, I was just happy to be there, riding the wave of these incredible moments, fully aware that my career was shifting into something bigger than I had ever expected.

One of the celebrities at A Night at the Movies was Nancy Lee Grahn, an actress on the soap opera Santa Barbara.

Nancy was mesmerized by Phyllis Frelich and had to talk to her after the show.

So, Phyllis pulled me backstage, and I interpreted their conversation.

Hollywood in Chaos: The Writer's Strike

At the time, Hollywood was in the middle of a writer's strike, and many shows had shut down. Except for soaps. Why? Because they had scab writers.

(Scab writer: Someone who doesn't join the Writer's Guild, therefore making them available to take writing jobs while the union members strike.)

Nancy was frustrated.

She leaned in conspiratorially and said, "Some of our scripts are being written by actors, actors' parents… and possibly the NBC janitor."

I don't think she was joking. But having seen how quickly soap scripts were churned out, I wasn't entirely sure.

Nancy told us she was going to pitch Phyllis to the producers. Phyllis and I exchanged a look—the kind that says stay cool, but oh my god, this could be huge.

NBC loved the idea. And just like that, Phyllis was cast as Sister Sarah—a nun with a sketchy past.

I was Phyllis' interpreter for all 31 episodes of Santa Barbara. And let me tell you—this was an education. Phyllis was fearless - which was good, because the storyline was all over the place, thanks to the strike-induced game of musical chairs happening in the writer's room.

One of the perks was she only had to wear a nun's habit. No worrying about endless costume fittings. No stressing over whether today's wardrobe was flattering. Just black. Every day. Kind of a dream scenario.

Working on a soap required a completely different muscle than episodic television.

For a one-hour drama, you get eight 12-hour days (sometimes 14 or 15 hours) to shoot a single episode. On a soap, that one-hour episode is shot in one day.

A Typical Day on a Soap Opera:

7:00 AM – Blocking rehearsal

Actors roll out of bed, show up with their scripts, and get told exactly where to stand, when to turn, and when to exit.

8:00 AM – Hair & Makeup - Actors try to become human while caffeinating.

9:00 AM – Camera Rehearsal

This is where actors fine-tune their blocking and figure out where the cameras will be.

The director runs through which camera will be used for which shot.

12:00 PM – Lunch

Because even in the chaos of daytime television, you must feed the talent.

1:00 PM – Shoot the show

No time for perfectionism. It's basically live theatre with cameras. If you mess up? You keep going. I was blown away by how well the actors memorized their massive amounts of dialogue. In primetime TV or film, an actor might have a few scenes to study for the day. On a soap, they were handed pages of dialogue, daily. They had one take, maybe two. There were occasional flubs, but they were rare. Soap actors don't get nearly enough credit. They make it look effortless.

And for 31 episodes, I got a front-row seat to just how hard they worked. After just a few days on Santa Barbara, Phyllis started getting the hang of it. But it was an adjustment. She was a consummate stage actress, used to weeks of rehearsals before an audience ever saw her work. But on Santa Barbara you were handed pages of dialogue, given moments to rehearse, and expected to go. It was like being thrown into a river and told to swim.

One day, she turned to me, eyes twinkling, and signed, "I think I'll make Sister Sarah... crazy." We both smiled at each other. "Yes!" I signed back. "Do it!" The writing was already silly and unbelievable, so Phyllis decided to fully commit to making Sister Sarah a little offbeat. And you know what happened? Nothing. No one stopped her. Not a single director, producer, actor or writer said, "Wait, why is the nun acting like she's a character out of One Flew Over the Cuckoo's Nest?" They just went with it. And we had the best time.

I was invited to a dinner party at Lisa Davis's house. Lisa was the sister of Beryl Davis, a well-known singer (and one of my favorite guest performers on Princess Cruises). I almost didn't go because I had just spent the weekend in Palm Springs, where I had gotten way too much sun, and I really considered canceling.

But then I thought, Lisa is the kind of person who probably has place cards. It would be rude to cancel on the Hostess with the Mostess. So, I went. And I had a fantastic time. I ended up seated next to Jeffrey Epstein. (Not that Jeffrey Epstein.) We spent the entire evening talking, about his life in New York, his late parents, his move to LA, and everything in between. At some point, someone played the piano, I sang, and the night turned into one of those unexpectedly perfect evenings. I was so glad I had decided to go.

A few days later, Jeffrey called me. "Hey, I'm having a dinner party. You should come." "Oh, nice to hear from you! Sure, I'd love to. I'll bring some wine." Jeffrey lived in Van Nuys in the cutest little house on Califa Street.

It had a white picket fence, two massive orange trees out front, and in the backyard was pomegranate, lemon, and lime trees, basically a Whole Foods produce section.

The front-yard trees along with the enormous Rosemary hedge were so huge they practically hid the house. I walked up, knocked, and stepped inside. Jeffrey was there. His two dogs, Bianca and Bosco, were there. And in the dining room was a beautifully set table… for two.

I glanced around. "Do I have the right day?" I asked. "You do," he said, smiling. "The dinner party is just for you."

Jeffrey was a great guy. We spent the next year growing closer and closer, until finally, after exactly one year of knowing each other, he said, "You're here all the time. Why don't you just move in?" And so… I moved again. And this time? It felt like home. Life on Califa Street was good.

I was busier than ever, SCRIPT had grown, and coming home to a well-cooked meal and a house full of people was exactly what I needed.

Jeffrey's friends became my friends, including Merry Moore, who, fun fact, was Lisa Davis's niece and Beryl's daughter.

The dogs were a happy handful. The parties were legendary. Friends were constantly coming and going, and everyone loved that house. About a year later, I got a call from Terrylene's agent. Which was odd, considering I didn't even have an agent anymore.

I was so busy interpreting that auditions had become a thing of the past. (They always happened last minute, and I had too many commitments to drop everything and run to a casting call.)

But apparently, this agent had seen me work at the Mark Taper Forum and on set with Terrylene, so when a new television show came up, he thought of me.

The show was Reasonable Doubts and it starred Mark Harmon and Marlee Matlin. Marlee had never mentioned this show to me. Later, she told me she wanted to keep it quiet in case it didn't go anywhere. But come on, Mark Harmon and Marlee Matlin? Yeah, it was getting picked up.

I didn't even hesitate. "Thank you for thinking of me! Call me with the details, and I'll be there!"

The audition was at Warner Bros. in Burbank. The moment I walked into the lobby, I knew almost every guy sitting there. We were all auditioning for the role of Ben Douglass, Tess Kaufman's courtroom interpreter. (Tess being Marlee's character, and Dickie Cobb being Mark's.)

Robert Singer, the creator and showrunner, had named all the male characters after baseball players. This was completely lost on me, because unless it's Damn Yankees, I don't follow baseball.

We all grabbed copies of the scene, a few pages pulled from the pilot's script. We had a few minutes to look it over before going in to read for casting director Tony Sepulveda.

I took a deep breath. It had been a long time since I'd auditioned for anything. But something about this felt... Big.

The role of Ben Douglass called for someone in their early to mid-thirties. That was me. Strait-laced, buttoned-up courtroom interpreter. I could do that. The lines were pretty funny, and Tony Sepulveda, the casting director, put me at ease right away. I was immediately impressed by the size of his office and all the posters on the walls. "Wow," I said, looking around. "Nice office, but I don't think it's big enough." Because flattery never hurts.

Tony smiled. "Ready?" Tony read the character's role in the scene, and I interpreted as though Tess/Marlee was standing right there. When I finished, he leaned back in his chair and asked, "How do I know what you just signed was real?" Without missing a beat, I said, "You don't." He laughed. "Well, how did it look?" I asked. "It looked real." I shrugged. "Then my job here is done."

We shook hands, I said goodbye to the other actors still waiting to audition (may the best 'Ben' win!), and I left. A couple of days later, Terrylene's agent called. "You've got a callback." Okay, here we go.

This time, I went to Bob Singer's office at Warner Bros. Now, Tony's office was big. Bob's office? Twice as big. I was given the same scene from my first audition, plus two more.

Then I was informed that I'd be reading with Marlee Matlin, Bob Singer, three other producers, and a couple of guys from NBC. Gulp.

I did my thing. Then I went home and told Jeffrey, "Now it's a waiting game." At first, I was anxious. Then, after a few days, I just forgot about it. I was too busy interpreting to dwell on it, so I figured they'd picked someone else. Oh well. Bummer.

About ten days later, the phone rang. I picked up, expecting it to be just another work call. It was Terrylene's agent. "Hang on," he said. "I want you to hear something." He pressed play on his answering machine (remember those?), and I heard Tony Sepulveda's voice. "We would like to hire Bill for the role of Ben Douglass. We need him to fly to Chicago to film part of the pilot, and the remainder will be done here in town."

He kept talking about contracts and flights and dates, but I didn't hear any of it. Because my brain had stopped at "We would like to hire Bill."

I hung up, walked into the next room where Jeffrey was, and calmly said, "I got it." Jeffrey jumped up, immediately dialing the phone. "We got it! We got it!" he yelled. It was like when husbands announce, "We're pregnant!" Except in this case, I was the baby.

It was a wonderful evening.

Later, after we shot the pilot, Tony pulled me aside. NBC and the producers loved the rapport that Marlee and I had. They said I fit the description of the character perfectly. And, this part stuck with me, they loved my voice. Hearing my voice as Marlee's character was very important to the network. Apparently, all those years of singing and voicing for Deaf performers had paid off. And just like that… I was going to be on TV.

Reasonable Doubts was a dream. Being flown First Class to Chicago. Staying in a gorgeous hotel, acting alongside an Academy Award winner who taught me so much about working in front of a camera. Having Mark Harmon (aka People Magazine's Sexiest Man Alive) take me under his wing. It was all just… a high. And I loved it.

When we returned to LA to finish shooting the pilot, Bob Singer pulled me in for a meeting. "I need your help," he said. Well. Mark's character needed to sign, and I was a good teacher. So just like that, I became Mark's sign coach.

Let me tell you, this was not easy. Mark had played football in college and had broken several fingers as a player. Mark's fingers had zero flexibility and were not interested in the graceful, precise movements of ASL.

To save time and make things easier, I recorded all of his lines on VHS (this was the '90s), signing everything so he could watch and practice whenever he had time. (He rarely had time.)

Because here's the thing, he wasn't learning to sign for a stage play, where you get four to six weeks of rehearsing the same dialogue over and over. This was episodic television. His signs changed from week to week. And on top of memorizing his lines, staying in character, hitting his mark, finding his camera, and not blocking someone's light, he also had to sign. Oy vey.

We did the best we could. Mark would watch my VHS tapes when he could, and then, bam, the script would change. Lines would be cut. New lines would be added. It was like playing whack-a-mole with dialogue.

And you know who suffered the most? Marlee. She relied on knowing his signs to deliver her lines. So when Mark's signs changed, Marlee had to adjust in real time. Mark was frustrated. Marlee was frustrated. And Bob Singer would just look at me, waiting for me to fix it. (No pressure, Bill. No pressure at all.)

Meanwhile, it became painfully obvious that it was easier for me to be Marlee's on-set interpreter as well as the character of Ben. I was already in every scene with her. I was always sitting next to her. Why have someone else run over every time she needed something relayed when I was literally right there? NBC and Lorimar, the production company, agreed. They realized this was a separate job, so they paid me separately. (Thank you, Hollywood gods.)

At least now, amidst all the sign language whack-a-mole, rewrites, and finger-inflexibility battles, things were finally flowing smoother. You can imagine that working on a television show took up all of my time. SCRIPT was on pause. Freelance interpreting just couldn't exist anymore.

Now, I was waking up before the crack of dawn, in hair and makeup by 5:30 or 6 a.m., and on set for 12 to 14-hour days. By the time I got home, I was wrecked. And yet, there was no crashing on the couch with a glass of wine and a home-cooked meal.

Jeffrey hadn't been feeling well for a while, so in addition to filming all day, I was now taking care of Jeffrey and the dogs, cleaning the house, studying my lines for the next day, making sure Mark had his signing tapes, and attempting to get some sleep before doing it all over again.

The only glamorous part of show business is walking a red carpet. Yeah, well... I never got to do that. But there were perks. I got interviewed by a few publications.

I had a segment air on Entertainment Tonight (because nothing says "You've Made It" like Mary Hart talking about you).

People told me, "You should get a publicist! Milk this job for all it's worth!" And then I started getting recognized, which was weird.

The morning after Reasonable Doubts premiered, I went to Acura to pick up my car from the service department. I'm on TV now, so I traded up from my Toyota Tercel!

A man and a woman kept staring at me. Finally, they walked over and said, "Are you on TV?" I was not used to this. But then it started happening more and more. Because that's the power of millions of people seeing you every week.

Then the fan mail started rolling in. Letters were sent to Lorimar or NBC and delivered to me in bulk. At first, I thought, Oh no. I have to respond to all these people? But Marlee and Mark shut that down immediately. "Don't do it," they warned. "It could open a can of worms." And they were right.

Actors at their level had designated people to deal with fan mail. These people would sort through it, weed out the suspicious letters, and, if necessary, forward red-flag mail to law enforcement. I was never in that league. I did end up writing back to one or two people, though. They seemed harmless and sincere. At least, I hoped they were. One fan kept sending me letters written on the side of a grocery bag. I should've sent her money for stationery.

Making History, And Making People Think

Despite the exhaustion and the newfound weirdness of being recognized, I loved this new chapter in my life.

I was the first person in history to play a professional sign language interpreter on a weekly TV series. And that mattered. Because millions of people who had never seen an interpreter before were now watching Ben Douglass every week. Most of the fan letters weren't just, "Hey, you're great on the show!" They were curious. People wanted to know more. They had never thought about interpreting as a profession. They had never considered accessibility in the way the show was presenting it.

And if Reasonable Doubts could open that door for even a handful of people, then, to me, it was all worth it.

One of the hardest parts of the job, though, was having to memorize everyone's lines. Not just my own lines as Ben Douglass, but Marlee's lines too. Why? Because I voiced for Tess, her character, and on television, there's no room for lag time.

In real life, an interpreter waits before voicing a deaf person's signs. We take a beat, process the concept, and then start speaking. But that can't happen on TV. That would be dead air. And dead air is the worst thing imaginable on television.

So my job was to speak while Marlee signed, in real time, flawlessly, seamlessly, and without hesitation and still make it look authentic - like I didn't know the line that was coming next.

And it worked both ways. If an attorney or judge was speaking, my signs had to be right on top of their words. The interpreting had to be seamless, perfectly timed, and done while acting. When the camera was on Marlee, she signed, and I voiced off-camera. If she ever forgot a line, I'd sign it to her, subtly helping her keep going. We never wanted to stop a scene if we could help it. When the camera was on me, Marlee was off-camera signing, and if she forgot, I kept voicing. (Because, of course, I had everyone's lines memorized.) Whenever I saved her, she'd mouth "thank you" to me. And I'd give her a little nod, like, Yeah, yeah, I got you. That was our rhythm. We had each other's backs.

Sometimes, though, no matter how professional you are, things just go off the rails. In one episode, Marlee and I got the giggles. Big time. There was an actress on the witness stand who delivered her lines the exact same way every single time. Something about it just hit us funny. Actually, we lost it. So the scene starts. The camera is on me. I hear, "Action!" I begin my lines, the scene is rolling… Then the actress said her line. And that was it. I lost all self control. Marlee had her back to the camera, and I could see her shoulders shaking as she tried to keep it together.

Her face was red, her whole body trembling, and she was desperately trying to hold in a laugh. Which only made it worse. It was awful. And by awful, I mean hilarious. The actress on the witness stand thought we were laughing at her. (Technically... we kind of were.) (But not in a mean way!) (It was just, funny!) If you've ever seen blooper reels of actors cracking up mid-scene, trust me, It's real. And once you start, it's impossible to stop. They actually had to call lunch early because we just couldn't get through the scene.

To this day, if Marlee and I are together, we can be reduced to tears over the stupidest things. People around us think we're bonkers. And they're probably right.

Another reason it was essential for me to have Marlee's lines memorized was because sometimes disasters strike. Case in point: The night we wrapped Marlee too early. Now, let me tell you, Marlee is an absolute pro. But she is also the Queen of the Quick Exit. Every single morning, the first thing she asked the assistant director was "What time am I wrapped?" (Priorities, people.) So this night? We had spent the entire day filming in the courtroom, which meant pages and pages of dialogue and monologues. It was exhausting. Finally, Ken Collins, our First AD, announced "Marlee, you're wrapped!" Which meant I was wrapped too. And before anyone could even process that information, Marlee was gone. Like, vanished. A driver had her car waiting outside the stage door, and she was just a blur exiting the sound stage.

I was mid-tie removal, heading for my dressing room, when I felt panic sweep across the set. Turns out... They forgot to get coverage of the judge. This wouldn't be a huge problem, except, I was in all of those shots. (Of course I was.) The judge's coverage required the camera to pan back and forth between him and me. Which meant I had to be there. Marlee, on the other hand? Not in the shot. But still very much needed. Because this was the era of pagers, not cell phones, and Marlee would throw her pager in her bag the second she left for the night. So there was no way to reach her. Ken, our First AD, stood there frozen, probably wondering if he was about to get fired.

Silence. Then, finally, I said "I can do the scene. I can do it without Marlee." The entire courtroom, jurors, crew, other actors, just stared at me. Ken: "Are you sure?" Me: "Sure, I'm sure. I mean… I think I'm sure. Let's try." I had to be sure. We had just done the scene five or six times. It was fresh in my head. I knew Marlee's blocking, where she moved, when she moved. So… We set up. The makeup department rushed in to touch me up. Everyone held their breath. Then "Roll sound. Speed. Action!" And just like that… I became two people.

The scene was almost three full pages of Tess's closing argument. Three pages is a lot to memorize, especially when your usual cue system (Marlee's signing) is gone. I had nothing to go off of. No prompts. No subtle hints. Just me, standing in a full and anxious courtroom, delivering a monologue that wasn't even mine. I forced myself to remember everything. I moved left, just like Marlee had. Then right, exactly as she did. Back to the left again. I mirrored her blocking precisely, making sure everything would seamlessly match when the scene was edited. This was her moment, and she wasn't there. So I had to pretend she was. I sort of channeled her performance. I felt the weight of her final words. The closing words of her monologue were coming up and it was like a bright light coming at me in a dark tunnel. And when I delivered the last line, I held my ground, standing tall.

Silence. Then, "CUT!" The entire courtroom, crew, cast, extras, stood up and applauded. Ken, our First AD, had tears in his eyes. Then he hugged me. I had saved the production a lot of money and probably his job. One take. I earned my paycheck that day.

One of my favorite memories from Season One was the night Marlee turned to me and said "Hey, want to come with me, Ruthie, and David Kelley to see Liza Minnelli at the Greek?" Liza Minnelli. At the Greek Theatre. For its 60th anniversary celebration. A star-studded event. Oh, let me think about that, YES.

Now, before we go any further, you need to understand something. I was obsessed with Liza Minnelli. This was not a casual appreciation. This was a full-blown teenage fixation. Let's rewind to the summer of my 14th year. I was on a cross-country road trip with my brother Welby in his Volkswagen Sun Beetle. We eventually ended up at his place in Bloomington, Indiana, where he took me to see Cabaret, which had just opened. And let me tell you, when Liza's face appeared on that screen, something clicked in my brain. I was transfixed. It was like she reached through the screen, grabbed my soul, and said, "You're one of mine now." That was it. I was done for. I joined her fan club. I collected every photo, article, and magazine clipping I could find.

My bedroom walls were Liza. Everywhere. I bought every record. And when she came to Atlanta in 1973, I begged my parents to let me go. To their credit, Mom and Dad said yes. I went with Evelyn and two friends from Eastman, and it was pure magic.

And Now, Years Later... Fast forward to me, standing across from Marlee, being casually invited to see Liza Minnelli at the Greek Theatre. Fourteen-year-old me would have died on the spot. Of course, I said yes. On August 30, 1991, after wrapping on set, we climbed into the stretch limo that David E. Kelley had provided and headed to the Greek Theatre. Because that's just how things went on Friday nights in Hollywood. David, of course, was already one of the biggest television writers at the time.

He and Marlee were a power couple, and our tickets had been given to him by some industry connection but David had never seen Liza perform.

I had seen Liza perform six times before, but I had never arrived at her show in a limo. That was new. Our seats were in the third row. A prime location to watch Liza Minnelli sweat in real time. I turned to David and said, "You are going to love her." He smirked. "Just don't be too big a fan when we go to the after-party." I stopped breathing. "I'm sorry, what?" After-party? Liza's after-party? No one had mentioned this part of the evening. The audience was packed with celebrities, but I didn't care. I never took my eyes off the stage.

And Liza, as usual, was phenomenal. This was her big Radio City Music Hall show, taken on tour, A full-blown Broadway-caliber production. One of the most touching moments was when she performed a song in sign language. She signed and sang about two people in love, communicating in a different language, which was a touching effort. And when the show ended, David, David E. Kelley, the man who had written some of the sharpest TV scripts ever, was on his feet instantly. "You were right," he said. "She's amazing." (Obviously.)

The party was buzzing with the biggest stars from the audience. Liza's sister, Lorna Luft, came over to say hello to Marlee and David. Then came the L.A. Law cast, David's show at the time. (Side note: David later named the mayor on Picket Fences "Bill Pugen." When I asked why he didn't spell it like mine, he said he didn't want to pay me royalties. Typical.) But back to the party. We mingled. We waited. And then, Liza arrived.

Here's the thing. I had met Princess Diana. I had met Elizabeth Taylor. But this? This was Liza Minnelli. My teenage idol. Liza worked her way through the crowd, eventually reaching us. She was smaller than I expected! She chatted with Marlee and David while Ruthie and I stood there like starstruck statues. Then Marlee said "Liza, this is Bill Pugin. He plays my interpreter in my show." Liza turned to me, eyes sparkling, and asked, "So you know sign language? How did I do?" What could I say? "You were perfect." Then, with that trademark Liza enthusiasm, she hugged me. "Thank you! That means a lot!" Then she hugged me again, And vanished into the crowd. And just like that, My life was complete.

Jeffrey was getting sicker. Hospitals became a revolving door. And through it all, Marlee was a lifeline, not just to me, but to Jeffrey too. He adored her. Marlee, of course, loved his sarcasm, his bluntness, and their shared Jewish upbringing, full of eye-rolls, guilt, and family stories too absurd to be fiction.

Jeffrey had been an only child, born to older parents who hadn't exactly planned on a kid. His relationship with his father was strained. His mother was his idol, even though she was tough as nails. They were gone. Both of them, by the time he was a teenager. Leaving him with an inheritance, a sense of freedom, and an overwhelming sense of loss. He had an aunt and uncle in Elmira, a few cousins, But the second he turned 18, he left home and never looked back. Had I met him then I think his life would have been very different.

At that time, medical advancements for AIDS patients were still frustratingly limited. People were still sick. Still dying. We tried everything. Anytime a new medication was announced, Jeffrey was on it immediately. If hope came in a pill, we were first in line. I was still filming every day, and the hours were brutal. I needed help.

This is when I met Gary Webber. Gary was a man whose calling in life was to be there for people exactly when they needed him most. He was an angel in human form and he knew what to do and when to do it. And, maybe most importantly, he knew how to take care of me, too. Caregiving is not just about the patient. The ones standing beside them need help, too. I'd be on set, acting, filming, doing my job, and my pager would go off. Jeffrey, wanting to talk. Needing to talk. Gary shielded me when he could.

Intercepting calls, making sure I could stay focused, keep working, and still come home to Jeffrey when it mattered most.

He had it covered.

Along with Marlee helping to keep my life sane, was friend and fellow interpreter, Jann Goldsby. She, Marlee and Jack were friends before I met any of them, and Jann helped keep my ego in check once I ended up on television. She and Jeffrey also shared that Jewish bond that I didn't grow up with.

None of my Jewish friends are religious, or orthodox. I call them "over-the-counter" Jews... but there is definitely a shared connection - food and family - and I loved when Jann was around. She truly brought out the best in Jeffrey.

The way Jann and I met is a story I'll never forget.

Once I left Princess Cruises, I started getting a lot of work interpreting around LA. Apparently, when interpreters called the various agencies to let them know they were available for a job, they were often told, "Oh, sorry. Bill Pugin got that job." Jann would commiserate with Jack and other interpreters after missing out again and again. She would exclaim, "Arrgh! Who is this Bill Pugin and why is he getting all the jobs?"

Well, one day Jann learned that she would be working a job and her team would be… Bill Pugin! She couldn't wait. She told Jack that she was finally going to meet me and she was really ready to hate me for swooping into town and gobbling up all the jobs.

We both fell in love within the first five minutes of our job. We had the same sense of humor and Jann was so upset when she couldn't announce to the world how she "hated Bill Pugin"! Jann helped me through so much in my life that she even came to my Dad's funeral at Arlington National. She's a true friend to this day.

Back to Jeffrey and Gary Webber.

Tim Galardi: The Friend I Never Knew I Needed

One of the greatest things Gary ever did was introduce me to Tim Galardi. Tim had hired Gary the year before, when his partner, James, was sick. As fate would have it, Tim lived right around the corner from me. And every single day, he'd come over to see Jeffrey and me. Tim was a landscape artist, and he'd bring cuttings from his garden, filling our space with color and life. A quiet, steady presence in the middle of the storm. Tim and I are still close friends today. He's still creating beauty wherever he goes. (Marlee even had him design her garden in the Hollywood Hills, which, naturally, led to jobs with other celebrities.) Because when you're the best at what you do, word gets around.

When Reasonable Doubts wrapped for the season, Marlee landed a movie shooting during our hiatus. And guess where it was filming? Portland. Uh-oh. Portland, you again? Alright. Let's try this one more time. The movie was Hear No Evil, a mystery-thriller starring Marlee, D.B. Sweeney, and Martin Sheen. Marlee wanted me to come along as her interpreter, and I wanted to say yes. But, Jeffrey was failing. I wasn't sure if I could leave him.

"You Need a Break"

Jeffrey insisted. "Go." "It'll make Marlee happy, and you need a break." I looked at him like he had lost his mind. A break? Let me walk you through my daily routine.

12 to 14 hours on set. Come home. Take over for Gary. Laundry. Always laundry. Prepare whatever food Jeffrey could keep down. Walk Bosco and Bianca separately (because those two giant beasts were impossible to walk together). Organize Jeffrey's medications. Administer his daily IV treatment through the Hickman catheter in his chest. Sit on the bed and talk with him while administering the treatment. (Sometimes he'd doze off, sometimes he'd want to hear every detail of my day.) Feed the dogs. Clean up after them. Fold the laundry. Again. Make something for myself to eat. Take a shower. Memorize my lines for the next day. Wake up. Do it all again.

"You need a break," he repeated. He wasn't wrong. But how do you step away from someone you love when they need you most?

Gary promised me that Jeffrey would be taken care of. And I believed him. I was making good money on the show, so I upped Gary's contract to have him there 24 hours a day. It was expensive, and I was grateful I could afford it. Jeffrey, of course, hadn't worked in over a year. So I was covering everything. The house, The gardener, Hilda, our cleaning lady, The utilities, The car payments…

And speaking of cars, Soon after starting on Reasonable Doubts, I upgraded my Acura to a brand-new BMW. I had loved my first Beemer, the one that had lived in Brian's garage. But now I could afford a new one. So I bought it. I was thrilled. I drove it home, excited to show Jeffrey. "Come on," I said. "Let's go for a ride." He tried. He walked slowly to the passenger side. Sat down. Looked around. "I love it," he said, smiling. But he was exhausted. He needed to go back inside and lie down.

Jeffrey had bought a little Toyota when he could still drive. The payments were still being made and I kept making them. Not because he needed the car, But because I needed the hope. The idea that maybe, one day, he'd be well enough to drive it again. But that day never came. Eventually, I sold it. And that day felt heavier than I ever expected it to.

While I was in Portland, Los Angeles was on fire. The Rodney King verdict had come down, and the riots exploded across the city. I watched the news in horror. Buildings burning. People running. The city I called home was unrecognizable. I called Jeffrey every day.

"How are you? Can you see the smoke?" "Yeah," he said. "I can smell it from the house." "How's the movie? How's Marlee? Are you eating? You better be eating." Jeffrey, even in the middle of everything, still being the Jewish mother.

Being in Portland and working on the movie was a lot of fun and a welcome escape. I befriended one of the actresses in the film, Christina Carlisi. Tina played the character "Grace," who was the best friend of Marlee's character, "Jillian." When we had time off, Tina and I loved exploring Portland, its wonderful shops and restaurants, and we are still great friends today.

The director of the film, Robert Greenwald, told me he needed two small roles to be played and asked if I'd be interested in either the doctor or policeman role. I asked him if either character had to wear a hat.

"That's an odd question," he said.

I explained that I looked ridiculous in hats, any hat. I can't even wear a baseball cap without someone asking if I'm a chemo patient. Performing on Princess Cruises always found me in a hat, an English Bobby helmet, a Mexican sombrero, a sailor's cap, a cowboy hat… every time I walked out on stage, I would get a laugh from the audience.

"I'll play the doctor, thank you."

So, I appeared as "Dr. Tucker," wearing no hat. My one line was pivotal! My character informed the audience that Grace would survive her terrible accident! And scene.

Then, near the end of May, I got the call that changed everything. It was Gary. "It's time to come home." I had a contingency plan, just in case. I put it into motion. Kayelle Morgan, my friend and colleague from the TDD Distribution Center, flew up to Portland to take my place. Marlee understood. She knew I had to go. When Kayelle arrived, I ran her through everything she needed to know, gave Marlee a hug, and left for Van Nuys.

Everything moved fast when I got home. Too fast. Gary held my hand through all of it. We did everything we could to keep Jeffrey comfortable. Jeffrey was only 30 years old and terrified. He wasn't ready. Who would be at that age?

One day, he told me about a dream he had. His mother was calling to him, motioning for him to come closer.

"That's good, right?" I asked.

"No! I've always been scared of her!"

And we laughed. For the first time in a long time, we laughed. Then, he looked at me, serious now, and said he had two things he wanted me to promise him.

"Anything," I said. "Promise me you'll take care of the dogs." "Of course." "And promise me you'll buy the house." I was confused. "Buy the house?" I asked. Wouldn't he just leave me the house?

After three years together, Jeffrey told me a secret he had never shared. He didn't own the house. His accountant, Penny, did. I had known Penny through Jeffrey. She did our taxes. She never once mentioned that she owned the house I thought Jeffrey owned.

He explained that when he got his inheritance, he wanted to buy the house, but he had no credit history. So, Penny came up with a plan. Jeffrey gave her the down payment, and she put the house in her name. Jeffrey paid her like a mortgage. But legally, he had been renting from her.

"So, you've been renting the house from Penny this whole time?"

He nodded.

I didn't press it. I didn't want him to feel bad. But I wished I had known him before he made some of these big financial decisions.

I had never owned a house before and I made the promise. So, I bought it. And I stayed there for 18 years. Taking care of Bosco and Bianca until their last days.

Jeffrey had a yellow legal pad stuck to the side of the fridge. His wish list. The list was a running tally of things he wanted for the house. Things that, over the years, I actually managed to complete. It took time. It took eighteen years, in fact. But one by one, I crossed them off:

New roof ✔ Central A/C (because we were not going to suffer through another LA summer like peasants) ✔ New hardwood floors (only the best for Jeffrey's high standards) ✔ New appliances ✔ Interior and exterior painted in his favorite Dunn-Edwards colors ✔ Electric gate installed ✔ Fountains added ✔ A cactus garden (thank you, Tim!) ✓ A primary suite and bath with a raised tub and separate shower And, of course, the most important thing: ✓ A walk-in closet Because priorities. ✓

Jeffrey had been in a coma for three days. People called, wanting to come visit. I told them no. He wasn't able to see anyone. But our friends came over anyway, for me.

It was Saturday, June 27. We were sitting in the living room, maybe six or seven of us, when Jeffrey appeared in the doorway. Standing. Awake. We froze. He just stood there, holding onto the door frame. Finally, I said the only thing that came to mind.

"Hey, sleepyhead!" Jeffrey then said, "I'm hungry. I want Chinese food." Of course he did.

Jeffrey loved to eat, and he loved to cook. He must have owned over 100 cookbooks! When we met, he had been pushing 200 pounds. Now? Eighty-six. So, if he wanted Chinese food, then we were getting Chinese food.

"Then we shall order Chinese food!" I said, as if I were granting a royal decree.

Everyone jumped up, helping Jeffrey into the living room. We ordered everything. When it arrived, we sat back and watched in awe as Jeffrey devoured plate after plate of sweet and sour everything. I had never been so happy to watch someone eat.

Finally, when he was too tired to keep going, I sent everyone home. And I put him to bed.

At 5 a.m. on Sunday morning, the Landers earthquake decided to shake us all awake with its 7.3 Richter scale tantrum. Landers, California, out in San Bernardino County, was miles away from the Valley, but still managed to make itself known. The bed shook. The windows rattled. Jeffrey startled awake, wide-eyed and terrified.

"Should we turn on the TV? Check the magnitude?" he asked, his voice weak but urgent.

"No," I said. "Let's go back to sleep. We'll check in the morning." He paused, looked at me, and then... "Oh. Thank you for the Chinese food. Thank you for everything." And with that, he closed his eyes. He never woke up again. At noon on Sunday, June 28, Jeffrey was gone.

I had already made all the arrangements long before he passed. But that morning, the house was a disaster. Empty Chinese takeout boxes everywhere, tipped over cartons of rice, half-eaten dumplings, the remnants of last night's celebration still lingering. I hadn't bothered cleaning up before bed. I was too happy. Too grateful that Jeffrey had been awake, talking, eating, alive.

But when I woke up, I knew. I knew that day would be the day. Gary had told me about Cheyne-Stokes breathing, the irregular, labored breathing pattern that comes before the end. It was happening now. I tried speaking to him. No response.

I called Gary. I called Merry Moore. Merry took charge, picking up the phone to call my parents, because at that moment, I couldn't speak. Then, she turned to me, phone in hand.

"Your dad wants to ask you something."

My dad was a true Southern gentleman, born in Savannah, raised in Nashville, and a firm believer that family was everything. If there was a fourth cousin, three times removed, by marriage, living in San Diego, my dad expected me to track them down the next time I was there.

"They're family!" he'd insist.

So when I took the phone from Merry, I was still surprised by what came next. Through the receiver, I could hear my mom crying. Then, Dad's voice.

"Where are Jeffrey's parents?" "They died," I told him. "Where are his siblings?" "He's an only child."

There was a long pause. Then my dad said something I will never forget as long as I live.

"You go in there and tell him we will be his parents." "Tell him he has parents who are alive and who love him. Tell him."

I put the phone down. I went to Jeffrey's bedside. I told him. Someone once told me that hearing is the last thing to go. I hoped that was true. Because I needed him to hear it.

Gary watched over us like a guardian. "Go make a pot of coffee," he said.

I walked into the kitchen, mechanically measuring the grounds, filling the pot. And then, before the coffee had even finished brewing, Gary appeared. Softly, he said -

"It's time to call Aftercare. He's gone."

You brace yourself for the inevitable. You think you're prepared. And then, when it finally happens, it doesn't feel real.

For so long, caring for Jeffrey had been my life. My routine. My purpose. And just like that, my job had been taken away from me.

I made the call.

Gary, ever the guardian angel, took me by the hand and led me to the cupboard, where bottles upon bottles of Jeffrey's medications lined the shelves.

"We need to clear these out," he said.

One by one, I threw them into a grocery-sized bag, the sheer weight of it startling me. All that effort. All those pills. And now, none of it mattered.

Gary reached in and pulled out one bottle. "Keep the morphine," he said. "You might need it." I nodded, not knowing exactly what he meant. I watched as the body bag was zipped up and Jeffrey was taken away. That image would stay with me forever. I will always be grateful for Gary and my late friend, Merry, for being there in the moment I needed them most.

The next day, my sister Evelyn and her then husband, Mike, both longtime Delta employees, flew me to Georgia to be with Mom and Dad. I probably should have stayed longer. But I couldn't shake the feeling that I needed to be back at the house. Bosco and Bianca were waiting for me. And honestly? I think I was waiting for Jeffrey to walk through the door, too.

Two weeks later, I filled the house again. I invited everyone who knew me and Jeffrey, over one hundred people came for Jeffrey's memorial. Mom and Dad flew in. Mom was sick with cancer, and she would pass away the following year, but she insisted on being there. Jeffrey's childhood friend, Susan Boedicker, came all the way from Elmira. His cousin, Kate, too. They helped me go through his things, closets, drawers, every small reminder of the life he had built. We donated everything to charity. I couldn't have done it alone.

The house was happy again, buzzing with voices and laughter. One by one, people stood up, sharing stories about Jeffrey, who he was, what he meant, why he mattered. Marlee was there. I had Francine interpret for her and for the many Deaf friends who came to support me. At the end of the afternoon, we wrote messages to Jeffrey, private words we weren't ready to say out loud, tied them to white balloons, and let them go. Most of the balloons got caught in the wires in the backyard. Jeffrey would have thought this was hilarious.

As the last guests trickled out, someone turned to me. "Do you think you would have been with Jeffrey for the rest of your life?" I smiled. "Who knows? All I know is that I was with him for the rest of his."

Everyone at the Season Two table read was buzzing with excitement, hugging, laughing, catching up. It all felt awkward. I was faking it. I wanted to be just as excited, but I had a grief-sized weight sitting on my chest.

Bob Singer, Mark, the producers, everyone knew. Word had spread and they were nothing but kind. Their sympathy wasn't forced or performative. It was genuine, and I appreciated it.

But what I really appreciated?

Bob and Lorimar gave me five days off to fly to New York and scatter Jeffrey's ashes.

This was no small task on television. Schedules were airtight, and the slightest shift meant ripple effects for an entire production.

Still, they made it work.

I packed my bags and flew to Elmira, where Jeffrey's aunt, uncle, cousins, and childhood friend, Susan took me to Keuka Lake, one of the Finger Lakes in upstate New York.

This was the only place from Jeffrey's childhood that he talked about with joy. It was quiet as I stood at the edge of the lake, bag in hand. The others had already begun crying. I told myself I would keep it together. I took a deep breath. Opened the bag. Began to pour. A gust of wind. An ill-timed, completely predictable, Jeffrey-style gust of wind. His ashes did not scatter into the lake. They blew all over me. I was covered. In pure Jeffrey fashion, he refused to go quietly. If he had been there, he would have shrieked with laughter. And then dusted me off while still laughing.

Back in LA, it actually felt good to be working again. This season, they gave Ben more to do. There were even talks of giving him an apartment and a personal life in Season Three. Yeah. That didn't happen. In Season One, we were stuck in TV purgatory, Friday nights at 10 p.m. That's where shows go to die. NBC agreed to move us to Tuesday nights at 9 p.m. Great, right? Not exactly. We were now opposite Roseanne, a.k.a. the number one show on television.

By spring of '93, the writing was on the wall. Our ratings were too low. The fans we had were loyal, but there just weren't enough of them. If we had lasted just one more season, we would've made it to syndication. And that would have meant healthy residuals for years. But after 45 episodes, it was over. Canceled. Cut to black. It was strange not driving to Warner Bros. anymore.

I wasn't waking up at 5 a.m. to sit in a makeup chair, or running lines in my dressing room, or trying to coach Mark Harmon's football-injured hands into some kind of legible ASL.

So, I did what any newly unemployed actor does. I called GLAD and told them I was available again.

Oh, how the mighty have fallen.

I went from primetime TV to interpreting at doctor's offices in about five seconds. But Hollywood didn't forget me.

Word got around, and soon I was back on sets, but this time as an ASL tutor, interpreter, and technical advisor. When they needed someone to make sure people weren't signing gibberish, they called me.

And when I wasn't on set, I was reviving SCRIPT, my little interpreting business that had taken a backseat while I was playing Ben Douglass, TV's first full-time interpreter character.

It didn't take long before my calendar was just as packed as before.

Freelance interpreting has always been my favorite. I loved meeting new people, being in wildly different environments, and occasionally being recognized in the waiting room of a gynecologist's office.

(Yes, that happened. No, I wasn't the patient.)

I'd walk into a classroom, a courtroom, or a hospital and inevitably hear "What's it like having to drive around and interpret when you used to be on TV?" At first, it was tough. I missed the creative energy of television. I missed the paychecks (oh, how I missed the paychecks). But the truth was I loved this work. It was different every day. The people, their needs, the situations, no two were the same. And for someone like me, someone who thrived on new adventures, this was exactly where I was meant to be.

When the Northridge earthquake shook all of California in 1994, a new adventure certainly happened for me.

The epicenter was only a couple of miles from my house in Van Nuys, and talk about a rude awakening! The grand piano shifted from one part of the living room to the other. All dishes and glasses were broken, and LA was a mess.

Dad called me to report on the damage because there was no electricity for television. My landline stayed operational, which was very important. After my conversation with Dad, the phone rang with KTLA, Channel 5 calling asking if I could drive to their studios in Hollywood to interpret live.

I couldn't shower, shave or look anything resembling "professional", but I said I would come. I had to pry open the electric gate to get my car out, and the drive to Hollywood was like driving through a war zone.

Once at the studio, I was fitted with a headset so that I could hear the reports from all over the city. The heavy lights hanging above would rattle and threaten to drop due to all the aftershocks, but I stayed at my desk - even while the anchors dove underneath theirs.

I kept thinking to myself, "Well, Bill... you wanted to be in entertainment. What a way to go... interpreting while being crushed by studio lighting equipment crashing down!"

Medicine fascinated me. In particular, I was drawn to the mental health field, two days a week, I worked at Saint John's Mental Health Clinic in Santa Monica. The drive was a nightmare, but the work was endlessly fascinating. My role was to interpret staff meetings for the two deaf therapists and, more importantly, interpret therapy sessions between non-signing therapists and psychiatrists treating Deaf patients.

These patients came from all over Los Angeles because St. John's was the only place for treatment in ASL. Some traveled three hours by bus just to have a 20-minute session with a doctor. There should have been more accessible clinics across the city, but the ever-reliable excuse of "We don't have the funding" meant that St. John's was the only option.

It made my job incredibly challenging because Deaf patients, like all patients, had a vast range of diagnoses such as schizophrenia, depression, bipolar disorder, borderline personality disorder. But what made it even trickier was that so many of them had stopped taking their meds. And let me tell you, that's when things got really interesting.

Ever tried interpreting for a Deaf person experiencing auditory hallucinations? How do you explain the voices they're hearing?

I became hyper-aware of facial expressions and body language. Some patients were more unpredictable than others, so I learned to spot warning signs fast. If I sensed danger, I had a go-to phrase: "Interpreter unsafe." That was my cue to bolt for the door. And it happened more than once.

One major issue was that patients sometimes struggled to separate me from the doctor. I would position myself directly behind the doctor's left shoulder, physically as close as possible without touching them, trying to steer the patient to look at the actual person treating them. But it didn't always work.

If the doctor said something upsetting, the patient would glare at me. I'd subtly nod toward the doctor, trying to signal "Him! He said it, not me!"

That didn't always work either.

One session, I kept signing the word "computer", but it wasn't the choice of the sign that this particular patient used. I didn't know this until he'd had enough. He lunged at me. The doctor had to physically pry him off me, and, well... session over.

Note to self: Sign "computer" his way next time.

Another day, another awkward medical exam.

This time, I was in the exam room with a husband and wife. The wife had been experiencing some, uh… itching down there, and they needed to get it checked out. Simple enough. After some tests and a thorough examination, the doctor turned to them and, with all the finesse of a man who had done this far too many times, announced -

"You have an STD."

Awkward.

Now, I'm not saying I could feel the temperature in the room drop, but let's just say I'm very glad I wasn't riding home in their car with them.

One of the most poignant moments of my interpreting career happened at a hospital appointment with an elderly gentleman seeing his urologist. I arrived early, as usual, so I could assess the patient's language needs and make sure my interpretation choices were the best fit. His wife was with him, and we had a lovely chat in the waiting room. They were adorable. Married 55 years and still holding hands like teenagers.

When the doctor was ready, I followed the patient in, taking my usual position next to the doctor so the patient could see both of us at the same time without having to shift his gaze.

The doctor didn't waste any time. "I have your results. Your PSA number is off the charts, and we found cancer. We need to schedule surgery immediately."

The man nodded, keeping the same pleasant smile on his face. "Thank you for letting me know, but no thank you for the surgery." The doctor blinked. "I don't think you understood what I said. You have cancer. Your prostate must be removed."

"I understood you," the man said. "We have an interpreter here who was very clear. I don't want the surgery. I have a friend who had this surgery, and he told me it ruined his sex life."

Good for you, old man!

The doctor looked at me like I had somehow mis-interpreted "cancer" into "mild indigestion."

"Are you sure you're interpreting exactly what I'm saying?" I nodded. As an interpreter, we're asked this quite often. The doctor excused himself and left the room.

Now, this is a crucial moment for an interpreter. When the doctor leaves, we're supposed to leave, too. Otherwise, the patient might start talking to us, and suddenly, we're holding onto information we shouldn't have. We're neutral. We're not part of the conversation, we just carry it from one person to another.

I got up to go, but the elderly man caught my eye and signed, "Please stay with me." So, I stayed.

Then, with a quiet confidence, he told me that he understood exactly what he was doing. He knew the consequences, but he was determined to live out the rest of his life as is. No surgery. No long recovery. No missing out on life. And most importantly?

"There's a deaf bowling event in Las Vegas next month, and I refuse to miss it." I mean…priorities. Then he asked me something interpreters dread hearing. "Do you think I'm making the right decision?"

This is why we leave the room. It puts us in an impossible position. We're not supposed to have opinions. We're certainly not supposed to share them. I knew I couldn't answer, so I did the next best thing, I deflected.

"I'm not into bowling, but Las Vegas is fun."

He caught the dodge. His face told me as much. But he didn't push.

The doctor returned with a piece of paper, documenting everything. The diagnosis, the recommendation, the patient's absolute refusal to move forward with surgery. His frustration was evident, but he maintained professionalism as he once again urged the man to reconsider.

The patient simply nodded, signed the paper, and stood up. He shook the doctor's hand, signed "Thank you for your time," and we walked out together.

In the waiting room, his wife put down her book, tucked her glasses into her purse, and stood up. She looked at her husband.

"Everything okay?" "Everything's fine. Are you ready to go?"
Then she turned to me. "Is that true? Is everything okay?"

I looked at them, this couple who had spent decades together, who had built an entire life side by side. I took both their
hands in mine, gave them a reassuring smile, and signed -

"It was a pleasure meeting you both."

Then I watched as they walked down the long, narrow cor-
ridor, his arm wrapped around her shoulder, until they disap-
peared from sight.

There were probably thousands of jobs I interpreted in the
field of medicine, but the most exciting, by far, was being part
of the interpreting team for a deaf medical student at UCLA.
This was a three-year commitment, and I teamed up with my
good friend, Roberta (RJ) Munsey. RJ was a powerhouse in medical interpreting. She had experience, confidence, and the kind
of stomach that could handle anything, a crucial quality when
you're about to spend years up close and personal with the human body in all its less glamorous states.

Our student was brilliant. She had been raised oral and took
an entire year off from her medical studies to learn ASL. That
alone impressed me. Most people don't take a year off from anything to learn a whole new language, much less the one they'll be
using to navigate med school. The first part of her training was
easier, lots of virtual lectures, self-study, and online modules all
with captions. But when she started her rotations, she needed us
there.

RJ and I basically became medical students by proxy, except we never had to take an exam (thank God). We wore scrubs every day and followed her through every rotation, witnessing things that made me rethink my entire existence.

One of her rotations was in the ER of a South Central Los Angeles County hospital. And let me tell you, this was not the ER of a Hallmark movie where the doctor stitches up a single cut and falls in love with the patient. This was full-on trauma. The ER was always packed, not just with patients, but with as many police officers as doctors. The cases that came through were intense. Gunshot wounds. Gang violence. Knife attacks. Car crashes. Drug overdoses. Domestic abuse. That was a Tuesday morning.

One late-night shift, they wheeled in an entire family, stabbed by their house renter. I remember standing there, completely stunned, watching the doctors triage the scene like a highly organized war zone. That night, I walked out of the hospital with a whole new level of respect for ER doctors and nurses.

Another rotation took us to the Operating Room. And this was a completely different world. If the ER was chaos, the OR was choreographed chaos, complete with a god complex headliner.

Operating Rooms are tight spaces, surgeons, anesthesiologists, nurses, machines, beeping monitors. Add two interpreters into the mix, and suddenly, you've got a room with about four too many people. But the real showstopper was the surgeon himself.

This guy was treated like Elvis. I was half-expecting someone to throw a cape over his shoulders when he walked in. The nurses practically dressed him, holding out his gloves, adjusting his gown, while he stood there like he was about to descend from the heavens. Then, without missing a beat, he barked for the Rock music to be turned up.

The patient was an elderly woman, fully prepped, unconscious on the table. The surgeon glanced at her, barely registering that she was a human being, announced her name and procedure, and then, with the grace of a man flipping a pancake, flopped her over like a dead fish.

And suddenly, all those unexplained bruises I had after my own surgeries made sense.

On the very first day of filming Reasonable Doubts, Marlee walked right up to a cop, threw her arms around him, and gave him a big hug. There was just one small problem, this man was not the cop she thought he was.

Now, in those days, if Marlee wasn't wearing her glasses, she was basically wandering the world blind as a newborn. Turns out, the police officer she had just warmly embraced was not her longtime friend, but an entirely different and very confused Burbank cop named Kevin.

Marlee, absolutely mortified, started apologizing profusely. Kevin, meanwhile, was not complaining.

They got married two years later.

But I'm skipping ahead, so forgive me. This is a fantastic medical interpreting story, and I promise it's worth it.

In 1995, Marlee and I had just wrapped filming The Outer Limits in Vancouver when she called me over to her house. She opened the door, pulled me inside, shut it behind us, and with the most serious expression on her face, said -

"I'm pregnant."

Now, given all the insane situations I had been roped into over the years, you'd think this wouldn't shock me. But it did. And before I could even say congratulations, I realized exactly what this meant.

I was about to become her personal pregnancy interpreter.

I was there for everything. Every medical appointment, every test, and yes, every single Lamaze class. Kevin, of course, was her official coach, but I was at their side interpreting everything into ASL.

So, if you ever need highly detailed instructions on breathing techniques, birth positions, or the exact moment when a woman is ready to kill everyone in the delivery room, I'm your guy.

In our Lamaze class was a woman named Mia Radcliffe. I loved Mia. She had this fabulous New Zealand accent, and we spent most of the classes cracking jokes and getting to know each other. Mia was the first in the class to give birth, and I was genuinely sad that we hadn't exchanged numbers.

Fast forward 13 years, I'm out walking my dog in Studio City, and who do I randomly run into? Mia. Turns out, she had been living in the building right next to mine. We immediately picked up where we left off, and now we're in touch all the time.

The call finally came. It's time. I met Marlee and Kevin at their house, and we all rode together to Cedars-Sinai.

Now, I have been in my fair share of intense situations, multiple hospitals, multiple high-stress environments, but nothing quite prepared me for childbirth.

Marlee was in labor for hours. I stood next to the machine, watching the contractions spike and letting her know when one was coming, because after finally receiving an epidural, she had no idea when they were happening.

Finally, early on January 19, 1996, Sarah was born. It was an incredible moment. Beautiful. Emotional. The miracle of life. And also? Absolutely, 100% not for me.

The second it was over, I turned to Marlee and said, "If you ever have another kid, I highly recommend finding another interpreter." She went on to have three more. I went on to never interpret a birth again.

When Sarah was nine months old, Marlee landed a movie in Toronto with James Garner. And just like that, we were off to the Four Seasons in Yorkville, a neighborhood so upscale it practically came with a personal shopper and a faint whiff of Chanel in the air.

Let me tell you about Yorkville. This place is the destination for affluent shoppers, full of high-end boutiques, swanky galleries, and designer studios. Bloor Street's "Mink Mile" was dangerous, not because of crime, but because our credit cards practically begged for mercy every time we walked past a storefront. The side streets were lined with stunning Victorian homes with meticulously manicured gardens, and it was the kind of place where even the pigeons seemed more refined.

Marlee and I, of course, took full advantage.

The thing about doing location shoots with Marlee is that the work is fantastic, but the hanging out is even better. If we weren't on set, we were either laughing until we cried or shopping until our wallets did. And if we were shopping outside the U.S.? Well, that wasn't real money... right?

This particular movie was especially fun because we worked with a lot of local Deaf kids and their interpreters. Canadians primarily use ASL, but they have quite a few signs that are different from ours. So, half the time, I wasn't just interpreting, I was also learning.

Now, let's talk about the Four Seasons Experience.

Marlee and I were on the same floor. She had a suite, because, well, she's Marlee, and I had a perfectly nice room next door. Every morning, without fail, there would be a knock at my door. I'd open it, and there, sitting on the floor, would be Sarah. Beaming. Toothless. Adorable.

Marlee, of course, had placed her there, knocked, and then ducked around the corner like some kind of mischievous elf. And just like that, my day would start with the best possible greeting.

We also befriended the legendary head concierge, Randy Ross. Randy was the guy. He was the kind of concierge who could make things happen.

When he learned I liked a specific brand of vodka for my evening martini, he had it brought in from New York. This brand wasn't available in Canada yet, so they couldn't serve it in the bar, but Randy had it delivered to my room.

So, there I was, sitting alone in my hotel room, a perfectly chilled martini appearing at my door nightly, feeling both incredibly sophisticated and a bit like a lonely lush because I had to drink it in my room.

At the end of our six-week stay, Randy gifted me the martini shaker.

Madonna had stayed at the same Four Seasons while shooting a film in Toronto and insisted Randy be at her beck and call, even on his days off. The man had a reputation for excellence, and it wasn't long before he was recruited to The Pierre in New York and later Miami. We still keep in touch, and yes, I still have the martini shaker.

Marlee and I worked in Canada many times over the years, Vancouver, Montreal, Toronto, New Brunswick.

One of the movies we worked on in Canada was Freak City in 1999. This film had a stacked cast, but what made it extra special was that singer Natalie Cole was making her acting debut. And she was nervous.

Now, let's be clear… Natalie Cole. As in Unforgettable. As in This Will Be (An Everlasting Love). I couldn't believe I was sitting next to her at the cast welcome dinner hosted by director Lynne Littman.

Marlee, on the other hand, was unfazed. She wasn't really familiar with Natalie's music and had no idea why I was so excited.

Natalie, being the absolute queen that she was, leaned over and explained to Marlee, "Bill is talking about This Will Be. It was my first hit. It put me on the map."

I mentioned to Natalie that I always had trouble remembering the lyrics to the fast part of the song. Then, as if the universe decided to reward me for all my good deeds, Natalie took a sip of water, set down her glass, and sang the fast part of This Will Be right there at the dinner table… to me.

I got a private Natalie Cole concert and a free meal!

In total, I've worked on 28 projects with Marlee. If I went into detail on every single one, this book would be longer than War and Peace. On many of these projects, I wasn't just her interpreter, I was also the sign language coach and tutor for the actors working with her.

Some highlights?

Eric Roberts (It's My Party), a hoot. Olivia Newton-John (also It's My Party), an actual goddess. She even invited me to her house in Malibu to sit in her hot tub, which jutted out over the Pacific Ocean. Why didn't I go? I have no idea. That is a regret I will carry to my grave.

But of those 28 projects, the most unforgettable one was Askari, a movie about elephants, filmed in South Africa.

Marlee and I were flown First Class on South African Airways. I had flown First Class before, but never like this. I never wanted to get off that plane. The movie also starred C. Thomas Howell, and, yes, we literally worked with elephants.

They are the most majestic, intelligent creatures on earth. We were given strict rules to never approach an elephant without a trainer, and never walk underneath them. The trainers could do it because the elephants trusted them. We were just a couple of clueless Americans with a script.

And trust me, when an elephant the size of a two-story building doesn't trust you? You learn quickly.

During our downtime, we were taken to a crocodile farm and a private lion preserve. Because, you know, what else does one do on a day off in Africa?

The man who owned the preserve turned to Marlee and asked if she'd like to hold a lion cub. She politely declined. I, on the other hand, did not hesitate. "Absolutely," I said, picturing myself in some kind of Born Free moment, bonding with wildlife.

That fantasy lasted exactly four seconds.

The cub they brought out was not so small, and those tiny, adorable paws came with razor-sharp claws. As I held the little guy, he extended one of those claws right into my t-shirt, slicing through the fabric and straight to my chest.

The owner, unfazed, clapped me on the back and said, "Well, now you can tell people you've been attacked by a lion." Perfect. Just what I wanted, another great travel anecdote. Also, it happened to be one of my favorite t-shirts!

When the movie wrapped, we flew home in First Class again. A week later, my friend David Fader and I flew to Australia for a two-week vacation. This time, I was in the middle seat of Economy Class. Again, how the mighty have fallen.

I worked on plenty of projects without Marlee, but let's be honest, they were never as much fun. When Reasonable Doubts was canceled in 1993, I had a few months of licking my wounds and recalibrating. Then the phone rang.

It was the office of Ilona Herzberg, an executive producer looking for a sign language tutor and interpreter for a deaf actor. Ilona explained the film, where it would be shot, and what she needed. At first, it sounded straightforward. The lead actress needed to learn to sign because the actor playing her father was deaf, and there were a few scenes where she would sign to her young son as a secret form of communication.

Then, casually, like it was no big deal, Ilona added, "Oh, you'll have to be on location for four months." Now, let's review.

My show had just been canceled. I was broke. Every dime I had made in those two years had gone toward Jeffrey's care. And now, a job offer on a silver platter.

I would have to leave the dogs again, but this was exactly the kind of opportunity you don't think about. You just say yes.

There were still plenty of unanswered questions, but Ilona assured me that all the details, travel, lodging, per diem, and, most importantly, who I'd be working with, would be coming later in the day.

When the production office sent over the information, I skimmed through the logistics, then landed on the crucial piece. The film was called The River Wild, and it would star Meryl Streep, Kevin Bacon, and David Strathairn.

I did a double take. MERYL. STREEP. I needed to sit down. And possibly breathe into a paper bag.

Filming would take place in Oregon and Montana, and once I arrived in Grants Pass, Oregon, I'd start immediately. The actor cast as Meryl's father was none other than Vic Galloway, a man I had worked with at CSUN. In fact, I'd been Vic's personal interpreter for months, so this felt like an unexpected and wonderful reunion.

Vic wasn't an actor by trade, but he fit the role perfectly. He was a Deaf man in his late 60s or early 70s, over six feet tall, rugged, exactly what the production was looking for. His on-screen wife, Meryl's mother, was played by Elizabeth Hoffman, fresh off Sisters, which had been shooting just a few soundstages away from Reasonable Doubts at Warner Bros.

The interpreting and entertainment worlds are surprisingly small. Shortly after I arrived in Grants Pass, we had the table read. Everyone was already in the room. And then, she walked in. Meryl. Streep.

I stood up straighter, trying to maintain an air of professionalism. Every fiber of my being wanted to sprint over to her, grab her hands, and pour out my admiration. Instead, I just kept repeating to myself: You are a professional. You are here to work. Do not screw this up.

I took my seat next to Vic so I could track the script for him, and I did my best to focus. Kevin Bacon, playing the villain, added just the right amount of unsettling creepiness to his delivery. He was already in character. And then Meryl started reading. Just reading. No performance, no emotion, just words on a page.

At first, I was surprised, but over the next four months, I got to observe one of the greatest actresses of all time up close, and I learned that this was one of her techniques. She didn't perform at table reads. She simply let the words settle.

This was Meryl's only action film, and she had been convinced to do it by her son, Henry, who thought it would be cool for his mom to do a thriller with whitewater rafting and bad guys.

And she didn't hold back.

She did a lot of her own stunts, paddling through rapids, hanging onto rafts for dear life. I can't even begin to imagine what the insurance cost must have been. Of course, for the truly dangerous stunts, her double stepped in. Production wouldn't dream of risking Meryl.

But she was all in. And I was about to have a front-row seat to the magic. The day had finally arrived. Meryl Streep's first sign language lesson.

In The River Wild, Meryl's character, Gail, was the daughter of a Deaf man and a teacher at a school for Deaf children in Boston. That meant she couldn't just fake signing, she had to look like she'd been doing it her whole life. No stiff, uncertain hands. No hesitation. She needed to be fluid, natural, effortless.

Luckily, I had a knack for making actors look fluent. There were always little tricks, cheating movements, signing with one hand when possible, and just generally looking like you know what you're doing.

I drove over to the house… correction, mansion… that had been rented for Meryl in Grants Pass. When I rang the doorbell, she answered.

We had already met at the table read, so there was no awkward Hi, nice to meet you, I'm a huge fan, oh god, did I just say that out loud? moment. The first thing I did say, however, was, "Nice house."

She laughed. "It's too much. I don't need all this."

Meryl Streep, Academy Award-winning, actual legend… completely down-to-earth. She had that kind of infectious, hearty, guttural laugh that instantly put you at ease.

She poured two glasses of iced tea, and we headed outside to the enormous patio that overlooked the kind of view that makes you want to quit your job, write poetry, and start a lavender farm.

Oregon is stunning, and whoever picked this house knew exactly what they were doing.

I always start my lessons with a quick primer on deafness: pre-lingually deaf vs. post-lingually deaf, deaf vs. hard of hearing, ASL vs. oralism, the works. Most actors sit through it with the polite-but-glazed-over look of someone who just wants to skip to the good part.

But Meryl was engaged.

She asked questions. Smart ones. She knew that every detail helped shape her character, so she absorbed everything.

Once I confirmed she was right-handed, I got into the actual mechanics, dominant and base hands, proper form. It was a lot of information in a short time, but she was soaking it all in.

I thought, Piece of cake. It was not a piece of cake.

The second I started teaching her actual signs, she got flustered. Confused. She'd repeat after me, then immediately forget. I reassured her that ASL was a language, and it would take time, but I was there to make sure she'd get it.

Well… she didn't get it. At least, not that first lesson. After two hours of struggling, I finally felt comfortable enough to break the tension with, "Wow. You really suck at this." Meryl threw back her head and let out one of those deep, guttural laughs.

"This is fucking hard!" she groaned. I laughed, too. "Don't worry. I won't let you embarrass yourself on film."

While Meryl struggled, her on-screen son, Joey Mazzello (a.k.a. the kid from Jurassic Park), picked up his signs in one lesson. The first time through, he had everything memorized, fluid, and perfect. I could officially check him off my to do list and focus all my attention on Meryl.

And she had a lot to juggle.

In addition to learning ASL, she also had to master shooting a gun, fly fishing, and river rafting like a pro. This wasn't just a movie; it was Meryl's Outdoor Adventure Camp.

Since her schedule was jam-packed, I had to find ways to fit in our sessions. Fortunately, I had an in.

Meryl traveled with what was known as a Preferred List. This is a short, highly exclusive lineup of people who were essential to her success on set. These were the ones given VIP treatment.

There were only four people on that list. J. Roy Helland, her longtime hair and makeup artist; Maria, her personal masseuse; Maggie Pierson, her assistant; and me. Not too shabby for a guy who just told Meryl Streep she sucked at sign language.

The River Wild was a big-budget Universal picture. And when I say big, I mean big. Helicopters, remote mountain locations, roaring rapids, and a cast full of A-listers. None of it came cheap.

When a movie like this goes on location, studios will often pay families to temporarily move out of their homes so the actors can stay somewhere more comfortable than a generic hotel. Libby, Montana wasn't exactly overflowing with luxury resorts, so this arrangement was necessary. I have no idea what the families were paid, but I imagine it was enough to make them very comfortable somewhere else for a while.

For my accommodations, I lived with Vic, his wife Marilyn, and Elizabeth Hoffman in a stunning lakeside home, complete with a dock and a boat. The view was postcard perfect, the air smelled ridiculously fresh, and I had a lot of time off, with pay.

Meryl didn't have much signing in the film, which meant I wasn't needed on set every day. But she didn't want me to leave, either. Every now and then, she'd get inspired mid-scene and decide to add a bit of signing that wasn't in the script. So I had to be on call, ready to drop everything if she needed me.

Case in point:

I was at the house, probably drinking coffee and admiring the scenery, when the phone rang. The production office was on the line. "Meryl wants to sign something in this scene," they said. "We're sending a car for you." Sure enough, within minutes, a car pulled up, whisked me away… and drove me straight to a waiting helicopter. Helicopter?

Meryl, Kevin Bacon (Wade), and John C. Reilly (Terry) were in the middle of filming on a mountainside overlooking the raging rapids below. The fastest way to get me there was to airlift me in.

I'm not a fan of heights, and I seriously considered saying, "I'll do this, but I want hazard pay." But before I could think of a solid excuse, I was already in the air.

The helicopter landed on a clearing on the mountain... but that wasn't where the actors were. Nope. To actually get to them, I had to rappel down a rope to the ledge where Meryl, Kevin, John, and director Curtis Hanson were waiting.

I want to pause here and emphasize that I was rappelling down the side of a mountain just to teach Meryl Streep a sign. I barely had time to process my own life choices before I landed on the ledge, the wind from the chopper still whipping around us.

"Bill, what's the sign for, ?" Meryl asked.

I honestly can't remember what word or phrase she wanted to sign. I was too busy making sure I wasn't about to plunge into the rapids below. But I showed her the signs, she nodded, and just like that, my job was done.

I rappelled back up the mountain, climbed into the waiting helicopter, was flown back to the car, and driven back to the house. All in a day's work. And the funny part is they didn't even use that take!

But hey, at least I got a free helicopter ride and a very dramatic story out of it. I would find myself in a very similar situation years later working on an Anne Hathaway movie. But that's a story for another time.

Around the second week of filming, Meryl had to fly to Tokyo with her husband, Don Gummer, for an art exhibit featuring his work. Before she left, I went into a tiny studio in Libby and recorded all of her scripted signed lines onto videotape. Twice.

First, I faced the camera so she could see the full picture. Then, I turned around and signed everything from her point of view. I learned early on that actors do better when they can see the signs as they would actually perform them, rather than trying to mirror them like some kind of backwards game of charades.

This worked for almost every actor. Except Mark Harmon. Mark… had challenges. And I'm being kind.

I was still nervous about Meryl's signing skills, so I wanted to check in with her the moment she got back from Japan. We met for a class, and she immediately launched into her signed lines, flawless, fluid, confident.

I just stared at her. "What happened?" I asked. "I watched your tape," she said. I must have looked unconvinced, because she added, "I watched your tape many, many times." I was floored. Of course she did. This was Meryl Streep.

We started meeting in her trailer regularly to practice. I always loved glancing at the notes she scribbled in the margins of her script, little insights into how she built her characters. I wasn't above being nosy, I wanted to learn everything I could.

Meanwhile, my back was not cooperating. It had been giving me problems for a while, and finally, one day, it just… gave out.

Meryl took one look at me hobbling around and pulled me into her trailer. "Maria, get the table," she called out.

Maria, her personal masseuse, set up a massage table right there in the trailer, and before I knew it, I was getting worked on. I should have felt embarrassed, but it really helped.

Still, I felt a little guilty. This was Meryl's time, she had an emotional scene to film the next day, and I was in her space. Plus, she had her entire family with her. Her husband and four kids were on location, and while they weren't in the trailer at that moment, I knew she had a lot on her plate.

She told me she only worked in the summers so she could bring her kids with her on location. She didn't want to be away from them during the school year.

Her oldest, Henry, was 14, and the three daughters were still little. The youngest, Louisa, was just two. I'd see them walking through the small town of Libby, Meryl carrying Louisa in her arms, looking like any other doting mom, except, of course, for the fact that she was Meryl Streep. She told me that when Libby residents pulled out their cameras, it was time to go.

While we were alone in the trailer, I couldn't help myself. I had to ask.

I tried not to sound like a fan, but I was so curious about her process. "You're known for picking up languages and accents so easily," I said. "But with sign language... it seems like it's been more of a struggle. I'm just surprised."

She thought about it for a moment, then sighed.

"This," she said, wiggling her fingers in the air, "feels so different from anything else I've ever learned."

And with that, I finally understood, Meryl Streep could master any spoken language, any accent, but this was an entirely different kind of muscle.

And even Meryl had to work for it.

Meryl told me she was like a parrot when it came to accents. "I have to hear it right before I film it," she said. "I either have my lines on tape, or the dialect coach is standing just off-camera in case I need them."

This became our process, too. I would sign the line, then shuffle out of the way of the camera just before the director called Action!

We were talking about the emotional scene she had coming up, and I asked her, "What if you don't feel like crying at that moment when the script says you're supposed to cry?" She didn't miss a beat.

"I go stand in a corner and remind myself how much money they're paying me to cry." Then, completely deadpan: "Then I cry."

That summer, Montana had a horrendous bee infestation. People were getting stung left and right. It was a horrible thing.

I had never been stung in my life, and I was deadly afraid of finding out if I was allergic. Both of my sisters were, so I figured I was, too. I didn't want to test the theory in the middle of a film set where half the crew was already dropping like flies, pun absolutely intended.

Every day, we ate lunch outside, and every day, people were picking bees out of their food. The dessert table was carnage, bees swarming the tubs of ice cream like they had been personally invited. Meanwhile, Meryl, completely unfazed, would just reach in and pluck them out like it was something you did every day.

I kept my distance. Then came the day we were filming on the tarmac of a small landing strip.

The wardrobe department had given me jeans and a long-sleeve shirt to wear so I was completely covered. In theory, this would protect me from getting stung. In reality, it meant I was dying of heatstroke in 90-degree weather.

The boom mic operator kept getting stung on his fingers. One of the set guys moving scenery had to be rushed to the hospital after a bad reaction. My anxiety was at an all-time high.

The plane landed. The stairs came down. Meryl and the two kids hit their marks. The scene played out. Then, just as the director called Cut!, Meryl shouted, "Damn!" A bee had flown up her pants and stung her on the leg. And the woman never broke character. Of course she finished the scene.

By the fourth month of filming, Meryl saw that there was no more signing left for her to do, and I was sent home. Just like that, my river-rafting, bee-dodging, Oscar-winner-tutoring adventure had come to an end.

Years later, I was Marlee's date at an event at the Beverly Hills Hotel honoring Meryl, who was receiving an award from More Magazine. It was one of those fancy luncheons where everyone at the table has at least one Oscar, an honorary doctorate, and a personal driver waiting outside.

Marlee and I ended up sitting with Milton Berle.

I have never laughed so much during a meal. Milton was old, but still razor-sharp and absolutely filthy. He kept waving his hands at Marlee as if he were signing, except some of those hand gestures were unmistakably rude.

Marlee loved it. At some point, Meryl made her way over to say hello. "Meryl," I said, arms outstretched in mock betrayal. "No calls? No Christmas cards?"

She laughed and pulled me into a quick hug. "I know! I haven't seen you since we were standing on the bank of some river!"

And just like that, she was whisked away into a waiting car, with her best friend Carrie Fisher in tow.

Apparently, after Vic, Elizabeth, and I wrapped on The River Wild, Meryl, Carrie, and their families moved into the same lake house in Libby. I told you it was a great house.

After I was wrapped on the film, I flew to Georgia to spend time with Mom and Dad.

Mom was sleeping in a hospital bed set up in their bedroom, and she only had a few months left. She was so weak and frail, and I couldn't help but think about Jeffrey. It had only been a year since I lost him.

Mom needed Dad's help for everything, including going to the bathroom. This was devastating for her because she was so proper. She had spent her entire life setting the standard for grace and good manners.

For example:

If you needed to blow your nose and happened to be at the dinner table, you excused yourself and did it privately. She would close the bathroom door just to brush her teeth.

If she offered you a piece of gum, she'd hand you a napkin first, because chewing gum in public like some kind of barbarian was simply not done.

So, as you can imagine, having Dad help her to the bathroom was mortifying. Dad knew this, of course. And, in the way that only he could, he found a way to make it a little less unbearable for her. Whenever she needed to go, he would wrap her arms around his neck, pull her up, and say, "Miss P., may I have this dance?" Then, he would "dance-walk" her to the bathroom, set her down, and close the door. When she was ready, he would "dance" her back to bed.

Mom passed away on Thanksgiving of 1993. Dad died exactly eleven years later, on the same date. They're buried together at Arlington National Cemetery in Virginia.

I worked on the film Congo, based on Michael Crichton's book. My job was to teach sign language to Amy the gorilla. That's right, Hollywood was paying me to teach a fake gorilla how to sign. Of course, Amy wasn't real; she was played by an actor in a high-tech animatronic suit, but still, I had officially reached the peak of bizarre job descriptions.

I also tutored Dylan Walsh and Laura Linney with their signs. Laura, like Meryl, is an incredible talent. I remember watching the director, Frank Marshall, ask Laura to deliver a single line in as many ways as possible while the camera kept rolling. Over and over, she did it, each take completely different, yet each one equally brilliant and usable in the film. It was like getting a free master class in acting just by showing up to work.

Oh, and I was in Congo too.

In the beginning of the film, I play a character named William, born without vocal cords, fitted with a creepy little voice apparatus that speaks for me when I sign. If you ever watch Congo, go ahead and turn it off after my scene. It didn't exactly live up to the success of the book.

Watching Laura work reminded me of something the late, great, and very funny Leslie Jordan once said to me when we were filming Reasonable Doubts.

We were about to enter a scene already in progress with Marlee and Mark. When you do this, you stand off-camera (in this case, behind a door), staring at a cue light. The second that little red light goes off, you enter into the scene.

Leslie and I were standing there, staring at the light, waiting for our cue, when he turned to me and whispered, "They don't teach you this in acting school."

He was so right.

There are so many things you can't learn in a classroom. Whether it's acting or interpreting, no amount of training can fully prepare you for the real thing. I tell new interpreters this all the time, just say yes, jump in, let it scare you. That's the only way you really learn.

When I went in for my first day of work in Congo, the receptionist at the production office asked who I was and who I was with.

I said, "I'm the sign language guy."

It was at that moment that I realized something, I was so tired of explaining what SCRIPT was. People kept asking if we sold scripts. If we wrote scripts. Someone even called once thinking we were Scripps, the medical center in San Diego.

Right then and there, I decided to change the name of the company. I needed something clear, something that actually described what we did. So, I rebranded. SCRIPT became The Sign Language Company. It worked, mostly.

Now, instead of people asking if we wrote scripts, I got calls from people asking if we made signs. I can't win.

Still, with The Sign Language Company up and running, I went back to life as a freelance interpreter, working through my company, with other interpreters working through it as well. Life moved on.

Another genre I've always found fascinating is law. I've interpreted in law schools (hello, UCLA), for Deaf jurors on court cases, for Deaf attorneys in hearings, mediations, and depositions, and as a courtroom interpreter.

I have so much admiration for interpreters who work full-time in the courts. It's a high-pressure gig, constantly navigating a minefield of legal jargon, intense personalities, and the occasional judge who likes to pretend they've never met an interpreter before.

Attorneys always needed someone to blame when something went wrong, and it was usually the interpreter.

"Your Honor, the interpreter must have signed something incorrectly." Oh, sure. It's always the interpreter's fault. One case in particular stands out.

I was interpreting for a young Deaf guy who'd been arrested because of something to do with his motorcycle. If I recall correctly, the bike backfired and somehow started a small fire.

We weren't always given the full backstory, so we just did our best with whatever scraps of information we had. What I did know was that this guy was terrified.

He was shaking, sweating, and signing so erratically I could barely keep up. His nerves were contagious. I started getting nervous for him. Then came the moment. The judge asked him a question. The guy nodded. Well, that's a problem.

Court reporters can't record a head nod. As interpreters, we are not supposed to voice "yes" or "no" based on a nod, but ideally, the person needs to sign their response. The judge asked another question. More nodding. Then, the final question.

I could see the guy was completely confused. I signed the question again, slower. He nodded, but I wasn't convinced he actually understood what was being asked. So, I made a choice. I said, "No." The judge nodded, shuffled some papers. "Thank you. Case dismissed. You may go." Just like that.

The guy lit up, grinning ear to ear. His shaking stopped immediately. He grabbed my hand in gratitude and bolted out of the courtroom like he'd just won the legal lottery.

In hindsight, I should have asked for clarification. But hey, he left a free man. Everybody was happy!

Bread, Butter, and Brilliant Comebacks

I was the preferred interpreter for Alexis Kashar, a Deaf attorney in Los Angeles. Alexis worked at a law firm specializing in cases where parents were locking horns with school districts, and she always had hearings and mediations that were straight out of a courtroom drama. I loved working with her because, simply put, she was exceptional at her job, poised, razor-sharp, and the kind of professional who made you want to raise your own game.

One of the cardinal rules of interpreting is to know your audience. This is why I drill into interpreters, usually more times than they're ready to hear, that they need to arrive early, meet the client, and learn their language preferences. Because communication isn't a one-size-fits-all gig. Some folks want pure ASL, others prefer interpreting in English word order. Some want Oral interpreting. Some want more visual cues and clarity on the lips. The point is it varies, and your job is to adapt.

Alexis came from a Deaf family, so in casual conversation, we were fluent in ASL. But when it came to her work she insisted on English. That meant I had to interpret exactly what I heard, no conceptualizing, no summarizing or simplifying. Every idiom, every slang expression, every awkward metaphor the opposing attorney trotted out, I was signing it all.

Which brings me to one particular mediation that remains seared into my memory.

The opposing attorney was filled with, what I can only describe as, linguistic flair. Her speech was laced with flowery language, double entendres, and idioms that would make Shakespeare raise an eyebrow. And while she might have been a handful for the average listener, I felt that I was in my element.

The discussion turned heated, always a bonus in my book, since it makes the interpreting way more fun. Neither attorney was backing down. I imagined the Roman Coliseum, two legal gladiators in a battle of wits. And I was thrilled to be there.

Then came this moment of absolute, idiomatic gold. The opposing counsel, in her best dramatic voice, said, "Well, we certainly know which side your client's bread is buttered." Without missing a beat, Alexis shot back: "Yes. And your client is about to be toast."

Brilliant.

If I had chosen to interpret just the concept, the gist, of what she said, and not her exact words, Alexis wouldn't have had the setup for that perfect comeback. It's moments like those that remind you why precision matters. Language has rhythm. Comedy has timing. And interpreting, when done right, lets those things land exactly where they're supposed to.

Eventually, Alexis moved to New York. But thanks to Zoom and the wonders of remote interpreting, I'm still her voice, and she's still the highlight of any legal battle I get to witness.

Champagne, Celebrities, and a Little Jitterbug

Sometime in the late '90s, I'd just wrapped another on-set job. I was tired, cranky, and in desperate need of a vacation that didn't include a call time. My friend, Dave McCallan, and I decided to blow a substantial amount of money and hop aboard the Windstar, departing from Rome. It was indulgent, unnecessary, and absolutely earned.

I was used to working on the big ships during my Princess days, those floating cities with over a thousand passengers, formal nights, casinos, production shows, and lines for everything. The Windstar was something else entirely. It felt more like a private yacht than a cruise ship, carrying only 288 passengers. Every one of its 144 cabins was identical, which meant no one could play the "who-has-the-bigger-balcony" game. No showgirls, no tuxedo expectations, just a week of luxury sailing the Mediterranean, and the promise of actual relaxation.

We hadn't even made it to our staterooms before a glass of champagne was placed in my hand. I took a sip, turned my head, and froze. Standing nearby was a woman who looked familiar.

Beside her? Another face I recognized. I did a quick mental Rolodex flip.

Wait a second.

That's Barbara Walters. Standing next to Senator John Warner. I'd read they were a couple, or friends, or some ambiguous, jet-setting blend of both. Whatever they were, they were definitely traveling together.

I downed the rest of my champagne, not the classiest move, but I needed courage, and told Dave I was going in. I walked directly toward him, not her. That alone got Barbara's attention. I said, "Hello, Senator. I'm sure you don't remember me, but twenty years ago, I sat on a sofa with you and your then-wife for an interview done in sign language at Gallaudet College in D.C."

Before he could respond, Barbara jumped in with, "Gallaudet? Marlee Matlin went there! Hello, I'm Barbara." Marlee didn't actually attend Gallaudet, but I decided that wasn't the moment to correct her. We'd be at this floating cocktail party together for a week, and I didn't want to start things off with a fact-check.

The Senator smiled and said, "Wow, you have a good memory! I remember that day."

Did he? Probably not. But I gave him the benefit of the doubt.

"Well," I said, "it's not every day a 19-year-old ends up on a sofa with a U.S. Senator and the most famous movie star in the world."

I was glancing at Barbara throughout all this, trying to gauge her reaction. For all I knew, she might suddenly decide to swan-dive overboard in a jealous fit. But she stayed put, intrigued, and smiling.

I kept it brief, I wasn't looking to become that guy. "Great seeing you again, Senator. Lovely to meet you, Ms. Walters. See ya around the ship!" And just like that, I turned, retrieved another glass of champagne, and returned to Dave, who of course was dying to know what we talked about.

He reminded me of the crew on the Royal Princess who were desperate to know what Princess Diana and I had said to each other. There's a pattern in my life, apparently.

"We're going to be friends with them on this cruise," I told him. "Just wait."

Most of the 288 passengers on that ship skewed older, by a decade or four, which is probably why a younger couple came over to us for a chat. The woman introduced herself as Jackie and her partner, Mark. Not sure if they were married or just vacationing blissfully without paperwork, but they clearly saw Dave and me as kindred spirits in the "not quite retirement age" category.

Jackie, ten years younger than I was, apparently thought I looked youthful. Or maybe I just looked younger compared to everyone else onboard. Either way, I took the compliment.

We chatted about how they ended up on the Windstar. Jackie said her mother was on board with a male friend and wanted them to come along. "So, it was all paid for by Mom," she said.

I tilted my head and asked, "Is your mother's name…Barbara?"

Jackie froze for a moment, then smiled. "Yes. But she's trying to fly under the radar."

I laughed. "That's kind of hard to do when there are only 144 cabins on the ship. And I met her the minute we came aboard."

I filled Jackie and Mark in on the sofa interview with the Senator and Elizabeth Taylor at Gallaudet. She seemed relieved I wasn't some overzealous fan or aspiring biographer. Just a guy with a memory, a few stories, and a decent sense of timing.

Jackie and Mark were sweet. She opened up a little about how her relationship with her mother hadn't always been smooth sailing, and agreeing to come on this cruise made Barbara happy. I liked that. I liked her.

It was time to get ready for dinner, so we said we'd see them on deck later that evening. There wasn't a ton to do on that ship, outside of enjoying the deck, listening to the combo, and watching the Mediterranean do its thing. But sometimes, that's the absolute best thing to do.

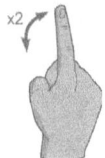

High-Profile Encounters

"Please Don't Drop Me": A Dance with Destiny (and Barbara Walters)

After dinner, Dave and I made our way up to the deck where the music was playing. It was one of those impossibly perfect Italian evenings. The food was excellent, the breeze gentle, and the whole evening carried that delicious potential that something was about to happen.

And something did.

The music started, and with it came a familiar itch. I wanted to dance. I needed to dance. I'd been dancing my whole life, on stage, on ships, and anywhere else music dared to play. I missed it, especially partner dancing, so I began scanning the deck for a willing partner.

Most of the women on board looked like my Jitterbug might send them straight to the ship's infirmary. But then I saw Jackie.

I walked over, extended my hand, and without hesitation, she sprang up like we were about to compete in the finals of Dancing with the Semi-Famous. Jackie was much taller than I, so the under-the-arm twirls were a bit of a challenge. But we owned that dance floor. It was like the gym scene from Grease, and the crowd gave us our space accordingly.

Dave, of course, was snapping photos like the cruise ship paparazzi. Then he glanced over at Barbara and John, gave her a little nod, and mouthed "you're next."

He wasn't wrong.

When the song ended, I returned Jackie to her seat, both of us winded and laughing. Then I did what any reasonable person would do next. I turned and extended my hand to Barbara Walters.

She took it. As she rose, she looked me dead in the eye and said, "Please don't drop me." "I'll do my best," I promised.

The crowd reacted like it was prom night. Every camera on the ship came out. I've always been a solid lead, women trust me to twirl and lift them without winding up in traction, but I was acutely aware of how very bad it would look if Barbara Walters ended up on 20/20 in a neck brace.

"Feet, don't fail me now," I thought.

We danced. I didn't drop her. I didn't even stumble. We moved like we'd rehearsed it in a past life, and I guided her back to her seat, where I knelt in front of her, holding her hands like a man proposing something dramatic.

"Barbara," I said, "now that we've shown everyone that we can dance, I would like to invite you and your family to dinner. My treat."

Keep in mind, the meals were included in the cruise fare, so the invite was entirely for effect. But she didn't skip a beat.

"Okay," she said. "I'll bring the wine." The wine was not included.

We agreed on dinner two nights from then. Dave stared at me like I'd just asked the Queen of England to split an Uber. "You actually invited her?" he whispered.

"She had fun," I said. "She probably hasn't danced like that in years."

Jackie confirmed as much later. She was floored that her mother had even considered getting up to dance. Apparently, Barbara didn't do anything without rehearsal or prep. That dance was entirely out of character. And yet, there she was, on a ship in the middle of the Mediterranean, twirling with me under the stars.

Later that night, I found the combo that had been playing and struck up a chat. I let it slip that I was a singer, too. They already knew I danced (the whole ship did), and they asked if I wanted to sing something one night.

"Absolutely," I said, without hesitation.

Word traveled fast. Suddenly, the guy who danced with Barbara Walters was going to sing in the lounge. Jackie promised she'd be there, and said she'd let her mom know, too.

The next evening, the lounge was packed, mostly for the combo, let's be honest, but I had my own tiny buzz going. The band gave me the kindest introduction. "As you saw last night, he dances and he sings! Please welcome Bill Pugin!"

Years of performing on Princess Cruises had trained me for moments like this. I stepped up to the mic, and just as I did, I spotted Barbara entering quietly from the back.

I sang I Dreamed a Dream from Les Misérables, and it went beautifully. Dave had heard the stories of my performing life, but this was his first time seeing it in action. He and the rest of the crowd gave me a wonderful ovation. Barbara clapped along, then slipped out without a word, classy, understated, and very much present just for the song.

I was honored.

Dinner with Barbara
(and the Seasick Secretary of the Navy)

The day of our dinner had arrived. And I'll admit, I was nervous. I didn't want Barbara to feel obligated, like she had to follow through just because we'd danced under the stars. I called Jackie's room with what I thought was a graceful out.

"No pressure," I told her. "If there's a change of plans, I completely understand."

"Are you kidding?" she said. "We're all looking forward to it!" Well then.

When Dave and I walked into the dining room, there they were, Barbara, the senator, Jackie, and Mark, all standing at the table, waiting for us.

Barbara immediately took charge, directing us like a network producer with a place card obsession. I was seated to her left, the senator to her right, with Dave, Jackie, and Mark across from us. It felt curated, intentional, and frankly, a little bit fantastic.

"I loved the song you sang last night," she said, as casually as if we were discussing the shrimp cocktail. "It's from one of my favorite shows."

"Mine, too," I said. "It's a powerful song to sing."

There are moments in life when you feel the glow of everything aligning, the music, the laughter, the wine, the right people at the table. This dinner was one of those moments.

Barbara had the sommelier bring two bottles of wine. She was sharp, funny, entirely engaged. We talked, we laughed, and for a woman who had likely dined with kings and kissed the Pope's ring, she made us feel like equals. Maybe even the interesting ones at the table.

Halfway through, the senator excused himself. He wasn't feeling well. When he was out of earshot, Barbara turned to us and said, "Can you believe it? The ex–Secretary of the Navy is seasick! Should I order another bottle?"

"Silly not to," I said. She did.

I asked about The View, about some of her interviews. She politely redirected, far more interested in asking Dave and me questions. She was fascinated by sign language, peppering me with questions like a curious student. Dave had recently sold his company for a healthy sum, Barbara wanted to know all about that, too.

This wasn't Barbara the journalist; this was Barbara the guest who wanted to learn, to listen, to connect. It was, dare I say it, intimate. In the very best, most human way.

Eventually, she glanced at her watch and sighed. "I need to take the senator's massage appointment," she said. "Though frankly, I don't want to go. I've had such a good time."

She looked at Dave and me, genuinely warm. "Thank you for treating us to dinner," she said. I grinned. "Thank you for actually showing up. And for the wine." She left with a smile.

Jackie and Mark lingered for a moment, watching her go, then turned back to us, almost in disbelief.

"I've never seen her this relaxed," Jackie said. "She's never had this much fun." We just sat there for a beat, letting the evening settle in like a well-aged Bordeaux. It was a great night. The next morning, we arrived in Capri.

This dreamy little island off the coast of Naples is known for its jagged cliffs, glamorous shops, and the kind of people who wear white linen well. It's also known for draining your bank account faster than you can say "limoncello."

I couldn't afford much, unless a touristy tank top counts as high fashion, but walking through those cobblestone streets, window shopping for a life I absolutely could not sustain, was worth every euro I didn't spend.

At one point, we wandered into a men's shirt shop and ran into the senator, flipping through high-end shirts with the focus of a man trying to solve a particularly expensive puzzle.

He leaned in and said, "Don't tell Barbara I was here. She'll have a fit if she finds out how much I'm spending."

The senator and Barbara Walters were counting their pennies? She was still earning a fortune, but we promised and zipped our lips.

About thirty minutes later, we ran into Barbara. "I'm looking for John," she said, slightly annoyed. "Have you seen him?"

"He was a couple streets over," we offered casually. Not a word about the shirts!

It's funny how the song I Dreamed a Dream found its way onto three separate cruises. Before the Windstar with Barbara and the senator, I was asked to interpret for about seventeen elderly Deaf couples on a cruise in the Caribbean. My friend and colleague, John Arce, was the other interpreter and we had a blast sailing with these folks. Our only rule was that we insisted on having our own table in the Dining Room. We would happily go over to their tables and interpret the specials or any announcements made while in the dining room, but we wanted peace and to rest our arms while eating.

A Talent Show was announced, and I asked John if he would sign while I sang I Dreamed a Dream. He knew the song and agreed! Luckily, we were placed last in the show - which is always a good sign (the puns just keep a'comin!).

We won!

Then, nine months after Jeffrey died, Brian convinced me to join him on a cruise to Mexico. He thought I could use the distraction and finally relax after Jeffrey and the cancellation of Reasonable Doubts. It was a good idea. Brian had known me for years as his friend, and was blown away by how many people recognized me from television. That was weird for him.

Again, there was a Talent Show, and this one was run by pianist Michael Orland. Michael was good friends with my friend, Candi Milo, who I performed with on Princess. Candi performed her cabaret act all around Los Angeles and Michael was her accompanist. Michael was also there for me the few times I sang in LA, so it was wonderful seeing him on the cruise!

In later years, Michael became the rehearsal pianist and vocal coach on American Idol and has played with some of the greats in Show Biz!

Like on the cruise with John, Michael put my song last in the show.

I changed the ending of the song to land on words of optimism and I introduced the song to the audience as a fitting tribute to Jeffrey.

I guess my words hit a nerve.

When I sang the last note, the audience was silent. I looked over at Michael for some sort of acknowledgement and he had tears in his eyes. When the lights came up, I saw many in the audience were crying - and then they broke into applause. I really had no idea it would get that sort of response from the crowd.

I won again!

Pickfair, Presidents, and the Secret Service Side-Eye

A few years after moving from D.C. to California, Janet Bailey and some colleagues launched a company called Sign Language Associates, SLA for short. Janet grew it into one of the top ASL interpreting agencies in the country, maybe the world. Had I not moved across the country, I'd have been in-house with them. But even from the West Coast, I felt like part of the family. SLA used my company, The Sign Language Company, for a lot of their California work. And when a high-profile job came up, they often asked for me specifically.

One of those jobs was interpreting for President Bill Clinton. Not once. Not twice. Three times.

The first gig was at Pickfair.

For the uninitiated, Pickfair is a legendary Beverly Hills estate, once home to Douglas Fairbanks and Mary Pickford, a place where Old Hollywood met royalty and had cocktails in the garden. This particular event was hosted to honor The Brady Campaign to End Gun Violence. On November 30, 1993, President Clinton had signed the Brady Bill into law, making good on his promise to "keep guns out of the hands of criminals."

The security for this event was... intense. Getting into Pickfair felt like applying for a passport and the CIA at the same time. We had to park miles away, shuttle in, go through metal detectors, and show two forms of ID. If your name wasn't on the list, you weren't getting in, not even with a magic wand and a good story.

The hosts for the evening were Beau Bridges and Whoopi Goldberg.

The guests were a who's-who of 1990s Hollywood: Brendan Fraser and his wife Afton, Jack Nicholson and Lara Flynn Boyle, Bill Maher, Carrie Fisher, Rick Hess, Rob Vinson, and Rebecca De Mornay. It felt like being dropped into an episode of Inside the Actors Studio, except with a much stricter dress code and armed personnel.

Now, here's what I learned very quickly at this event. The Secret Service does not like sign language interpreters. We're just another body on stage, flailing our arms, and they see us as a distraction, or worse, a threat.

I was told very clearly, by a man with a buzzcut and an earpiece, that when the President was introduced, I was not to be anywhere near the stage. I had to wait until he reached the microphone. Only then could I join him. My platform, a wooden box placed to his side, had already been thoroughly inspected, presumably for explosives, weapons, or possibly Republican propaganda. No deviations. Well.

Beau Bridges, bless him, decided to improvise. He wanted to make a short statement before introducing the President. He walked out, and, being the interpreter, I followed. Because that's my job.

What I didn't know was that this went against every carefully choreographed second of Secret Service protocol. I could see them in the wings, headsets crackling, visibly distressed. I'd become the twitchy figure in their nightmare scenario.

Suddenly, the unmistakable strains of Hail to the Chief began, and I felt a presence behind me. Not metaphorically, physically.

President Clinton brushed up against my back as he made his entrance. I froze. The space was tight, more cocktail tent than grand ballroom, and for one wild second, I was certain the Secret Service was going to shoot me. Or at least tackle me and throw me into a black van marked "You Were Warned."

They didn't. Thank God. Everything went off without a hitch.

Afterward, I got to chat briefly with Whoopi, mostly about our mutual friend, Marlee Matlin, but I never got a moment alone with the President. Still, I interpreted for him two more times after that.

The second time was at the memorial service for Lew Wasserman, held at the Universal Studios Amphitheatre. Lew was the last of the true Hollywood moguls. Described as "the most powerful and influential Hollywood titan in the four decades after World War II," he had famous friends in every zip code, including the Clintons.

The third time I interpreted for President Clinton was during a speech he gave in Calabasas, California.

By then, I was practically on a first-name basis with the Secret Service agents who, though still wary, at least stopped flinching every time I adjusted my stance.

President Clinton was a dream to interpret. Smooth, charismatic, a master storyteller. He spoke in full thoughts, didn't rush, and actually gave you something to work with. Some speakers ramble. Not Bill Clinton.

But if he was a dream, Hillary Clinton was a master class.

I interpreted for her at a women's group luncheon at the Beverly Hilton Hotel. I was the sole interpreter. She was seated right next to the podium, having lunch. When she was introduced, she calmly put down her fork, dabbed her mouth with a napkin, and walked up to the podium where I was standing and waiting to her left.

She spoke for almost an hour.

No notes. No teleprompter. Just pure, thoughtful, organized delivery. She thanked hotel staff by name, including the guys at valet, and acknowledged half the room without a cue card in sight.

Meanwhile, I can barely remember what I ate for breakfast.

As an interpreter, I'm hyper-aware of how people speak. The words they choose, the rhythm of their sentences, the ums, errs, and nervous "likes" that sneak in when someone isn't confident. Hillary didn't need fillers. Her inflection never rose unless it was a question. Her voice was steady, warm, commanding. She made you lean in.

Another incredible speaker was Maya Angelou. I had the honor of interpreting for her twice. She didn't just speak, she offered. Her pauses were intentional. Her silence was powerful. If you ever need a lesson in oratory, find footage of Maya Angelou. It'll change the way you think about language.

One piece of advice I always give speakers is that when you don't know what to say next, say nothing. Think silently. Don't fill the air with sounds that aren't words. Don't um your way into confusion.

Just pause. And then, speak.

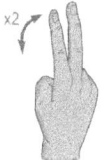

Global Assignments & Corporate Tech

Aloha to the Best Job That Never Happened

Thanks to Janet and Karen Johnson over at SLA, the dream gigs just kept coming. One particular job sent me to Honolulu, where I was to interpret for a Deaf bigwig from D.C. attending a week-long conference. The setting was The Hawaiian Hilton Hotel.

Because I was overseeing the team for this one, I called up RJ Munsey, my med-school-fun-to-be-with interpreter and a dear friend. She had never been to Hawaii, and just saying the words "you're coming with me" made her eyes well up. This wasn't just work. This was a dream come true.

We were set up with two stunning rooms, mine overlooked the marina, while RJ's faced Diamond Head like a perfect post-card. The plan was simple. We would work all day, explore all evening. But on Day One, the client didn't show up.

Turns out, he was stuck wrapping up last-minute business back in D.C. Which meant… a full day off.

RJ and I did what anyone would do. We lounged at the hotel, wandered around Waikiki Beach, soaked up some sun, and waited for a call with instructions. That evening, my phone rang, it was Karen.

"He's not coming tomorrow either," she said. "He still might make it out later in the week. Stay put until you hear otherwise." I hung up, turned to RJ, and said, "We're on hold. Time to explore."

The people running the event told me they'd call each morning to confirm if our client was arriving. Until then, we were free. So I rented a convertible, because, obviously, and became RJ's personal island tour guide.

We went everywhere. Pearl Harbor, Diamond Head, and even to Ewa Beach, where I was born. This was starting to feel less like a work trip and more like a sponsored honeymoon, minus the awkward matching outfits.

Each morning, we repeated the same routine. Call comes in. "He's still in D.C." And off we went, beach, hiking, Mai Tais, repeat.

It was heaven. The kind of blissful fluke that happens once in a career and never again. An all-expenses-paid tropical vacation with a friend, all because someone couldn't make their flight.

One day, RJ said she really wanted to watch some surfers. "Perfect," I said. "Let's head to the North Shore. We'll definitely spot a few."

What we didn't know was that the **Pipeline Masters**, the world's largest international surfing competition, was underway. The North Shore was teeming with surf gods, fans, camera crews, and boards everywhere.

"You said a few surfers," I told her, as we stood there blinking in disbelief. The client never showed. Not a single day.

And RJ and I ? We laughed, we tanned, we soaked up every accidental second of it. It was, and still is, the best job I ever had.

Merde, Machines, and Monsieur Sysplex

Fresh off the Hawaiian dream job, SLA sent me on another international assignment. This time, it was Montpellier, France. An important Deaf executive from IBM needed a team of interpreters for a computer technology conference.

I was told, "Steve is a nice guy, but very particular. If he doesn't like your interpretation, he'll tell you."

Great! Okay, Steve…I'm ready for you. I have no idea what will be discussed at this conference, but how hard can it be? I soon found out.

I met my team, Liz Brunett, at the hotel. She'd already met Steve and relayed the plan that he wanted to meet us for breakfast at 6 a.m., "ready to work." Okay, I thought. Maybe he's jet-lagged too. Maybe he'll be mellow. He was not mellow.

At breakfast, I politely said I needed a bite of something and a few sips of coffee before we started. Steve gave me just enough time to inhale a croissant, then we were off.

We walked to a massive auditorium where the first session would be held. So far, so good. What we didn't know, and no one thought to tell us, was what everyone would be talking about was "Parallel Sysplex."

Which, if you're wondering, is not a band.

A Parallel Sysplex is a 'Sysplex' that uses multi-system data-sharing technology. You can link up to 32 servers to create a clustered system that allows "near-linear scalability."

Clear as mud? Great. Us too.

Not only were these folks wildly enthusiastic about this tech wizardry, they were dying to present their findings. And since this was a global conference, the speakers came from every corner of the world, each with a new accent for us to decipher on the fly.

Liz and I sat there, white-knuckled and wide-eyed, like we'd just been dropped into a UN debate on astrophysics. In Klingon.

In normal interpreting situations, interpreters switch every 20–30 minutes. With this kind of content we were switching every 5 to 7. And even that felt too long.

Steve, for his part, seemed to follow us. Sort of. He gave us reassuring nods, though at one point, he said, "What you signed was completely wrong, but I knew what you meant."

Great. That's the kind of feedback that makes you want to walk into the Seine.

By the end of Day One, Liz and I were desperate for a monitor to see the overhead slides, because we were constantly craning our necks to catch context clues behind us. We were doing our best, but this was less interpreting and more interpretive suffering.

Steve, it turned out, was also on a mission to impress everyone at the conference by having constant, private one-on-one chats. Translation: no breaks for us. When the group had a scheduled break, Steve didn't. And neither did we.

He told me he expected me to accompany him into the bathroom in case he struck up a conversation at the urinal. Absolutely not.

I drew a hard line. "Hearing men don't talk at urinals," I said. "Especially not about Sysplex." He was not pleased.

At lunch, everyone walked to a nearby restaurant. Steve never stopped talking, which meant Liz and I had to interpret while walking backward on centuries-old cobblestone, dodging dog poop that was either aggressively abundant or strategically placed precisely where we needed to step. We couldn't sit, we couldn't eat, and we couldn't turn off our brains for even a second.

After lunch… More presentations. Then, because France doesn't believe in moderation, we were bussed to a vineyard for a wine tasting and dinner, an event that screamed "relaxation" for everyone except the interpreters.

Liz and I were not offered wine. We were there to work. We interpreted conversation after conversation, were bussed back to the hotel, and stumbled through the lobby at 12:30 a.m.

As we dragged ourselves to the elevator, Steve cheerily said, "See you tomorrow at 6 a.m. in the dining room." I looked at the clock. "You mean later today. In five and a half hours." I was ready to quit. Day Two? Even worse.

During a break, a friendly attendee approached Liz and asked her how she got into sign language. A perfectly innocent nice question. Harmless. Human.

Steve spotted it and beelined over - pulling me by the arm. He asked what the man had said. I told him what I had overheard. He turned to Liz, signed sharply, and ordered me to voice for the poor, unsuspecting innocent attendee: "The interpreters have no name and have nothing to contribute. If you want to know anything about the interpreters, come to me."

That was not easy to say out loud.

Then Steve silently screamed at Liz, furious she had "overstepped" by... answering a question about herself. It was dehumanizing, and she'd had enough.

Liz pulled Steve aside and unleashed hell, in the most professional, perfectly signed tirade I've ever witnessed. "You are disrespectful. This treatment is not acceptable. Life is too short to be this mistreated and this unhappy. I'm going home."

Wait, going home? You're not leaving me here for five more days with Captain Sysplex!

Steve stood there, stunned, shaking, his mouth dry, unable to respond.

Liz and I had one final short session that day, which I interpreted alone. Then I told Steve we needed to talk. Over very strong french coffee. My treat.

He looked like a little boy about to be grounded.

I sat him down and said, gently but firmly, "You're working too hard. You're trying to have constant conversations when people don't want to talk. When a group of hearing people walk to lunch, they don't talk the whole time. Especially when trying to avoid dog poop. Save the small talk for when you're seated."

I paused.

"And I've never had a business meeting at a urinal. Let's not start now."

I told him he had to stop punishing us for doing our jobs. This had to be a two-way street. Liz and I were not machines and we needed to pee and sometimes grab a coffee, too.

Steve just nodded. Silently. Taking it all in.

And then I signed, "Now if you'll excuse me, I need to stop Liz from catching the next flight out of here."

The Redemption of Steve (A.K.A. Hazard Pay, Please)

Liz stayed.

To this day, I'm not entirely sure how I convinced her, but I like to think it was a combination of sincere gratitude and the promise of a croissant and wine the second we changed planes in Paris.

The work remained brutally hard, tech-heavy presentations, multinational accents, and Steve's unique brand of high-maintenance marathon chatter, but something had changed.

Steve had changed.

He eased up. Just enough to be tolerable, maybe even, dare I say, workable. He apologized to Liz. Well, sort of. In the way certain people apologize without actually forming the word "sorry." But he clearly felt remorse. There was less barking. Fewer impossible demands. And most importantly, he no longer expected me to interpret urinal banter.

We made it through the week. Barely. But together. When I returned home, I called Janet.

"Thanks for the opportunity," I said. "That was... an experience. I'm honored. Oh... I never want to interpret for Steve again."

There was a pause on the other end. One of those too-long pauses that always means something's coming.

"Well," she said, "funny you should say that. Steve just requested you for a week in Chicago."

"Of course he did."

I told her I'd do it, but I'd need hazard pay. She laughed. I didn't.

Apparently, that little coffee chat in France had sparked something in Steve. He told SLA he'd never worked with an interpreter who was that honest, to the point of risking getting fired.

I didn't know whether to feel flattered or like a man who'd just been tricked into the football kicking scene between Lucy and Charlie Brown. But I took the job in Chicago.

And wouldn't you know, it was like working with a whole new person.

"Chicago Steve," as I would come to call him, was practically charming. He actually excused me and my team, Pam Carchio, from sessions midway through. "Go take a break," he'd say. "I'm heading to my hotel room for a bit."

What alternate universe had I stepped into?

Pam, who'd worked with Steve back in his D.C. days, was ready for the full France-level meltdown. She was geared up for tag-team interpreting, ten-minute switch-offs, mental exhaustion, and logistical acrobatics.

Instead, we got a mellow, considerate version of Steve. She was just as stunned as I was.

"We love this guy," I whispered to her at one point. "Let's not question it."

Apparently, Steve made it official. SLA was to use me exclusively for his interpreting needs.

I was a little apprehensive, sure. But flattered. So when the call came in for a job in China, I said yes.

Steve would be working with a bank in Shanghai, something to do with programming systems. Honestly, I still had no idea what he actually did, but at this point, I knew how to nod convincingly while spelling out "Parallel Sysplex" with dead eyes.

Fortunately, I now had Ann Apple running The Sign Language Company back home.

Ann was a gift from the interpreting gods. Capable, smart, and a grounding force. She kept the business humming while I gallivanted around the world, sometimes to interpret, sometimes just to recover from interpreting. Ann stayed with me and the company for 21 years. An absolute legend.

By that time, I'd also started a new relationship with Todd Curran. He was from Canada, and we hit it off immediately. How we met could be a book in itself. But he and Ann held down the fort while I headed off to Shanghai with Steve, Round Three.

We met at the San Francisco airport for the flight. And that's where I got my first reminder that this man, no matter how evolved, still had Steve-ness in his DNA. We boarded the plane. Long flight ahead. I looked around, searching for our Business Class seats. Nothing. We were in coach. Excuse me?

It turned out IBM would cover one Business Class ticket or two in coach. Steve, ever the team player, had opted for two coach seats, but was constantly reminding me that he could be in Business Class.

I gave him a long, slow look. "I've had back surgery," I said. "I can't fly halfway across the world in a seat designed for someone under five feet tall."

"From here on out, I'll pay to upgrade myself."

Steve shrugged. Settled in. And that's when I remembered that every job, no matter how cushy it looks on paper, has a middle seat with your name on it.

Welcome to Shanghai. Please Remain Seated Until the Ride Comes to a Complete Emotional Stop.

What an adventure, and we're only at the beginning. The flight was looooong. And guess who got the middle seat in coach? Yes. Again. I must have the worst flying karma of anyone I know. Maybe in a past life I was the guy who reclined his seat all the way during meal service.

Lots of movies were played. Lots of Chinese passengers on board. And, not sure I mentioned this, the flight was long.

Did I mention I was in the middle seat?

When we started our work - or Steve's work (I still had no idea what he was doing there), I thought I should share my adventures with friends and family back home. So, I sent emails to everyone trying to paint the picture of "Life in China" from an American's perspective:

Things are a little fuzzy now. It's my first full day here, and Steve and I just walked nearly six hours through the streets of Shanghai. But let's rewind a little, back to the glamorous moment of arrival.

We made it through immigration, where you're photographed to determine if you're running a fever (not entirely sure how that works, but okay), and customs, which involved waiting forever for the bags. Once reunited with our luggage, we were immediately approached by a "taxi" driver. I say "taxi" because it was more of a performance piece on how to overcharge obvious foreigners. We must've looked very foreign. Steve and I got shanghai'd, yes, literally in Shanghai, and charged 350 yuan for a cab ride that should've cost 100. Then, when Steve handed him 400, our new friend just… drove off. No change. No receipt. Just a blur of motion and regret. I thought, "Yuan's been robbed." Good thing IBM reimburses him.

My hotel room, actually, my home for the next month, is small, but nice. The hotel itself? Gorgeous. Pricey. And in a part of town that looks more like Europe than anything you'd expect to find in the People's Republic. This morning, though, we walked toward the real China, think Chinatown in San Francisco, but multiplied by 5,000 and sprinkled with enough noise to dislodge a filling.

My room at the Okura Garden Hotel had a terrific view of Shanghai. As I was settling in, there was a knock at my door. I assumed it was Steve wanting to give me the itinerary of our weeks ahead. Or he needed me to make a call, or he was lonely and wanted company.

No, it was someone from the hotel checking in on me. I mimed the best I could that I didn't need anything, but this person insisted on continuing their one-sided conversation with me in Mandarin…or Cantonese. I can't tell the difference.

She opened my closets…still talking…walked into the bathroom…still talking…and I followed her like a little puppy about to get instructions on how to use the soap and towels.

When she finally left, I hung the DO NOT DISTURB sign on my door. Five minutes later, another knock. Ok, this had to be Steve. No. Same woman. This time, bringing me bedroom slippers. I double checked the sign on the door making sure I hung it the right direction. It was a sign that had DO NOT DISTURB written in many different languages - including Mandarin…or Cantonese.

Steve and I were very jet-lagged, but we decided to hit the streets of Shanghai to explore our new city.

Steve, bless him, was wearing bright yellow and had his camera strapped around his neck like he was auditioning for the role of "Most Obvious Tourist in Asia." Think we stood out? I've never experienced so much noise and crowding in my life. If you're looking for a peaceful vacation, let me save you some time. Do not come to China.

Shanghai alone has 24 million people. Twenty. Four. Million. That's not a city, it's an entire planet. The population of China is over a billion. And if I make it through this trip without being hit by a car, bus, moped, or bicycle, it'll be a miracle. Pedestrians do not have the right of way here. There are horns honking at all times, bells of bicycles ringing, an ever-present layer of smog, and, forgive my jetlag honesty, millions and millions of not the prettiest population I've ever seen. I know, I know, that's not politically correct. But at hour five of our walk, I was tired, cranky, culture-shocked, and at the end of my rope. Judgmental? Maybe. Honest? Definitely.

(EMAIL) I woke up several times not knowing where I was. But then again, that's not new for me. I've been sleeping in my dining room since July. I'm trying to reframe this trip as a vacation, one from construction, and perhaps also from my bodyfat.

I expected the food to be terrible, but it's not. It's delicious. And the coffee is surprisingly great. We stopped at a tea house this afternoon, quite the ceremony. I haven't seen many white faces around. I thought it would be more touristy, but the few tourists here seem to be from other parts of China... or Japan. I get CNN and BBC on TV. That's about it.

Once I recover from today's impromptu marathon, I'll start using the gym. And one thing I will do when I get back home? Disinfect every pair of shoes I brought. This place is pretty dirty. Spitting seems to be the national pastime, with dodging moving vehicles a very close second. You can't put a bag down on the sidewalk without risking it coming back with a mystery substance fused to the bottom. I know, I know, gross. But what can I say?

WELCOME TO CHINA! When in CHOON-WAH... Duck

Well, it's time for another update. I've been here four days, and it feels like forty. Maybe longer. The only place you can truly be alone in this country is your hotel room, and even there, someone wants to come in and turn down your bed, deliver slippers, or otherwise make sure you're not suffering the devastating trauma of momentary solitude. There is no such thing as "personal space" here. It's not a concept.

Also non-existent? Politeness as we know it. "Ladies first," "be my guest," or "oh no, after you", laughable. When an elevator door opens, even if you're standing directly in front of it, someone will appear from the ether and body-check their way inside like it's the playoffs. Evelyn said my last email wasn't very PC, but you know what? No one here is. So, when in Rome. Or more accurately, when in Choon-Wah, which is apparently how you pronounce the Chinese word for China.

And now, I finally understand the "Asian driver" stereotype. It's not a stereotype. It's survival. For anyone who's driven a freeway in L.A. or visited Chinatown in the U.S., that's the training wheels version. Over here, it's like being part of a high-stakes, God-orchestrated traffic ballet. Pedestrians, bicycles, scooters, cars, and buses, all moving together in what I can only assume is divine choreography. Miraculously, no one dies. At least, not in front of me.

And the police give out tickets. To drivers and to people on bikes. And I'd love to know what the offenses are. Failure to signal? Spitting in a No-Spitting Zone? Disrespecting Chairman Mao's commemorative air freshener?

I don't want to harp, but I would honestly rather buy a vacation home in Iraq than deal with this traffic. Just when I thought I'd seen it all, I saw a guy on a motorcycle lighting a cigarette, talking on his cell phone, and balancing a toddler on his lap. I swear. In his defense, though, he was wearing a helmet. Not sure how he found the time to spit.

Work? Practically impossible. I'm holed up in a fluorescent-lit room, traffic and construction roaring through the window, trying to interpret for Little Miss Yang Yi, a woman whose voice could break glass and whose IBM tech jargon could break souls. Her accent is thick, her pace unrelenting, and her questions involve programming code. I'd need a PhD and a blood sacrifice to understand.

Just the other day, I found myself interpreting, "When the r.a.o.e. fox fox dumps partially to the TCB, the loop and hang from the TEB conforms to the PARB and not the cics safe area space dictated by the IMS transition development sequence."

Sure. Got it. Just say it in Chinese. I'm sure it would make as much sense.

At this point, forget the tall buildings. Just point me to the nearest curb, and I'll step off with my eyes closed. It'll be quick.

And then there's Steve. Bless his enthusiastic, slightly clueless heart. He still refers to me as "his interpreter." No name. Just a role. So, I've taken to referring to him as "my deaf guy." It's a private joke between me and… well, just me. The Chinese wouldn't get it.

Getting to and from work is a whole other ordeal. We have directions written out in Chinese characters for the taxi drivers, but honestly, I think they look at the paper the same way we do, a bunch of confusing sticks. There's a lot of guessing. And detours.

Today, Steve and I decided to brave a local restaurant for lunch. No English menus. No pictures to point at. But you should've seen the charades. I should've won an award. Acting out "chicken" was one thing, but "shrimp"? That totally got the attention of everyone in the restaurant!

The food? Absolutely delicious. And the entire meal set us back around eight bucks.

Later that day, we treated ourselves to an hour-long foot massage. And wow. It was amazing. Only thirteen dollars. They even scraped our nails. Not in a "clipping" way, more in a "here's a sharp knife, try not to bleed" kind of way. A pedicure with flair. Not quite inspiring enough for me to paint a SHANGHAI OR BUST sign... but close.

Steve's been asked to stay on through December. I'm sure he'll love his new interpreter. I still have 26 days left, but I think I'll start packing now... just in case.

More later, assuming I'm not taken out by a moped first.

Love,

Bill

Dim Sum, Department Stores, and Dressing Room Drama

Ni hau from the People's Republic.

It's my first weekend, and I'm not exactly sure how I'm going to fill the next three. I'm just trying to get through this one without losing my mind, or my footing, or my will to live.

On the bright side, the first workweek is behind me. And that's no small feat. Steve, a.k.a. "my deaf guy", hopped a morning train to a city that starts with "S" and ends in I'm-not-going-there. I figured more people and more traffic in a slightly different setting didn't qualify as adventure. So I stayed behind, determined to enjoy a fun-filled day alone.

Here's the shocker. Steve and I are actually getting along great now. He's still very much himself, camera strapped around his neck like a toddler leash, but there's a different energy this time around. In France, he was all business. Here in China? The man has discovered leisure. We start our mornings with a taxi ride to IBM China, then a perilous crossing of the street, and I do mean perilous. Picture me halfway across the street, dodging mopeds, while he's signing at me mid-crossing. Lesson learned. No sign language while navigating death intersections in Shanghai.

Breakfast is at a French pastry shop. Yes, really. And it's good, better than Starbucks, and cheaper than the hotel. It's a ritual now: coffee, pastry, near-death traffic experience. Then we're off to Pudong, across the river, which takes ages thanks to traffic that makes Manhattan look like Hooterville.

By the end of the week, Steve was calling it quits around 3:30 or 4:00 p.m. God bless him. I love this man.

The weather's been all over the place, hot, muggy, around 25°C most days, but today it dropped to 14°C and started raining. I ventured out anyway for a little shopping at the open market, where I was immediately accosted by more salespeople than exist in all of Macy's. The classic "Hey mister...wanna buy a watch?" pitch on loop. But thanks to a lovely young Chinese woman, I'd learned how to say, "I don't want any," and "I don't have any money left." You should've seen their faces when I busted that out. Sure, they were disappointed, but deeply impressed. I'll take the win.

After narrowly escaping with my wallet and dignity, I decided to try the hotel's swimming pool. That, too, was an experience.

The thing about being a foreigner in a land of hyper-specific, unwritten rules is this: no matter what you do, it's wrong. I should've just stood back and observed. But no, I charged in. Apparently, there are slippers for the pool. Different slippers for the dressing room. Towels for some things, not for others. Entry rituals that feel like interpretive dance. I was absolutely radiating ugly American energy, faux pas upon faux pas, and convinced every single person in the place was judging my every move.

And then I remembered. I could've been dressed like Carmen Miranda, dragging a flamingo behind me, and no one would've noticed. There's just too much going on in this city for anyone to care about me, this dirty blond speck in a storm of dim sum.

Speaking of dim sum... have I mentioned how good the food is? I found myself swept along by a crowd, not by choice, mind you, but by sheer momentum, into a department store. I had zero intention of going shopping, but the crowd moved, and I moved with it. I was like a rubber ducky in a human whirlpool. Next thing I knew, I was on an escalator heading directly to the women's shoe department. How? Why? Have I no free will?

I managed to escape and reward myself with my first non-Chinese meal, broiled chicken, a side of spaghetti, and a cold Tsingtao beer. It was... heavenly. So heavenly, in fact, I stopped by the Haa-

gen-Dazs next door for dessert. So much for my "maybe I'll lose weight on this trip" fantasy. R.I.P., abs.

I'm not sure what I'll do tomorrow, I assume it will involve the gym, a whole lot of walking, and dodging moving vehicles. Standard Shanghai Sunday.

I miss you all. Hope life in your time zone involves fewer near-death experiences and more familiar forms of footwear.

Love,

Bill

Duck Tongue, Death Wishes, and My Rise to Lunchroom Fame

Well, the end of Week Two, and I'm still alive!

But, as expected, the inevitable has happened. I caught a cold. At least... I hope it's a cold. I'm not having trouble breathing (yet), so I doubt it's SARS. Still, there are just too many opportunities to come into contact with the bodily fluids of others here, especially since public spitting is the national pastime. It was bound to happen.

And as it turns out, the surgical masks everyone wears? Yeah, those aren't just a smog statement. I'll be looking into local remedies, as long as they don't involve ingredients like toad gall, bat liver, or... human.

Speaking of Chinese medicine, I went for my second foot massage. Why this isn't a national mandate back home, I'll never understand. According to ancient Chinese wisdom, every pressure point on your feet connects to some corner of your inner workings. Depressed? Rub your second toe. Constipated? Press your heel. Honestly, my cold might've been caused by a rogue thumb to the wrong metatarsal. Don't care. Still worth it.

Work continues to be a challenge, now with the added flair of voicing for Steve from behind him. Which is as difficult and awkward as it sounds. And just to keep things spicy, Steve signs things like:

"When the r.a.o.e. fox fox dumps partially to the TCB, the loop and hang from the TEB conforms to the PARB and not the cics safe area space dictated by the IMS transition development sequence."

At this point, if anyone ever suggests interpreters are overpaid, I'll slap them.

But you know what isn't a challenge? Eating. The food continues to surprise and delight me. After my latest foot massage, I stopped into a restaurant and ordered something called "big fried egg with rice inside." Sounds like a dare, right? But it was... incredible. When I eat alone, though, I become somewhat of a spectacle. The Chinese don't really do solo dining. Meals here are group bonding exercises, large round tables, large quantities of food, large-scale synchronized burping and smoking. When a lone, pale, non-smoking, non-Chinese diner appears, everyone pauses. It's hard to be noticed in this city, but eating alone seems to do it.

Another cultural curveball is the check. Every day, Steve and I go to the same restaurant, and we're basically celebrities at this point. Two young waitresses in particular are... how shall I put this? Smitten. One more than the other. Okay, they're both smitten with me. Not to brag. (Okay, a little to brag.)

They love when I act out menu items in my patented game of Culinary Charades, duck, lamb, shrimp, I've got a solid repertoire. They also use it as a chance to practice their very limited English. I'm convinced one of them wants to be my Shanghai bride. Hey, if she can massage feet…

Now, when the bill comes, in Chinese culture, the person who asks for it pays. No splitting. So when Steve and I go through our usual ritual of digging around and trying to convert yuan to dollars while sorting who owes what, we become the lunchtime show. All talking, burping, and smoking stops. Everyone watches the two white guys discuss a lunch bill. Hey, if we can accept spitting on the restaurant floor, they can accept two guys splitting the bill!

Today, we ordered perch. And our waitress, Liu Yan, my future Shanghai bride, brought it to the table in a bag. A flopping, living bag. That's some serious farm-to-table. Or rather, river-to-mouth.

I've started thinking about what kind of gifts I can get for these two when we wrap up our time here. Every day as we leave, they beam at us and say, "See you tomorrow!" One of them may or may not be planning our wedding.

Taxi drivers? Still confused. But I've changed my mind, they're not bad drivers. They're magicians. The things they do with a car in this traffic, it's Olympic-level precision. The problem isn't skill. It's willingness. When we hand over our little paper with Chinese characters showing our destination, they look at it, look at us, wave their hands, and drive away. Apparently, if it's across the river, not close to their food stop, or just mildly inconvenient? They'll pass. With flair.

So, there we are, Steve and I, walking down dimly lit streets after work, hoping to flag someone down. At some point, I thought, doesn't IBM have cars? With drivers? At this rate, I may just hop onto the back of one of the gazillion bicycles and hope for the best.

Every time I make it across a street or into the hotel lobby alive, I want to drop to my knees and kiss the ground. Then I remember where I am, and decide against it. Last thing I need is a faceful of spit and soy sauce.

But I am getting bolder. The rosary beads are off my Amazon wish list. I've graduated from wide-eyed fear to tourist-jog confidence. Soon, I'll be strutting across intersections like a local, daring any vehicle to hit me. As for taxi rides, I've learned to look anywhere but out the window.

So to summarize Week Two:

The city is huge. There are many people. The food is incredible. And I'm so ready to come home.

If something else insane happens during Week Three (and let's face it, it will), you'll be the first to know.

Love,

Bill

Embracing Chaos, One Rickshaw at a Time

Greetings one and all, it's the beginning of my fourth week here. I'm still alive, and believe it or not, I've actually grown... fond of this place.

It takes time, and maybe a mild case of psychosis, but you eventually learn to become one with the chaos. That's something most people wouldn't get on a quick visit. Living here, or, okay, surviving here, teaches you things. I'm fond... but don't worry. I'm not staying. I'm looking forward to leaving on December 1st.

Last week started off with the remnants of a typhoon that hit Vietnam. We got all the weather without any of the headlines. Wet, cold, then weirdly sunny and warm again, Shanghai just can't commit to a forecast.

So there we were, Steve and I, back on our daily adventure of "Mr. Taxi Driver, please pick us up." One morning, a man with a motorbike-and-rickshaw hybrid, picture a Vespa hauling a covered wagon, kept motioning for us to get on. Steve is fearless. I've learned there's a fine line between fearless and death wish, and Steve dances on that line like a Rockette! I wasn't even sure the guy was saying "subway." He kept motioning with one hand sliding under the other like a magician in need of subtitles. For all we knew, he wanted to drop us off in the tunnel under the river. But before I could object, Steve grabbed my arm and, boom, we were on board.

The seat was designed for either two Chinese people or one American. When exactly did I get hippy?

I can only imagine what a sight we were, two guys in business clothes, backpacks in laps, clutching the sides of this... contraption... while careening through the streets. In the rain. I'd only just gotten used to not looking out the side window of a taxi, and now I was face-to-face with oncoming traffic like I was in the front car of a rollercoaster themed "Cultural Misunderstanding."

The Chinese stare a lot. And today, they had a real show.

Somehow, miraculously, we arrived at the subway station. It was our first attempt at navigating it, and of course, we had no idea what we were doing. That's when an angel appeared, a wom-

an who spoke a little English and had a daughter in Philadelphia. And just like that, she made us her life's mission. She pretty much took our hands like a crosswalk mom and guided us all the way through, pointing loudly at every sign along the way like we were two blindfolded Golden Retrievers.

She told us, no less than twelve times, where our stop was. The Chinese really do repeat themselves, especially when they think you're dumb enough not to understand them the first eleven times.

We made it. No fatalities. Just another day in this very, very big city.

That night, I needed a break from the Chinese everything, so I found an Italian restaurant near the hotel. Isola Bella, Beautiful Island. And it truly was. Elegant, modern, completely empty. I was the only customer, with seven waitresses so happy they had someone to serve!

The owner is from Milan. Speaks no Chinese. Speaks no English. So we spoke Italian all night, me, him, and a chorus of "xièiè" to the staff who probably had no idea what was going on.

By the time I left, I was mentally exhausted from the linguistic gymnastics. I barely speak English anymore. My mouth only seems capable of IBM jargon and international charades.

But the pasta? Glorious. The wine? Italian. I've had Chinese wine. Let's just say... don't rush off to your local wine merchant. Stick with the tea.

Later in the week, I went for another Chinese massage. This time I asked for someone "strong."

Mistake.

What I should've said was "someone sensitive to my cries of anguish." For those of you who've given birth, walk in the park. Passed a kidney stone? Child's play. You have not experienced pain until a master of ancient Chinese muscle excavation goes digging around the tendons behind your kneecaps. I didn't even know I had muscles there.

If I do it again, I'm bringing two Vicodin and a martini.

A few days later, I ventured out to an international bookstore, a literal oasis. Found it, wept tears of joy, and immediately bought two trashy paperback novels. Each one costs about $10, which is wild, because here you can eat like royalty for three bucks, but reading will bankrupt you.

But the best night of the week was the visit with two deaf Chinese artists, a married couple who met us in the hotel lobby. He's a sculptor, she's a painter. Lovely people. Another taxi (naturally) to another mysterious part of the city, and we found ourselves in their apartment, which they share with her mother and sister.

They use Chinese Sign Language, and we somehow made it work. We laughed, gestured wildly, drank tea, and admired their work. They had both attended Deaf Way II in Washington, D.C. the previous summer. Incredible talents.

We had to remove our shoes or wear surgical booties inside the apartment, a brilliant rule, honestly. I might adopt it when I get home. Shoes OFF. Forever.

After tea, they took us to a restaurant where you "cook" your food at the table in a giant, bubbling vat of... something. Things brought to the table included: raw goat meat, raw mushrooms, seaweed, duck tongue, squid, goat tendons (seriously), and a few other mystery items that might've been parts of creatures I don't wish to name.

I feigned fullness around the goat tendons.

Let's just say, I left dreaming of an In-N-Out burger.

Despite the culinary trauma, it was a beautiful evening. The next time you see "goat tendon" on a menu? Run.

We're almost at the end of our restaurant routine. I bought a few gifts for our two favorite waitresses and had a thank-you note translated into Chinese. Steve brought his camera (obviously), and we had our farewell lunch today. The chef made us two special dishes: squid with onions (shockingly good) and hot yams drizzled in honey (even better). The latter was on the house.

Photos were taken. Tears were shed, mostly on the inside. Tomorrow's our last day there. Either they'll miss us terribly... or *throw a party when we leave. Hard to read the Chinese emotional register.*

Next stop? Beijing. The Great Wall, The Forbidden City, Tiananmen Square... and Peking Duck.

This trip is about many things. But mostly it's about food.

I'll update you from the next chapter of this madness.

Love,

Bill

From Beijing with Bags
(and a Side of Peking Duck Drama)

Well, I couldn't let the trip end without one last email, this time from Beijing. Steve and I said goodbye to our beloved Shanghai, the city I'd come to feel weirdly fond of, with all her flaws, faults, foibles... and phlegm.

Getting to Hangzhou airport was, for once, a breeze. Free shuttle, no haggling, no drama. We were older, wiser, and seasoned veterans of at least three attempted taxi scams, four foot massages, and a dozen food-related emotional roller coasters. We checked in easily, found our gate, and even boarded the plane without incident.

Sort of.

It was a flight on China Eastern Airlines, and for a 1-hour, 45-minute hop, I have to say, they put the U.S. airlines to shame. We were served a snack with beverage service, then a full lunch (choice between pork and rice or noodles), then another round of drinks. In the States, we'd get a sandwich you have to fight a flight attendant for and a handful of trail mix you could fit in a thimble.

I chose the pork and rice. I think.

We landed in Beijing absolutely exhausted. Short flight or not, air travel nowadays is a full-contact sport, emotionally and physically. And right away, drama.

Beijing's the one place in China where people actually queue for taxis. That said, don't let your guard down. They'll still slip in front of you even while you're standing there. If there's enough of a gap where a body could be, they'll fill it.

So there we were, next in line, ready to go... and the driver took one look at our bags and started yelling. Apparently, our luggage was too big. I didn't know there were carry-on expectations for taxi passengers, but here we were. In my defense, I've been gone for a month. I do tend to over-pack. There are wardrobe changes.

One of the official-looking officers in charge of organizing this chaos insisted the driver take us anyway. That resulted in a Candid Camera-worthy moment involving six people trying to force our bags into a trunk, back seat, and front seat all at once. Loud, frantic, multi-lingual shouting ensued. We were the evening entertainment.

Naturally, I assumed the driver was furious and plotting our slow detour into a ditch.

Sure enough, when we finally got moving, he pulled over just outside the airport, stepped out, opened a door, and rearranged the luggage. Not to throw us out, but to give me more legroom in the back. I was speechless.

Never judge the whole movie until you've seen the credits!

Beijing is big, gray, and cold. If Shanghai is New York, Beijing is Baltimore.

The hotel, though, was stunning. I'm on the Executive Floor, which means plush bedding, a solid breakfast, and all the bathroom goodies I can stuff into my suitcase. Suddenly, I was forgiving everyone. Especially the driver. There's nothing like a down comforter to cleanse your soul.

Steve, of course, was ready to GO GO GO. He was pumped. Adrenalized. A man on a mission. I had just experienced a domestic Chinese flight. Eaten airplane pork. Lived through another taxi saga. I was ready to go-go-go… to bed. But no, Steve wanted to see The Forbidden City. Except... It closes at 4:00. Oops. So he redirected to Tiananmen Square! Except... too dark. And also closed. I was jetlagged, pork-lagged, and emotionally spent. I wanted one eggroll and the right to remain horizontal.

But Steve wasn't having it.

The hotel suggested a lovely nearby restaurant. Quiet, convenient. Sounds great, right? Steve wanted excitement. I wanted to be calm. He wanted stimulation. I wanted room service. He insisted on going out for Peking Duck, which, let's be honest, I should've seen coming a mile away.

So, forty minutes in a taxi later, we're dropped off... not at the restaurant. The driver just kind of... pointed. "Over there," we assumed. We were near Tiananmen Square (there, checked that box. Let's go home.), but definitely not at a restaurant.

And that's when the rickshaw drivers found us.

This time, no motors. No coverings. Just two elderly men and a pair of wheeled benches. Of course, Steve climbs aboard with the glee of a boy on Christmas morning. "Get on yours!" he signs to me.

And I do. Because what's life without more chaos?

So there I am, bundled in my coat, perched on this glorified barstool with wheels, zipping through Beijing by an old Chinese guy with thighs of steel. It's freezing. And not just "chilly", Jack Fong is nipping at more than just my nose. I can't even feel my nose.

I realize, mid-ride:

I don't have insurance for this.

Insurance wouldn't cover this.

My driver has opted for the left side of the road, the one facing oncoming traffic.

Meanwhile, Steve's guy is on the right side, which at least pretends to follow traffic flow (that's an oxymoron if ever there was one). I can see Steve smiling, pointing at buildings. I, on the other hand, am staring straight ahead, watching my driver ring a small bell at every single oncoming vehicle like it's a magical shield.

I don't know if it was to clear the way or to make us an easier target to hit!

We arrive, miraculously, at Quanjude Roast Duck Restaurant. *Famous. Historic. Opened in 1864. There's a giant counter at the front tracking how many ducks have been served since then. Over 101 million! Did you know it takes three days to cook a duck? The place was packed with people who looked like us!*

They hand us a glossy brochure, the kind with pictures of George and Barbara Bush, Fidel Castro, Yasser Arafat... and now, apparently, Steve and Bill.

Steve was in heaven. Tour buses of camera-toting foreigners snapping shots of roasted birds being carved tableside. I was internally whispering "Check please" in every language I know. I wanted to eat where the locals go, but Steve chose what turned out to be the Lawry's Prime Rib of Beijing.

We were given the choice between à la carte or a seven-course duck-themed dinner. Guess what we went with.

Now, here's the part where Steve decides that half a duck is just not enough duck. The waitress, via pantomime, explains we're getting half. Steve isn't satisfied. I say, "We're getting six other courses. We'll be okay." Steve, undeterred, wants a full duck.

Have you seen a duck? They're not small.

We got the whole duck.

We ate maybe half of it.

I wish I had known how to sign "I told you so" in Chinese Sign Language!

Steve was so giddy he snuck into the kitchen to take photos. I felt the whole place was just a notch above Sizzler, and it helped me realize that

 I'm ready to go home.

I want to eat with a fork again. I want to be in a restaurant where no one has to flop the main course onto my table while it's still wiggling.

Steve wants to do The Great Wall this weekend. I want to do nothing. I want to slowly, lovingly pack my bags. I've reached a point in this journey where I can confidently say there are three stages in life.

"I want to know."

"I know."

"I don't want to know."

As far as China goes, I've hit Stage Three.

And yes, I've heard the Great Wall is a fantastic place to buy Great Wall souvenirs. Like hats. And T-shirts. And more ducks.

Maybe if Steve gets an assignment in Egypt, I'll go and buy T-shirts at the pyramids. But for now? I'm more excited about Van Nuys than any ancient wonder of the world.

Happy Thanksgiving to one and all, and thanks for reading.

Love,

Bill

Fever Dreams, Fake Gucci, and the Interpreter Who Shall Remain Nameless

Sending those emails back to the States helped keep me sane. I'd hear from people saying they enjoyed living vicariously through me, "Keep 'em coming!" they'd say, like I was starring in some offbeat travel docuseries they didn't have to pay for.

In my hotel room, I had an actual wall calendar where I'd X out each passing day, like I was counting time in San Quentin.

Christmas was coming up, so I started going to the local marketplace to shop for knockoff gifts. I ended up with several Rolex watches, Burberry, Louis Vuitton, Dolce & Gabbana, all lovingly stuffed into a fake Prada backpack. I mean, the thing practically squealed "Customs violation" every time I moved.

Of course, I told everyone the items were fake. I'm sure I did. Okay... I thought I did.

As you can probably tell from my emails, Steve really did become fun once he loosened up in Shanghai. He loved to shop. The man could vanish into a tailor shop for hours having custom shirts and suits made. He bought tons of gifts for his kids and actually seemed to be having a good time.

He was definitely more adventurous than I was, which, I'll admit, helped me loosen up, too. Our days usually ended with us in the back of a taxi, laughing until we couldn't breathe. It was like our own twisted version of "Carpool Karaoke," minus the singing and plus the near-death turns.

But of course... the "old Steve" had to resurface.

It happened in Beijing, during a meeting. We were seated at a large round table with high-level Chinese bankers and IBM execs. Power suits. Poker faces. Not a lot of laughs.

Steve was seated directly across from me, and the meeting began with introductions. They asked Steve to start. He signed his name and position, and I voiced, like I'd done so many times before.

Then the intros continued around the table. Thankfully, name placards were present, because fingerspelling Chinese names wasn't exactly in my wheelhouse.

When it got to me, I was about to sign and voice, "Bill Pugin, Sign Language Interpreter."

But Steve, with zero warning and both hands raised like he was presenting the next prophet, signed:

"The interpreter shall remain nameless."

Oh, Steve. Really?

And of course, I had to voice that.

Now, instead of a smooth continuation around the table, everything stopped. Everyone looked confused. The spotlight slammed onto me like a Broadway solo. And Steve. They all wanted to know why the interpreter had no name.

This truly had the opposite effect of what Steve had intended.

Montpellier France Steve had officially returned from hibernation.

During the first break, people approached Steve to ask for clarification. He knew immediately the can of worms he opened. I considered telling him to handle it on his own. "You can explain why I don't have a name, I'll be in the bathroom."

But, of course, I stayed. I voiced Steve's explanation:

"We aren't people. We don't have a voice. We don't have opinions. We are there only for him."

Great.

When the trip ended, we returned to Shanghai. Steve stayed on for a few extra days while I waited at the airport for my connecting flight to San Francisco. But first, I had to pass through China's fever detector.

This isn't just a temperature check. It's a whole machine. If you register a fever, you don't fly. You stay. Possibly forever.

Now, I run hot. Always have. I was terrified the machine would read me as a biohazard. I didn't know what I'd do if they told me I couldn't leave. Cry? Scream? Fake a heart attack?

I closed my eyes, walked through, and... made it. No fever detected. Thank you, baby Jesus.

Then came U.S. Customs in San Francisco. Me. My fake Prada backpack. My luggage is full of illegal designer goods. Sweating. Again.

And again... I made it through.

I had not done my homework and I honestly didn't know bringing knock-offs into the country was illegal. I was informed of this by a fellow passenger on the flight. Well, a little late for me to do anything about it then - except pray!

I was pissed at Steve again. Told myself I'd never work with him again. I called Karen and Janet at SLA and told them, "Thanks, but no thanks."

They understood.

Then, of course... Steve had to go back to China. And he wanted me to come.

I said yes, with conditions. I'd go for two weeks, not a month. They'd fly another interpreter in to replace me after that. And that's what happened.

Before the second trip, Steve asked if I'd meet him at his mother's house in L.A. to interpret a very early phone call. I agreed, 5am, coffee in hand, professional hat firmly on.

Before the call, we talked.

I told him how I felt about what he did in Beijing. I reminded him of our conversation in France. I was calm. Direct. Highly caffeinated but very clear. And to his credit... Steve apologized.

He said he was genuinely sorry. That he couldn't imagine taking these trips without me. That he hoped I'd accept the apology. Of course I would.

I liked the guy. I liked to travel. And most of all, I liked the work, even when it got messy.

After that China trip, Steve told me the next destinations would be Japan and Turkey.

Back to the City Above the Water

The second trip to China was, surprisingly, better than the first. Familiarity helped. We knew the hotel, and the folks at the front desk remembered us. It was hard to forget two pale, blonde-ish guys communicating entirely with their hands. In Pudong, where tourists were a rare breed, we stood out like albino giraffes in a petting zoo. One man literally fell off his bike trying to figure out what species we were.

These are the emails I sent during that second trip.

Shanghai II – The Recline Button Strikes Back

Hello all, well… I'M BAAAAAACK!

Dear lovely Shanghai... the city above the water. That's what "Shanghai" means. And sure enough, to the west of me is a lot of water. More rain and flooding than this part of China has seen in 200 years. Add that to a bumpy plane ride thanks to a typhoon pelting Japan, and all I can say is how much I love the Orient.

I hadn't planned to send more "Letters from Shanghai" this trip, but it turns out writing these is my form of therapy. And what kind of friend would I be to deny you all a front-row seat to my ongoing adventures in the land of jade and questionable plumbing?

The trip started out like déjà vu with a head cold. Sitting at the airport in San Francisco is basically a soft launch into Shanghai anyway, packed with Chinese travelers already speaking at full volume, in person and on their phones. We are all part of the conversation. We are all one. We are the world.

Once I boarded the plane, I was offered water, juice, or champagne. I grabbed the bubbly. It was 2pm. No regrets. Champagne on an empty stomach is a great way to sleep through the safety video and forget you're in a steel tube hurtling toward Asia.

I like to think of myself as a seasoned traveler, but Business Class on an international flight to China is a whole other species. Everyone else seemed to know exactly what to do. And then there was me, pressing every button completely unsure of what would happen. Pressed one button, leg rest popped up. Pressed another, tray table smacked me in the knee. I tried to fix that, the screen flew out. Tried to put that away, summoned the flight attendant. I felt like Lucy Ricardo auditioning for Cirque du Soleil.

After my fizzy nap, I made my way to the bathroom, which on international flights, of course, features no helpful words like "occupied" or "vacant." Just little symbols. Color-coded, naturally, because this was going to be a test. In the dark. Plus, I'm color blind.

So there I was, standing and staring at the lavatory doors, like I was reading a wall-mounted newspaper. I took a gamble, pushed the door... OCCUPIED. Of course.

When I returned to my seat, which I decided to leave in one position for the entire flight, the guy across the aisle from me was giving me that look. I assumed it had something to do with the seat/bathroom performance. No. Then he said those five unforgettable words:

"I recognize you... from TV!"

I asked if he watched a lot of reruns, because if he knew me from TV, it was years ago and very few people did. "I'm not anyone you'd know," I told him. He was still excited. If he'd been Chinese, I'd have been really impressed.

It's a long flight to China. Long. Long enough that I started reading The Da Vinci Code, and finished it. 605 pages. Plus I watched a movie, ate two meals, and slept. I could've earned a liberal arts degree in that amount of time.

Once we landed, my bag was, of course, one of the last off the conveyor belt. Which meant I missed the airport shuttle. Which meant I decided, in my infinite jetlagged wisdom, to take a city bus. It was only 19 yuan (about $2). Adventure time.

The bus took me to the city center, where I attempted to hail a taxi.

Ah, the nostalgia.

I had my hotel reservation page with me, proudly printed in English. So helpful! Except it wasn't. I kept shouting "Okura Garden Hotel," and nothing registered. Showed the driver the page, still nothing. I even tried saying "Mao Ming Road" in my best faux-fluent Chinese accent. Blank stares.

Eventually, I resorted to international sign language, pointing frantically at the phone number on the page and then to her phone. Her response? Get out of the car. So we both got out, flagged another cab behind us, and she handed over the problem, me, to someone else.

This second driver also had no idea what I was saying. But, and here's where things turned, he called the number (brilliant), nodded, and said the magic words: "Mao Ming."

Didn't I just say that? OY VEY, how do you say that in Chinese?

I got to the hotel and was greeted by the same lovely reservation staff, who once again didn't want to honor my IBM rate because I didn't have an IBM business card. Explaining my situation was like trying to describe quantum physics to a plant.

So I asked to see the manager. He came out, took one look at me and said, "Oh... I know you." Didn't even flinch. Had he been watching old American TV shows, too?

He instructed the staff to give me the rate. THANK YOU VERY MUCH. NOW MAY I PLEASE HAVE MY KEY SO I CAN TAKE OFF MY SHOES AND BRUSH MY TEETH!

I grabbed my suitcase from the bellhop myself. I'd had enough human interaction for the day. I just wanted to get to my room, become horizontal, and question every life choice that brought me here.

Then, right on cue, my American-bought Citizen watch fell off my wrist. Not just slipped off, it shattered. Broke clean in two. Crystal popped out of the face. It was like the watch had been waiting until it landed on Chinese soil to self-destruct.

I started to laugh. A little manic, maybe. But sometimes that's all you can do. This wasn't a cheap fake Rolex from the Shanghai market, it was the real thing. And it still gave up.

Welcome back, Bill. Let's see what breaks next.

Love,

Bill

Mystery Breakfasts, Dead-Eyed Waiters, and the Return of the Charade King

I've mentioned before how fun it is to ride in taxis here in Shanghai. But let's go deeper, because the real treat isn't just the ride itself. It's the rules posted behind the driver.

They're probably written beautifully in Chinese, full of clarity and Confucian wisdom. But the English translations are pretty wacky.

I wish I could've written them all down, but usually I'm too busy clutching my backpack, my nerves, or the door handle, just in case I need to bail out of a moving vehicle like Jason Bourne.

Still, here are a few I managed to commit to memory:

"No psychos or alcoholics will be allowed without a guardian." *I mean... fair. Let's all just agree that if you're babbling nonsense or hammered, you need a chaperone. Safety first.*

"No spitting or dumping in the taxi." *Let's not even go there.*

"If you don't agree with the rule, there will be no conniving with the driver about them." *Got it. No conniving. Also not sure I've ever connived in a cab, but thank you for the heads-up.*

Even the newspapers here are performance art. China Daily never disappoints. Some recent headlines:

- *"Woman Finds Dieting Secret in Silkworms"*

- *"Snake on Shelves Scares Shoppers"*

- *"High-Income Beggar Cheats Passers-By"*

- *"Granny Gives Lesson to Lover-Seeking Netizen"*

- *"Six-Legged Piglet Has Two to Spare"* *Trust me, these make a lot more sense after two Tsingtaos.*

Anyway, my first day back at work in Pudong was, let's say... familiar. Everything came rushing back, the noise, the traffic, the smog, the gray. Especially the gray. It's like working inside a dust bunny.

Steve and I are now stationed in a small cubicle with two Chinese coworkers, two Australians, and a French guy. Out of the seven of us, I'm the only one I can consistently understand.

On Wednesday, we returned to the restaurant that made us lunchtime legends on our first trip. The owner spotted us from across the room and greeted us with a massive smile and handshake.

That alone was shocking. People don't smile here, not in restaurants, anyway. I don't know if it's cultural, dental, or existential, but smiling is rare. The waitstaff usually look like they're mourning something, possibly the death of joy.

Liu Yan, our old favorite waitress and my possible one-that-got-away is gone. Quit her job. It just wasn't the same without her. Even the food tasted...off. We still went back, because unless I smuggle in a peanut butter sandwich, I'm doomed to follow Steve like a well-heeled puppy. And yes, I shouldn't say "puppy", it might be on the menu.

On Thursday, I woke up to wet sidewalks, which isn't unusual (if you catch my drift). But this time, the wet came from the sky. Rain. Actual, meteorological rain. Which just made the traffic even more theatrical.

What I've figured out is it's apparently a sign of weakness to use windshield wipers here. Either that, or cars don't come with them. Visibility is for the weak. So is using the defroster. Why see where you're going when you can guess?

I'm convinced that driving should be added as an Olympic sport when Beijing hosts. Headline: Gold medal goes to Wong Wei, who successfully avoided hitting all but six pedestrians.

Steve, meanwhile, has now officially befriended a local deaf artist, someone he met during our last visit. She joined us for lunch, which made things extra fun, as I attempted to converse in a hybrid of American Sign Language, International Sign, and gestures that may or may not have meant "fish" or "death."

She's apparently quite well-known in China, a ceramicist or potter or something equally gallery-worthy. She once presented a piece to a top government official and now receives free housing and museum passes for life. My career planning suddenly feels very off.

During lunch, we tried to order fish. Steve and our artist friend went to pick one from the tank. My only request was please don't bring it to the table with the head still attached. The waiter promised. Sort of.

When the dish arrived, the head was not attached, technically, but was laid beside the fish like a garnish, mouth gaping open to the ceiling like it was singing opera. A dead-eyed fishy fountain.

Bon appétit.

I keep thinking that at some point, I'll run out of things to write about. And yet... here we are. More soon, I have a hankering for a foot massage and possibly a tetanus shot.

Love,

Bill

Final Foot Rubs, Exit Strategies, and a Farewell to the City That Hacked My Sanity

The week has flown by. A good sign, I guess. When the days feel long, but the week feels short, it usually means you're running on adrenaline, tea, and the faint promise of freedom.

On Tuesday, Steve and I headed back to the massage place we'd found during our first Shanghai adventure. We remembered it fondly. Good chairs, low lighting, a mostly trauma-free experience.

Well. We got there and were handed a laminated menu of services. They had names like "Full body Tui Na (Strong)," "Foot & Lower Leg (Energy!)," and, my personal favorite, "Special Kidney Care." I asked what the last one entailed. The receptionist gave me a look that was either confusion or deep concern and simply said, "Strong. Very strong."

Hard pass.

Steve opted for the full-body massage. I went with the foot massage.

It started out lovely. A warm foot bath, soothing music that might've been bamboo-based, and a young woman who happened to be blind. Then she started. And I discovered she'd either misunderstood "foot massage" or was seeking revenge for something I did in a past life.

She jabbed my arches like I owed her money. She used her knuckles. Her elbows. At one point, I'm pretty sure she used a forehead. And then, like a dramatic twist in a suspense film, she flipped my foot sideways, cracked something that definitely wasn't meant to be cracked, and said, very proudly "Relax."

My foot just disassociated from my body.

Afterward, I hobbled out of the massage parlor like I'd survived a mugging. Steve looked refreshed. Radiant. A man reborn. I looked like a war widow.

So naturally, we went for ice cream.

Wednesday was a travel day. We took the subway across the river, which I now navigate like a local, by the way. I still don't understand anything, but I move with purpose, and that's 90% of surviving in this country.

Wednesday marked my first day back at work at China Bank, Pudong. I had somehow forgotten the E-ticket thrill ride of the cab commute, now with the added pleasure of sweat. Ever had your skin peel off the seat of a non-air-conditioned car? Multiply that by the ghosts of every other passenger who left part of themselves behind.

That morning, I told Steve I wanted a real breakfast. Not green tea. Not mystery paste. Just eggs, toast, and coffee. He suggested Starbucks, he's from Seattle, after all, but I vetoed that. Instead, he recommended a nearby restaurant the hotel staff swore by.

I had immediate doubts. A nice Chinese breakfast, recommended by Chinese people, from a Japanese hotel. What could go wrong?

We went. We pointed. We regretted.

Three separate dishes appeared, each showcasing a trio of mysterious, oblong objects. The first plate arrived and we just stared at it. Then at each other. And burst into uncontrollable laughter.

These weren't food items, they were props from a low-budget sci-fi film. Picture three brown ovals with a thick coating of what looked like petrified horsehair. "Go ahead, Steve," I said. "This was your idea. You try first."

We think there was meat inside. Possibly. There's really no way to know.

The second dish involved some kind of lava-esque paste that oozed across the plate, over our hands, and threatened to become sentient. The third plate? Best forgotten.

The "soup" was not soup. It was a semi-translucent gelatinous substance with a single corn kernel floating in it, like a sad little buoy. Dessert was a clear jelly square that could've doubled as packing material. Steve ate it all. I ate the decorative parsley.

"Tomorrow," I declared, "we're going to Starbucks."

Back at the hotel, I found myself flipping channels on the TV, hoping to catch CNN or anything familiar. What I got instead was:

- **"Are You Smarter Than a Panda?"**

- **Chinese dubbed version of The Lion King**, *which was oddly more dramatic*

- *An infomercial for a belt that "melts fat through vibration" (tempting)*

My final days in the office were marked by more of the same: meetings, interpreting things I only pretended to understand, trying not to laugh at titles like "Lead Product Strategy Developer, Agile Agile Integrations Liaison."

I told myself I'd take it easy. Walk slowly. Breathe. Absorb the culture one last time. But that's not how Shanghai works.

The sidewalks are never wide enough. The air is never quiet. The tea is never just tea, it's tea with herbs, flowers, bits of root, and (possibly) ancient hallucinogens. One afternoon I took a sip and swore I saw the Ming dynasty flash before my eyes.

Because I can't really participate in conversations here (unless pointing and miming counts as discourse), I've become an expert observer. Here are ten things I've noticed. These are not broad generalizations. These are not clichés. These are cold, hard, lived-in truths:

1. Japanese women cover their mouths when they laugh. Chinese women do not. *Possibly because Chinese women don't actually laugh.*

2. Chinese children do laugh. *Until they reach the age where they realize this is not a vacation, this is their life.*

3. Chinese men under 30 all have 26-inch waists. *Over 30? They turn into Humpty Dumpty in a windbreaker.*

4. Chinese women have 20-inch waists. *Even while pregnant. No explanation.*

5. Chinese women walk like they just dismounted a horse and were forced to put on high heels before stepping onto a sand dune. *Picture it.*

6. Japanese women look down when they walk. *Centuries of foot-binding might have left a lingering fear of tripping. Or rebellion. Or both.*

7. All Chinese men smoke. *All of them. I've yet to meet one who doesn't.*

8. Chinese men don't hold their cigarettes between their index and middle fingers. *They use their thumb and index finger and clutch the cigarette as though trying to hide it, or perform a magic trick. There's a lot of cupping involved.*

9. There is always a cloud of smoke around Chinese men. *Always. Which completely defeats the purpose of #8.*

10. The smoke cloud is so dense it often appears these men are participating in a roaming Buddhist ceremony. *Every alley smells like incense and Marlboros.*

Okay, just a few more observations before I leave this beautiful, chaotic wonderland. If I could actually engage in conversation, I'd probably miss out on all this staring. I mean, they stare at me, so it only seems fair that I return the favor. Yin for yang.

The Chinese are kind, gentle, and warm people. Their language, however, often sounds like someone's about to unleash artillery fire. It's a little jarring.

Whenever I walk around, especially in Pudong, people are both confused and delighted. They often say "HELLO!" with immense pride, as if their third-grade English teacher just appeared and handed them a gold star. When I say hello back, it's a moment of pure joy. I'm like a walking Sesame Street episode.

Around the hotel, I don't get many stares, but in the neighborhoods, I might as well be eight feet tall and lime green. I find myself double-checking to see if something's dripping off me, or if I've accidentally tucked my shirt into my underwear. But then I remember, fashion here is... flexible.

Where is it written that plaid doesn't pair well with stripes? Who decided polka dots and checkered pants were a no-go? And if you can't find your favorite outfit? Pajamas are totally fine. For any occasion. Comfort is king.

Which is why, ladies, **old black ballet flats go with everything** *in China. Wedding? Funeral? A nice walk to the meat market? Always ballet flats.*

Mental note: next time I pack for Shanghai, I'll stop obsessing about matching shoes to belts. In the grand scheme of things, it's irrelevant.

Here are a few final truths I've come to accept:

- *Chinese men have shockingly long fingernails. I keep meaning to ask why. And then deciding I'd rather not know.*

- On the subway in China, I am not short. *Not tall. Not average. Just... not short.*

- All Chinese women are pregnant in September. *Hear me out. Last year in November? Not a single pregnant woman. None. I was starting to wonder how the population replenished itself. This year? September. Everyone's seven months along. It must be tied to the Mooncake Festival, three weeks of celebrating something (I'm unclear on what exactly) and eating expensive desserts called "mooncakes," which are gooey pastries with a duck egg yolk in the middle. Allegedly. I didn't stick around long enough to confirm. But hey, if the yolk represents the moon... I guess it all makes sense.*

- The Chinese don't look both ways when crossing the street. *They just walk. No hesitation. No fear. No head-turning. I, meanwhile, look like Linda Blair in The Exorcist, spinning around in full panic mode every time I approach a crosswalk.*

And speaking of traffic, again, someone needs to create a series of bumper stickers for China:

- *Honk if you're breathing.*
- *Honk if you have a horn.*
- *Honk… because you can.*

And one last revelation:

Chinese massage therapists are out for emotional blood. *They find your stress. They poke it. Prod it. Name it. Mock it. And then they break it apart like a cheap souvenir. It's less massage, more exorcism. And yet we in the West opt for Swedish massages. Why? What do the Swedes know about stress? Are they worried about their space program? Their military? Their two-car lineup?*

Inga and Sven need to fly over here and discover the true meaning of tension. And that leads me to observation number seven:

If your Chinese masseur suggests something called "cupping," you do not have to say yes. *I said yes.*

I now have red welts on my back the size of dinner plates. David, my masseur, oddly named, swears they'll go away. Eventually. Maybe. Do I have that kind of time?

Oh, and a final word of advice: if you want to learn Chinese, take a class. With a lot of practice. I tried to be clever and learn how to say "I live here." That way, when people tried to sell me DVDs or bootleg DVDs or more DVDs, I'd have a good response.

Turns out, tonal inflection is... important.

The looks I got told me I wasn't saying "I live here." I was probably saying "My water broke," or "Your doom is imminent."

Whatever it was, it was alarming. And now? I say it all the time.

And as I near the end of this trip, I find myself taking a moment to reflect. Cue the dim lighting and soft piano music. It's time to say goodbye. Not just to Shanghai, but to the many, many memorable characters who've made this journey what it was.

The nameless taxi drivers who never wanted to take us back to our hotel. The China Construction Bank employees who still don't know why we were even there. The 4.2 million DVD sellers I now consider extended family. David, my blind, tooth-challenged, shiatsu-obsessed massage therapist.

Yes, I will miss them all.

And let's not forget the lovely jazz trio in the hotel lounge. On my final night, I wandered in for a solitary nightcap, an Irish crème that cost what I assume was a week's salary for the pianist, and sat down to enjoy their music one last time. Piano. Bass. And our star: the female singer who resembled a Chinese Joanne Worley channeling Ella Fitzgerald.

She sang jazz. She scatted. And it was glorious.

She clearly learned the lyrics phonetically. I doubt she understood a single word she was singing, but that didn't stop her from feeling every note. Nobody clapped, of course. This is not a clapping culture. No tipping, no cheering, no standing ovations. Just... polite silence.

Except for me.

There I sat, the lone, possibly tipsy American, silently miming (is that redundant?) my applause like a mute game show contestant. She noticed. She bowed. I bowed back. It was a moment.

She absolutely killed "I Love Paris." ("I love Paris in the morning... I love Paris in the fall...") Huh?

But her showstopper, the emotional climax of the evening, was her powerful, soul-bearing rendition of

"Cly Me a Liver."

I felt her pain.

And so, dear Shanghai... I raise my fake Prada backpack to you, filled with contraband couture and a few questionable memories. You've been absurd, frustrating, hilarious, and unforgettable.

Said goodbye to the hotel doorman, who nodded once, his version of a tearful hug.

Time to go home.

Namaste,

Bill

Foreign Beds, Hollywood Sets, and Unwelcome Calls

There's something magical about coming home and sleeping in your own bed, especially after a business trip that required both a passport and a high tolerance for jet lag. Steve had been surprisingly delightful on our second trip to China, mostly because he wasn't particularly in the mood to work. We'd show up at the office in Shanghai or Pudong, wave the flag of productivity for a few hours, and then Steve would casually suggest an early departure. I, being no stranger to diplomacy, fully supported this approach. All in all, a successful trip. Steve and I bonded. Next stop: Japan. I was looking forward to it.

Now, pivoting from China to Wisteria Lane, I had the pleasure of working on Desperate Housewives twice. Once for an episode featuring a deaf kid, and again for one with Marlee. I adored the cast and crew, especially Felicity Huffman. Months earlier, I had worked with her husband, William H. Macy, on The Wool Cap, a film in which he played a mute man who communicated using ASL. He was an outstanding student, completely committed.

We worked at their Hollywood Hills home. And when we weren't working, we were... talking. Macy enjoyed chatting. He also enjoyed giving the full tour of the house, the grounds, and most importantly, the woodworking shop. With the flair of a proud land baron, he gestured at the surrounding property, explaining how he bought the two adjacent lots for the sake of land and privacy.

So when I walked into the hair and makeup trailer on Desperate Housewives, Felicity turned to me and said, "I know you. You've been in my bathroom!"

"Yes, I have," I replied, without missing a beat. "And I'm going to call Entertainment Tonight after seeing all the medications you take!"

We laughed. It was a fun gig.

But not all phone calls in trailers bring good news.

While visiting Marlee's trailer during that same shoot, I received a phone call from Steve Bock's brother. There'd been an accident. Steve was in the hospital in Seattle. I was, of course, concerned. I asked to be kept in the loop.

The loop didn't last long. Steve died two days after that phone call.

I flew to Washington for his memorial. His family, his mother, brother, wife, and two kids, were grieving. They were kind and deeply appreciative of the support. I couldn't stop thinking about all the memories of our work together. They came rushing back. He was tough, no doubt. But I liked him a lot. I respected him. He would be missed, certainly by me.

Performance, Politics & Pop Culture

Juggling Accents and Gin Games

In the summer of 1989, I was invited to Washington, D.C., to interpret for the entertainment segment of a landmark event called DEAF WAY. It was the first festival of its kind, a worldwide showcase of Deaf talent, hosted at Gallaudet and other venues. The fact that I was asked to fly in from California, even with a sea of qualified interpreters up and down the East Coast, felt like a real honor. Ed Waterstreet and Jane Norman, the brilliant minds on the Entertainment Planning Committee, wanted me specifically. Flattering and mildly terrifying.

They housed me in a campus dorm. My roommate was a Deaf juggler from Poland. We didn't speak the same language, but we communicated the best we could using charades, gestures, wild guesses. He even tried to teach me to juggle. Considering I work with my hands professionally, you'd think I'd be better at it. I was not. It was pathetic.

I was thrilled to be assigned to work with Phyllis Frelich. I had loved working with her on Hunter and during our long stretch on Santa Barbara, so I was excited to reunite. But no gathering of interpreters would be complete without one gloriously awkward moment. During an event honoring both Marlee and Phyllis, the organizers, bless them, placed the two of them side by side. Jack Jason interpreted for Marlee. I interpreted for Phyllis. And as Jack and I looked at each other, we both had the same thought "Wouldn't one interpreter make more sense?"

It was a bit nuts. It must've looked ridiculous. Fortunately, Marlee and Phyllis had a great sense of humor. All four of us ended up laughing through the whole thing. It was one of those moments where absurdity meets camaraderie, and the result is unforgettable.

After the festival, Phyllis and I stayed in touch in L.A. I told her we'd be working together again soon. She smiled, but she wasn't overly optimistic. Ever the realist, Phyllis felt her moment in Hollywood had come and gone. Marlee was the new face of deaf representation in entertainment, and Phyllis figured her spotlight was dimming. She returned to her first love, the stage. Theatre was home, and she made herself cozy at the newly formed Deaf West Theatre in Los Angeles.

Her first production there was The Gin Game, and I interpreted the rehearsals for that show. It marked the start of a long collaboration between Deaf West and The Fountain Theatre, which often produced works exploring deafness or starring Deaf actors. It felt like the right place to be.

Around that time, Mark Medoff, the genius behind Children of a Lesser God and The Hands of Its Enemy, both starring Phyllis, was working on a new play titled Gila. It was ambitious, layered, and destined for Broadway, but would start with out-of-town tryouts in New Mexico. Enter Andrew Shea, the director, who asked me to tutor him and a young actress named Heather Tom in sign language. Heather, at just 21, was already a star on The Young and the Restless and had an Emmy to her name. I agreed.

Heather was a delight. She was enthusiastic, hardworking, and shockingly quick to learn. We spent long hours working on her signs and how to play an interpreter convincingly. She nailed it. I was genuinely impressed. Andrew, well… Andrew did his best. He was good-humored about it, but sign language didn't come quite as naturally to him. Still, he was determined to communicate directly with Phyllis during rehearsals without relying entirely on an interpreter. Admirable. Ambitious. Occasionally awkward.

As Mark continued tweaking the play, our lessons went on for months. I eventually turned down the job as the rehearsal interpreter due to scheduling conflicts, plus, the rehearsals were happening in New Mexico, so they found someone local.

I flew in for the workshop performances and watched with pride as Heather commanded the stage, signing fluently, voicing for Phyllis' character, and interpreting for the hearing actors. She was terrific. Phyllis was flawless, as usual. The play got mixed reviews from the local press, but the momentum was promising.

Next stop was the west coast tryouts at the Odyssey Theatre in L.A. Phyllis was back on stage, right where she belonged. It was shaping up to be another Medoff-Frelich Broadway moment.

And then, it all stalled. Mark got busy with something else. "Just a pause," he promised. The play would return. We just had to wait.

He was working on a film, co-written with Andrew. It turned out Andrew would direct. And this film would bring Phyllis and me back together again, this time, with cameras rolling.

Auditions, Crayons, and the
Parking Space That Vanished

So, Andrew was about to direct his first feature film, Santa Fe. The premise was hilarious, and Andrew wanted Phyllis to play a psychiatrist, Dr. Joyce Ginsberg, who was just a few beats off from reality. I would be playing her loyal interpreter, Ed, who dutifully went along with all her eccentricities. We had already test-driven a version of this dynamic in Santa Barbara, when Phyllis played an eccentric nun. Channeling that energy again would be easy. The movie starred Gary Cole and Lolita Davidovich. It was shaping up to be a riot.

Phyllis and I flew to Santa Fe for the shoot. The filming was as fun as you'd imagine. Watching Phyllis lean fully into the role of an off-kilter psychiatrist was worth the price of admission alone. She was magnetic. We laughed through the takes and reveled in the madness of the script. It was some of the most fun I've ever had on a set.

And as it turned out, someone important took notice.

Courtney Conte, who was producing a new sitcom with Marcy Carsey and Tom Werner, the powerhouse duo behind Roseanne, Cybill, 3rd Rock from the Sun and many others, saw the film. He thought the chemistry between Phyllis and me was hysterical and unique. He was determined to get us both into this new show called Damon, starring Damon Wayans, David Alan Grier, and Andrea Martin. A sitcom dream team.

Courtney lobbied hard. The producers offered the role to Phyllis. I, however, had to audition. Typical.

I thought I was walking into a casual meeting. What I walked into was a room full of... everybody. Producers galore, Damon Wayans himself, and several suits from Fox, the network airing the show. I was told the show had already been picked up for 13 episodes. The pilot was merely a formality. Whoever landed the role of Bobby, the interpreter, would sign a contract for a six-year run.

No pressure.

I read the lines. Got a few laughs. Damon then leaned in and asked, "Can you camp it up?" He wanted the performance to be a little more flamboyant. I said, "Certainly!", delivered with an exaggerated, slithering "s" that could have melted sequins. Huge laugh.

So I did the scene again, this time with flair, bigger, brighter, fabulous. The room erupted. I remember falling to the floor when it was over, Damon actually helped me up. I felt like I was already part of the gang.

And I was. As I left the Universal lot, my agent called. No callback needed. The part was mine.

Phyllis and I dove into prep. This was major. At the time, I was also working on a film in Toronto called His Bodyguard, starring Anthony Natale and Mitzi Kapture. But I had to fly back to L.A. to sign contracts. And no, this couldn't be done by mail. Apparently, the drama wasn't limited to the screen.

A car met me at LAX and whisked me off to the Universal lot, where I signed the contracts in person. The deal was official. The money was the kind you daydream about.

I was able to finish the film in Toronto before production on Damon kicked off. So, back I went to a very frigid Toronto, warmed by the thought of what was waiting for me in sunny L.A.

When I returned, Phyllis and I were sent to wardrobe. We were ready to figure out how these characters, hers, a police psychologist; mine, a flamboyant interpreter named Bobby, would look on screen.

Phyllis was easy. She'd wear a collection of professional suits. Done.

Then came Bobby.

The wardrobe team had assembled what I can only describe as the Love Child of a box of crayons and Liberace's vacation closet. Brightly colored, patterned shirts. Pants loud enough to get you flagged by the FAA. I tried them on and looked like I had either lost a bet or the wardrobe supervisor was having an LSD flashback.

I voiced some gentle concerns. Namely, that no real interpreter would dress like this.

The wardrobe folks nodded sympathetically, and then said the choices came straight from the producers, and Damon. Damon was one of the executive producers, alongside Marcy Carsey and Tom Werner. In other words, "Take it up with the big wigs."

Phyllis was thrilled. "Bobby would never follow convention," she said, delighted by the idea that he was breaking interpreter fashion norms with reckless abandon. Meanwhile, I could already hear the letters coming in from interpreters around the world.

This wasn't new. Back on Reasonable Doubts, I'd received letters from interpreters who took issue with what Ben Douglass, my character, did or didn't do. I couldn't respond to every letter, but I once addressed it during a televised interview. I explained that I was an actor, not a producer or writer. I couldn't tell the bigwigs at NBC or Lorimar to rewrite scenes because something might offend people. The show wasn't a documentary on sign language interpreting. It was a fictional drama. Period.

So, yes, Bobby wore the shirts.

On our first day of rehearsal at Universal, Phyllis and I saw our names on our parking spaces and our dressing rooms. It felt real. It felt permanent. The cast was incredible, Damon, David, Andrea, all from the elite ranks of improv. In Living Color, Second City, SNL. These were comedy heavyweights. Phyllis and I kept pinching ourselves.

We were in her dressing room, running lines with her husband Bob Steinberg quietly observing. Bob, who had a look on his face like he'd just walked into the second act of Death of a Salesman. Cautiously optimistic, but prepared for tragedy.

"I just don't want to jinx it," he said, brow furrowed. "Things don't always work out."

Oh, Bob. We had contracts! Dressing rooms! Parking spaces! Wardrobe fittings! What could possibly go wrong?

Cue dramatic irony.

Cancel Culture (Before It Was Trendy)

So there we were, Universal Studios, shiny parking spaces with our names on them, dressing rooms with real doors and actual mirrors with lights around them. We were in. Official. And from where I stood, it looked like this show would run forever. The cast was pure comedy gold, Damon, David Alan Grier, Andrea Martin, all veterans of improv stages and sketch shows. You could practically feel the Emmys being molded backstage.

Phyllis and I were over the moon. Bob, ever the cautious realist, kept side-eyeing our good fortune. "Things don't always work out," he warned, perched on the couch in her dressing room.

Bob had a point. A point I desperately wished he didn't.

Our names were finally called. Time to head to set and rehearse our scene. Excitement? Off the charts. What we didn't know was our dreams were about to walk face-first into a brick wall called "Improv."

This cast didn't rehearse like we did. They didn't run lines or block scenes the old-fashioned way. They improvised. Damon, David, and Andrea would toss the script into the air and follow their instincts. The writers sat nearby, jotting down the best ad-libs, incorporating the changes on the fly. It was brilliant and electric.

It was a nightmare for us.

Phyllis was a Tony Award–winning stage actress. The kind who rehearsed for six weeks before curtain-up. She knew her lines. She always knew her lines. I was pretty much the same. There weren't many on-the-fly changes on episodic television, and I could handle the occasional change of dialogue if it happened. But usually, I'd memorize every word, every beat. But the moment one of the actors went rogue and made up a new line, I had to interpret it in real time. Phyllis had no idea how to respond, because that wasn't the line she learned. If I just signed what was scripted, it wouldn't have made sense to what one of the actors just said. Phyllis had no choice but to look like a deer in headlights.

We were stuck. Pinned to the script. The others were jazz musicians; we were sight-reading Bach.

It didn't take long to see we were in trouble.

That was a Friday. We were told to go home, enjoy the weekend, and report to set Monday morning.

I didn't make it to Monday.

Saturday, I was sitting in a dark movie theater, ironically watching someone else live their dreams, when my pager went off. It was Sid Craig, my agent. I scrambled to the lobby pay-phone and called him back.

"Bill," Sid said gently, "Don't report to work Monday."

He quickly added "Don't worry. You and Phyllis are still part of the show. Your characters will be introduced in a later episode. You're just not in the pilot."

Uh-huh.

I told myself it was fine. Shows shuffle things around all the time. No big deal. I even decided to show up for the pilot taping to support the cast, to be a part of the Damon family. After all, families stick together. Right?

I invited my friend Candi Milo and drove to Universal, pilot script in my heart and parking placard on my dashboard. As we rolled onto the lot, I headed toward my space. It was empty. That was good. But the sign? My name? Gone.

I parked in the spot and entered through the stage door, not with the audience. I still had some dignity. One of the producers spotted me. "Bill! What are you doing here?" she asked, voice full of chirpy surprise.

"I'm here to support you all," I said, still trying to sound like the guy who believed this show would run forever. She smiled, then added, "Oh. Would you mind moving your car? One of the actors needs that spot."

And just like that, I knew. We weren't being introduced in a later episode. We weren't in the pilot. We weren't on the show. The Deaf psychiatrist and the flamboyant interpreter had been cut.

If there was any consolation, and it was a thin one, we got paid for the pilot anyway. Even though we weren't in it. The show only lasted 13 episodes. Cancelled. There was something poetic in that, I suppose.

Standing Ovations and Silent Exits

I soon recovered from sitcom heartbreak, and started working on other projects. Twenty one television and films later, I worked on the film, A Lot Like Love, starring Ashton Kutcher and Amanda Peet. Ty Giordano, fresh off his star turn in Deaf West's Big River on Broadway and in L.A., played Ashton's brother. I served as Ty's on-set interpreter and Ashton's sign language coach.

Ashton was a quick study. Years later, I'd work with him again on Two and a Half Men, where his character had to sign. He picked it up like he'd been doing it all his life. Some actors need flashcards and patience. Ashton needed ten minutes and an iced coffee.

A Lot Like Love filmed in both Los Angeles and New York, glorious New York. Being on the streets there, I reconnected with old friends from Gallaudet who'd moved post-graduation. My very first ASL teacher, Jackie Roth, among them. It was like walking through a city made of memory.

While I was still in New York, I learned that Gila, the Medoff play Phyllis and I had worked so hard on, had been reborn as Prymate. Why the name change? Why the "y" instead of an "i"? Who knows. Something about a gorilla, I think. (Primates... Prymates... spellcheck never stood a chance.)

Phyllis knew I was in town and invited me to a preview performance. The play had changed significantly since its New Mexico and L.A. incarnations. This was Broadway now. The Longacre Theatre. The same one where Children of a Lesser God had made her a star. A true homecoming.

The house was full. The lights dimmed. The play unfolded. I watched.

And… I was confused. So was the audience. At the end, when the lights went out, there was an awkward silence, like the collective version of "Wait, was that it?" Eventually, the actors came out for the curtain call. The applause was hesitant. Tepid.

Until Phyllis walked out. Then the audience stood.

I met Phyllis and the cast at a bar next to the theatre afterward. Heather Tom was there. James Naughton. Phyllis' husband, Bob. Everyone looked drained. Not just physically, but emotionally. Like the air had left the room and no one had noticed until it was too late.

They asked what I thought. And I remembered that old story, Judy Garland seeing a friend in a play that was truly awful. When asked her opinion, she said, "Oh, honey… you should've been in the audience!"

That's exactly how I felt.

"Phyllis, you were great. You too, Heather. The play itself…
not so much." I meant it with love. And I think deep down, they
all felt the same way.

Children of a Lesser God ran for 887 performances at the
Longacre. Prymate opened on May 5, 2004. It closed May 8.
Three performances.

The critics were merciless. It was heartbreaking. Especially
for Phyllis. Especially for Heather, who had worked so hard on
her character.

Then, out of nowhere, a small bit of sunshine. Phyllis and I
were cast in Boston Legal. She played a schoolteacher. I played
her interpreter (again, are you sensing a theme?). It was a
well-written one-hour drama by David E. Kelley, spun off from
The Practice. David had always been good to me, bringing me
in on shows like Picket Fences and The Practice. And this cast
included James Spader. William Shatner. Candice Bergen. Betty
White even popped in for 16 episodes.

Bill D'Elia, the director, had worked on Reasonable Doubts
and Picket Fences with me and Marlee. A good guy, a good friend
of David's, and one of the most competent directors you'll ever
meet. He called me before the episode aired.

"Bill," he said, "I wanted you to hear it from me… the deaf
storyline was cut."

It happens. Episodic dramas run long all the time. Entire sto-
rylines get scrapped. Phyllis and I were cut. We were paid, but we
weren't credited. No residuals. We just… vanished.

The last time Phyllis and I worked together was on CSI in 2011. The episode was called "The Two Mrs. Grissoms." I played a police interpreter. Phyllis and Marlee were both in it, along with Anthony Natalc and Ty Giordano. It felt like a family reunion. I also tutored Jorja Fox in ASL for the episode.

It was a great shoot. Fans loved it. CSI had a massive following. I didn't quite realize how massive until people started reaching out from everywhere.

But something was different.

Phyllis, always fearless and willing to throw herself into any physical scene, seemed... tired. She needed help getting up and down the trailer steps. She mentioned taking more naps. That wasn't like her.

And then there were the lines.

Phyllis had never struggled with lines. She was the kind of actress who could memorize a rewrite over lunch and nail it by call time. But this time she had to do take after take. She couldn't hold onto the changes. I heard quiet conversations between the director and producer. They'd fix it in editing. They had to move on.

She was frustrated. And it showed. But she still gave it her all. That was the last time we worked together. After that shoot, I asked Bob to keep me posted. To let me know how she was doing.

He promised he would.

Dancing, Private Jets, and Shaved Heads

In 2007, Marlee was asked to be one of the contestants on Dancing with the Stars, and Jack and I put our heads together to figure out the best way to support her during the show. Given my dance background, (remember my past life with jazz hands), it made perfect sense for me to work with Marlee and her pro partner, Fabian Sanchez, during rehearsals. Jack would take over interpreting for the live broadcasts.

I absolutely loved my side of the gig because it meant I was back in a dance studio, and working while wearing jazz shoes! Fabian was amazing and relied on me to spot mistakes Marlee made that he couldn't see. It was nearly impossible to get through a full rehearsal because we spent most of the time laughing. Fabian might just be one of the funniest people alive, and that's not a title I hand out lightly. More importantly, he knew how to draw out the best in Marlee, even when she wasn't sure she had it in her.

If the celebrities had to make a public appearance somewhere during the season, their pros would tag along so they wouldn't miss a day of practice. Marlee was no exception. One such appearance was a speech she gave in Washington, DC, and naturally, Fabian and I went with her. Jack came too, as he was interpreting the speech. This wasn't just any event, it was for the Marriott Corporation, who graciously sent a private plane for us.

Let me just say that once you've flown private, commercial air travel becomes something you squint at from afar like an old ex you're embarrassed you ever dated. I now knew how the other half flew, and I wanted to be part of that "other half" forever!

Marlee's speech was scheduled for the evening, so she and Fabian rehearsed all day. The DWTS production team could find a dance studio in the middle of a desert if they needed to, and this time they secured one in Virginia. When it was time for Marlee to switch gears and get ready for her speech, Jack stepped in, and I was free to reconnect with my old friend Mary Ruth from my District Heights Theatre of the Arts days. A little walk down memory lane, minus the dance belt.

The next morning, I arrived at the private terminal of the airport earlier than anyone else. I parked myself with a cup of coffee, surrounded by people who only fly private, people who, I assume, think turbulence is a myth. At one point, the pilot strolled over and asked, "Bill, do you want to get onboard now or keep drinking your coffee?" I stayed put. There were no lines. No elbowing strangers for overhead bin space. No one asked if I'd like to check my bag "for free." This was, I decided, the only way I wanted to fly for the rest of my life.

Another time, during DWTS, we jetted off to Guadalajara, Mexico, for an event Marlee had with the Starkey Foundation, distributing free hearing aids to underprivileged adults and children. Naturally, rehearsals didn't stop, so the skeletal crew went along. Once we landed back in Burbank, customs boarded the plane, checked our passports, and waved us through. That was it. No forms. No lines. No customs-sniffing dogs. When we descended the plane stairs (the kind with actual steps, not a jet bridge), our cars were lined up in a neat little row, trunks popped open and engines were running. Did I mention this is the only way I wanted to fly?

Soon after, I started interpreting for Marlee on Switched at Birth, filmed out in Santa Clarita. For those unfamiliar with the geography of Los Angeles, Santa Clarita is a lovely place… if you enjoy long commutes and soul-crushing traffic. Many shows were being shot there at the time, including NCIS, starring Mark Harmon. His character, Leroy Jethro Gibbs, signed with Pauley Perrette's character, Abby, in a few episodes. I drove out several times to tutor them both and, I'll admit, it was fun to be back with Mark. He joked often about our Reasonable Doubts days, good times. But those drives killed me.

After four years of Switched at Birth, I'd had enough of the gridlock. I loved working with Marlee, of course, but spending two to four hours a day in traffic made me develop a condition I'll call Chronic Bad Mood Syndrome. The tipping point came on April 10, 2014. I was standing on set when I received a text from Bob Steinberg. It read: "Phyllis died today." That's all it said.

Something came over me. Call it shock, call it grief, call it a mid-life style crisis, but I calmly walked into the hair and make-up trailer and asked them to shave my head. From a curly perm in the '70s to full Marine crew cut in 2014. I didn't know what else to do. I just needed to feel something else, something different. I stayed on the show until 2016, but that moment stuck with me. Grief has a strange way of sneaking up on you and it's really dangerous when you have full access to a hair and make-up trailer.

The Mark Taper Forum held a beautiful memorial for Phyllis. Fitting, really. That's where Children of a Lesser God had its out-of-town tryouts back in 1979 before going to Broadway. That's also where her Tony Award lives today. I saw the play when I first moved to Los Angeles. I had no idea then that Phyllis and I would become such close friends. Mark Medoff spoke at the memorial, one of many who did, and I was asked to interpret. But I declined. I've learned over the years that interpreting funerals is hard for me. The second I see someone cry, the waterworks begin. Interpreting while sniffling and snorting isn't exactly ideal.

So, I sat in the audience like everyone else, mourning the trailblazer she was. Mary Anne drove in for the memorial and sat beside me. Phyllis meant so much to so many in the community. It was an honor to know her, work with her, and be her friend.

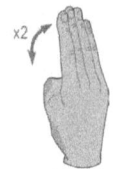

Milestones Beyond the Podium

Real Estate, Exams, and a Dash of Dalai Lama

Back at home, Ann was keeping The Sign Language Company afloat, actually, not just afloat. We were cruising. We suddenly had more contracts than we knew what to do with. School districts, universities, major studios. Interpreters were being sent out everywhere - including to jobs in other parts of the country. Meanwhile, I was enjoying life with Todd and our Wheaten Terrier, Jesse, and things were humming along quite nicely.

After 18 years, I decided to sell the house on Califa. A bittersweet goodbye. So many memories, Jeffrey, the dogs, remodeling mishaps turned into home improvements. But it was time. And, well, once I moved... I just kept going. It must be a genetic thing, or maybe I just enjoy the smell of fresh paint and new escrow forms. I'd buy a place, fix it up, sell it, and then do it all over again. I really should try to count how many toilets and washer/dryer sets I've bought over the years.

Eventually, I thought, "Why not just get my real estate license?" I wanted to know more about the business side of all these transactions, and having the license felt like an adult thing to do so that I knew what I was actually doing. I'd heard whispers that California had the hardest exam to pass, but thankfully no one told me before I took it. Blissful ignorance.

The day of the test, we were given three hours to complete it on individual computers in a room that looked like it could double as a NASA mission control center for wannabe agents. About 200 of us, all under strict examination protocols. You couldn't bring in anything, not jewelry, not cell phones, not your lucky pen or spiritual support bracelet. Everything went into a locker. And once you sat down at your computer, you weren't allowed to glance anywhere except straight ahead. I'm convinced if I had even sneezed, they would've tackled me to the floor.

People were sweating bullets. Nervous energy everywhere. Meanwhile, I felt oddly calm. I had studied the best I knew how, and I felt ready. The test lets you skip questions and return to them later, which I did one or two times, and when I got to the final question, I looked up at the timer: 0.59 minutes left. Finished in just under an hour.

I logged out, turned off the computer, stood up, and realized… I was the only one done. The rest of the room still looked like a war zone of concentration. In the lobby, the woman checking us in raised her eyebrows. "Are you finished?"

"Well, I answered all the questions, so... I guess so?" She smiled and told me to collect my things from the locker and return. "Congratulations! You passed."

That's how I became a licensed real estate agent.

Of course, I've always been too busy to actually be a real estate agent. The license was more of a bucket-list item, or maybe a party trick. "Want me to interpret and explain your mortgage options?" I never had any intention of leaving the world of interpreting, but my first brokerage, Rodeo Realty (thank you, Niki Rosenfeld), was happy to have me. I'm fairly certain they didn't have another agent fluent in ASL, and I made sure to let them know that. Turns out I was right.

Sometimes I look back at this winding road I've traveled, about fifty years in a career I stumbled into and I surprise even myself. Where did the time go? Some days, I still feel like that seventeen-year-old just discovering the art of sign language. Other days, I'm the seasoned mentor, guiding newer interpreters who remind me of, well, me back then. Full circle.

Things have certainly changed. Technology, in particular, has both improved and complicated our lives in ways nobody saw coming. When I was at Gallaudet, communication was charmingly analog. We used old Western Union machines that screamed as they printed on yellow paper. You'd think someone was sending Morse code from the trenches. These were used for deaf-to-deaf or deaf-to-hearing phone conversations, either that or a real live interpreter like myself was needed like when I moonlighted for extra cash.

Then came the smaller, portable TDDs (Telecommunication Devices for the Deaf), the sleek, sexy younger cousins of those noisy machines. I used to hand those out when I worked for AT&T, back when Bell telephones were still a thing. Now we've got smartphones, texting, FaceTime... Deaf people, and everyone else, for that matter, can communicate instantly, from anywhere, with or without being fully dressed!

And don't even get me started on social media. When did all of this happen?

But for all the changes in tech, the most profound part of my career has always been the people. I've met presidents, five of them, in fact. First Ladies. Governors. Mayors. Royalty. His Holiness The Dalai Lama. Now that was a day to remember.

Being in the same room with the Dalai Lama, you really feel something. I'm not a religious person, but there's a presence. A hush. A shift in the air. It's not something I can describe, it's just... there.

His Holiness was not the easiest person to interpret. His ability to speak English wasn't always consistent. Sometimes he'd start answering in English and halfway through would toss it to his language interpreter, who also had a thick accent and a zen-like disregard for speed or clarity.

An audience member asks a question. His Holiness furrows his brow, tries to understand. Then he turns to his interpreter, who whispers something. Then he either answers directly or repeats something back, which the interpreter then translates. It was like a spiritual game of telephone, and a challenge to put into ASL.

One question stood out. "Is it okay to kill a mosquito?"

The Dalai Lama, known for his unwavering reverence for all living things, gave a classically Buddhist answer, until he didn't. "When mosquito lands on my arm, I shoo it away. If mosquito comes back... I kill it!"

Naturally, I was dying to ask - "But Your Holiness, how do you know it's the same mosquito?"

Smoke-Filled Meetings and a Week in the Life

Earlier in my career, I'd often interpret AA (Alcoholics Anonymous) and OA (Overeaters Anonymous) meetings. These were always fascinating to me, the stories, the emotions, the rawness of people laying their lives bare in front of strangers. I didn't just interpret the words, I felt them. I couldn't help it. I seem to carry around more empathy than luggage on a trip to China.

But there was one thing I hated, hated, about interpreting those AA meetings in the '80s and early '90s. Everyone smoked. Apparently, when people gave up one addiction, they substituted with another. Alcohol out, cigarettes in. And let me tell you, those rooms were thick with smoke. You could barely see the person you were interpreting for, let alone breathe. I used to joke that it looked like they were electing a new pope.

Eventually, I waved my white flag, well, I would have if I could find it through the haze, and decided I would only interpret non-smoking meetings. I figured if I left every session coughing like I'd spent the weekend in an airport smoking lounge, it probably wasn't worth it.

OA meetings were just as surprising, but in a different way. I had gone in expecting a room full of people who, let's say, were on the larger side. But many of the participants were rail thin. I was confused at first, until I heard their stories. Bulimia. Eating disorders. Eye-opening doesn't even begin to describe it.

My career as an interpreter has taken me places I could never have imagined. Places most people wouldn't find themselves unless they were trying to win a very eclectic version of The Amazing Race. In fact, a typical week for me could look like this:

Monday – I'm at a lawyer's office for the reading of a will. I don't know these people, have no connection to them, and yet somehow, by the end, I've become "part of the family." Just like that.

Tuesday – I'm at UCLA, interpreting a law class. I swear, after the number of classes I've interpreted, someone should've handed me an honorary law degree, or at least a membership to the Bar Association.

Wednesday – County Jail. Interpreting for an inmate. These jobs had a very specific effect on me:. They made me very committed to staying on the right side of the law. There's nothing quite like hearing someone explain their poor life choices in ASL to drive home the importance of good behavior.

Thursday – On set for a national commercial with two Deaf lead actors. And here's the thing about working on set, whether it's TV, film, commercials, music videos… The food is incredible and plentiful. I'm not even a foodie, but I suddenly become very invested in craft services when they're offering gourmet sliders and chocolate chip brownies.

Friday – Interpreting Shabbat services at a downtown temple. I'm not Jewish, but I've always loved the ceremony and ritual of religious services. I've also interpreted Catholic mass, which has its own flair, candles, incense, the occasional Latin. There's something about the pomp that brings out the theatrical side of me. I'm easily entertained.

Saturday – Off the coast of Redondo Beach, interpreting for a Deaf woman getting her sailing certification. While she's mastering the ropes and sails, I'm mastering SPF and positioning my face toward the sun like a solar panel. Not a bad gig.

Sunday – Universal Studios. Interpreting for a Deaf family visiting the park. After a while, I became so familiar with the tours, I could've led them without the tour guide.

And just when I'd think I had a rhythm down, the next week would roll in, completely different. That's the beauty of this work, it's never boring. The people change, the environments change, the stories shift. I used to explain our role as interpreters as being "the uninvited guest at every party." And I stand by that. We're there, in the room, part of the moment, without technically being on the guest list.

One morning, Ann answered the phone and said, "Bill, England is calling."

The whole country? Sounds important. Sure, put them through.

I've had plenty of mysterious calls over the years where the lack of context was just as thrilling as the job itself. This was one of those. The gentleman on the line had been given my name for a project, very hush-hush. He needed someone to tutor a song to two actors for a recording… at another actor's home. In Beverly Hills. Naturally.

Okay, can you give me a little more?

Turns out, Paul McCartney had recorded a song called "My Valentine," and his daughter, Stella McCartney, thought it would be lovely, maybe even moving, to have it performed in ASL by two of her friends. Her friends were Natalie Portman and Johnny Depp.

Sure. Why not?

Once we negotiated the rate, England emailed me a direct link to the song and lyrics. My first step was to schedule time at Natalie Portman's house.

Natalie Portman's Doorbell
and the Beatles at the Gate

Ok, set a date to visit Natalie Portman's house in Los Feliz.

Natalie had won the Oscar for Best Actress for Black Swan in 2011. Her performance was incredibly impressive and I was looking forward to meeting and working with her. On my list of working with Oscar winners, she was one of my favorites.

Her home was in Los Feliz-a pocket of Los Angeles that feels like old Hollywood with gated mansions, lush greenery, and that gentle air of quiet money. When I arrived, I rang the bell and, just like Meryl did in Grants Pass, Natalie Portman answered the door herself. I always expect movie stars to have a small army of assistants or at the very least, a butler with a British accent. Not Natalie. Just her, being delightfully normal.

It reminded me of another experience, when I worked with Ann-Margret on the film A New Life, co-starring Alan Alda. Ann-Margret's character played a schoolteacher of deaf children, and I was brought in to tutor her on the little bit of signing she needed. The whole arrangement had been set up by her husband, Roger Smith, who gave me step-by-step directions to their house.

He told me, "Turn left at the mailbox and keep driving until you hit the gate." The man was not exaggerating, after that gate, it was a journey. Their home, which happened to be Humphrey Bogart's old estate in Benedict Canyon, was less of a house and more of a compound. Four homes, garages that looked like a small car dealership, and enough landscaping to require its own zip code. Roger added, "Ann-Margret herself will be waiting at the door so you know where to go." Thank God, otherwise, I might've wandered into a guesthouse and found myself tutoring ASL to the gardener.

And one last request from Roger. "Please don't call my wife Ann. Her name is Ann-Margret. Say the whole thing."

I knew the drill. Mary Anne had always hated being called just Mary. And after getting corrected by Senator Warner for referring to Elizabeth Taylor as "Liz," I wasn't about to mess it up.

Sure enough, Ann-Margret stood at the door of one of the houses with a tiny white dog nestled in her arms and greeted me warmly, pointing to where I should park. Inside, my jaw hit the floor. Floor-to-ceiling windows opened up to a sweeping view of Los Angeles. A grand piano sat in the living room, draped in fresh flowers. Gardeners moved like stagehands behind the glass.

She offered me a drink, and I asked for water. She pushed a button on her phone and said, "Hi. Bill will have water, and I'll have strawberry soda, please. Thank you." Moments later, a maid appeared in a crisp uniform and apron, carrying our drinks on an actual silver tray.

I laughed and said, "You live like a movie star should live."

She laughed, too. Then she gave me a tour of her office, which she was especially proud of, a bold red room just off the entry, with walls covered in photos from her legendary career. Posters, candid shots, her entire life in showbiz on display. She lit up talking about her Elvis photos. Her office was part shrine, part scrapbook, all heart.

She learned the signs for the film, thanked me graciously, and left me feeling like I'd just worked with royalty who happened to make strawberry soda feel classy.

Back to Natalie Portman's house. It was also beautiful, but in a more youthful, minimalist way. Less old-Hollywood, more modern chic with baby bottles. Her husband and child were there, and the whole vibe was relaxed, almost like I'd just dropped in for coffee with a friend. A friend who happened to have an Oscar.

Natalie already knew the lyrics to Paul's song and had clearly done her homework. Her ability to memorize and retain the signs was honestly impressive. We spent two hours going through everything, and by the end, we both felt confident. She was ready.

And then came the big one. Paul McCartney's house. The day I was scheduled to work with Johnny Depp. There was no time to meet with Johnny in advance like I did with Natalie because he was on location filming The Lone Ranger. This made me a bit nervous because it meant I'd have a short amount of time to work with him. I had no idea if he had started working with someone in New Mexico on the ASL... I had no idea of anything.

You would think after four decades of meeting celebrities, I'd be immune to nerves. But I woke up with what I call a "mini migraine", not full-blown, but just enough to remind me that something big was about to happen. The last time I felt that kind of tension was the day I met Elizabeth Taylor at Gallaudet. So yes, this was familiar territory.

Paul's house was in Beverly Hills, of course. As I pulled up to the gate, several security guards checked their list. My name was on it. (Always a relief.) I was told where to park, and after making the walk back to the gate, they radioed ahead and opened it. I was instructed to follow the long and winding road (see what I did there?) and to meet everyone at the top.

Security cameras blinked at me from the trees. It felt like being watched by very expensive owls. I started getting genuinely nervous. I've worked with a lot of famous people, but this was Paul McCartney. A Beatle. A global icon. The soundtrack of my childhood.

Growing up in the '60s, my sister Evelyn and I would fantasize about meeting the Beatles. Their first album was literally titled Meet the Beatles, and here I was… about to.

I had no idea what I'd say when I met him. Don't freeze up. Don't do Princess Diana. Don't sound like a fanboy, but don't act too cool either. You're here to do a job. Be professional. But also… it's Paul McCartney.

As I reached the top of the driveway, I saw people milling about, production team, assistants, the usual quiet chaos of a set. Paul's manager, Scott Rodger, spotted me and came over, hand extended. We'd talked by phone before, and he welcomed me warmly.

Then he turned to Paul and said, "Paul, please come over and meet Bill Pugin."

I was now standing inches away from Paul McCartney.

And without missing a beat, I blurted out, "Is it as big a thrill for you to meet me as it is for me to meet you?"

It just flew out.

Paul threw his head back and laughed. "Bigger!" he said.

Ice, broken.

So, I followed up with, "Oh, and my sister Evelyn wants to know if you got the letter she wrote to you when she was eight?"

He nodded. "It's the only one I've kept."

From there, we were off and running. Paul was charming, funny, warm, exactly the person you'd hope he'd be. We talked about his friendship with Princess Diana, my own moment with her, the Beatles, and how my parents woke us up to watch them on The Ed Sullivan Show. It was one of those surreal, pinch-me moments that you don't forget, especially not when the Beatles are involved.

But I wasn't just there for nostalgia. I was there for Johnny. And Johnny was... not there yet.

Feathers, Deadlines, and Sir Paul's Shoulder Rub

Back at Paul's house, we were all on a schedule. Paul had a private flight out of the Van Nuys airport that evening, headed for the Caribbean to start a tour. The airport had a curfew, closed at 10 p.m. back in 2015, unlike now. So, while the vibe was friendly, there was a growing tension underneath it all. We were running out of time.

Still no Johnny. His private jet coming in from New Mexico was late.

Natalie's segment had already been filmed, and I got to watch the playback. She nailed it. Didn't even need me there. True professional. And of course, she was wearing Stella McCartney designs. There was a whole rack of options set up just for her and Johnny. The fashion was worthy of a runway, though I don't think Johnny ever noticed it was there.

When Johnny finally arrived, everything kicked into high gear... sort of. He and his entourage walked in like they'd just strolled out of a Rolling Stones video, starving and half-dazed. Paul had laid out a massive vegetarian spread, and naturally, we all ate. Because what else do you do when Johnny Depp arrives late? You feed him and hope he starts learning sign language soon.

I kept glancing at my watch. Tick-tock. Time was not on our side.

I have always been a fan of Johnny Depp's work. He's a complex guy and an undeniably good actor. In person, he was nice. Gracious, even. But I couldn't, for the life of me, figure out what accent he was using. Born in Kentucky, raised in Florida, and yet somehow, he sounded like a British pirate trying to order a latte.

Also, he was... decorated. Covered in feathers, wrapped in leather, and wearing enough metal around his wrists and fingers to set off metal detectors everywhere. I said out loud, because someone had to, "It's a good thing he flies private and doesn't have to go through TSA. He'd never make it to the gate." After eating, I assumed we'd finally get to work. Nope.

Johnny decided he wanted to jam with Paul instead. He took out his guitar and started strumming. And really, who says no to that? Certainly not Paul. He grabbed his own guitar and offered to show Johnny the opening chords to Blackbird. Apparently, no one ever gets them right. I stood there thinking, "This is a disaster... but also, wow." Paul McCartney. Guitar in hand. Singing Blackbird. Live. Three feet from me.

Pinch me harder.

Finally, someone, thankfully, called us to action. It was time to start filming. The wardrobe team brought Johnny over to the clothing rack. I followed, wondering if the feathers would come off. They didn't.

Johnny picked something simple and then headed into a tiny bathroom where his makeup would be applied. And that, as it turned out, was our moment. That was our time. In the cramped, poorly lit bathroom, with him seated on the closed toilet lid and me kneeling in front of him like some sort of well-dressed ASL disciple, I began to teach him the signs.

We had twelve minutes. Twelve. I asked him if he'd worked with anyone in New Mexico, maybe started learning the song beforehand?

"Bill," he said, "not only have I not worked with anyone, but I also don't know the lyrics, and I've never heard the song." Excuse me?

PAUL, could I see you in the kitchen for a moment?

I'd had over two hours with Natalie. I now had ten, make that nine, minutes with Johnny. The makeup artist was hovering. Time was ticking. My migraine, once "mini," was threatening to become a full-blown opera.

Truthfully, Johnny didn't have a natural knack for sign language. Some actors do. Others don't. Johnny was firmly in the "don't" camp. Paul wanted him to play guitar in part of the video, which Johnny loved. Signing the lyrics? Less so. I made a last-ditch executive decision to forget the full lyrics, forget the words (since he didn't know them anyway), and instead, just give him something dramatic. Choppy. Stylized. Something he could pull off visually, if not linguistically. I pulled Paul aside and explained my concern and the decision I had just made. He agreed and said "Good. Johnny will contrast with Natalie's performance. I like it." Oh boy.

We filmed in a tiny outbuilding on Paul's property. The room held Paul, the camera operator, Johnny, and me, perched on an apple box directly beneath the camera. For those unfamiliar with film sets, an apple box is the Swiss Army knife of Hollywood, used to prop up lights, gear, actors, egos. That day, I used it to try to prop up a miracle.

I sat there, take after take, signing the lyrics in front of Johnny so he could see me in his peripheral vision and follow along like a glorified ASL karaoke screen. He never learned the lyrics. He never memorized the signs. But we got something. Was it great? Not in the least. Was it salvageable? Maybe.

Midway through, I mentioned to the group that I'd woken up with a migraine that morning. Paul, being Paul, came over and asked how I was doing. I told him I still had a bit of a headache, Johnny wasn't helping. And then, Paul McCartney placed his hands on my shoulders and started giving me a massage.

Let that sit with you.

And he was good at it! He believed in clean eating, massage, acupressure, so, of course, he was a natural. "I can't believe I'm getting a massage from the cute Beatle," I said.

Paul laughed. My head felt better. Temporarily. We did the best we could with Johnny. Truly. We just didn't have the time.

When the video came out? Oh boy. The internet had thoughts. I became the poster child for "Why are hearing people teaching ASL?" Critics popped up left and right, saying this person or that person should've been hired instead.

To this day, I'm not convinced anyone, hearing or Deaf, could've made Johnny Depp look good in the ten minutes I had. And I did tell Johnny that teaching him signs while kneeling in front of him on a toilet was beneath my pay grade.

And then came the cherry on top. Scott called me from back in England. He said, "Bill, British Deaf people are really upset, they can't understand the signing in the video."

I explained calmly - "That's because Natalie and Johnny signed in ASL. American Sign Language. If they'd wanted it in BSL, British Sign Language, they should have hired two British actors."

Scott paused. "Oh, there's a difference?"

"Yes, Scott. There's a difference."

I asked him to explain it to Paul. He said he would.

And yes, the video received criticism. But it was still an extraordinary experience. One for the books. As Marlee always told me - "You can't please everyone."

She was right.

Tour Guides, Law School, and a Life in Translation

After all the dust settled from the "My Valentine" whirlwind, I went right back to work, because in this business, the world doesn't stop turning just because you got a shoulder massage from a Beatle.

Looking back, I'm often amazed at the good fortune I've had. The timing. The people. The doors that opened, some gently, some with a dramatic swing. Sometimes I still feel like that kid just getting started in sign language. Other times, I feel every bit of the decades I've been doing it.

And still, it's never boring.

I've lived many lives in this career. I've interpreted wills and weddings, arrests and award shows. I've had my hands in motion in the most unexpected places, speaking for people who couldn't, and saying nothing of myself.

But if there's one thing I've learned, it's that language is more than words. It's presence. It's humanity. It's showing up. And if I've done anything right in all these years, it's that I've shown up.

Not long after the Paul McCartney job, I received another call from England. What is it with this country? Why do they keep calling me?

This time, it was from the office of Ilona Herzberg, the executive producer who had hired me for The River Wild. Apparently, she was producing another film, and lo and behold, it involved a brief moment of sign language. And Ilona, bless her loyalty, wanted only me to handle it.

Let me tell you, one of the best things you can do in the entertainment industry, aside from not stealing the craft services, is to make a good impression. People remember. And more importantly, they call you again. And again.

Ilona told me the lead in the film was Anne Hathaway. Her character, Josephine, was a glamorous con artist who could dazzle in multiple languages, including ASL. The movie co-starred Rebel Wilson, who also had a producer credit, and was being shot in several picturesque countries. This particular scene would be shot in Majorca, Spain.

Ilona gave me the line that Anne's character was supposed to sign. Half-joking, and I really did mean it as a joke, I said, "Well, Anne Hathaway deserves an in-person tutor and not just me showing her over Zoom."

Without missing a beat, Ilona said, "Oh absolutely. We need to send you to Majorca and be there in person."

Come on. It's one line. Really?

One line, yet I was flown First Class to Majorca, Spain.

First Class on Lufthansa is no joke. I found myself seated next to Jamie Foxx, who slept the entire flight. I walked into the airplane bathroom and laughed out loud. It was the size of a small apartment. There were makeup lights around the mirror. A full-sized sofa. In the bathroom.

Of course, fate, as it often does, decided I was having too good a time and needed a little reality check. My luggage, apparently more adventurous than I am, rerouted itself to Tel Aviv.

So for seven days, I navigated the sun-drenched cliffs and coastal charm of Mallorca without any of my belongings, improvising like a survivor on a luxury reality show. No razors. No fresh clothes. Just me, my resourcefulness, and a growing bond with the only shirt I had. Ok, the producers took me shopping the first day I arrived, so I managed to shave, brush my teeth, and change my underwear!

The moment that truly defined the trip, though, had nothing to do with the hotel, the sunsets, or even Anne Hathaway's completely disarming charm. It was standing on a cliffside with

Anne, the director, and the writer, all of them looking at me with quiet intensity.

They didn't like the line that was written. "Bill," the director said, "can you come up with something else? Something better?" (I looked to the writer hoping she wasn't insulted).

And maybe it was the salty air, or maybe I was just running on the delirium of wearing the same socks for six days, but inspiration struck. I gave them a new line. Half-joking, I said:

"If you use this, I want writer's credit."

They laughed. (Thank God.) And truthfully, I was so relieved they didn't take me up on that, because, well, the film turned out to be... not great. The original line was "You're a bag of dicks." I didn't get it. Still don't. It felt juvenile, like something scrawled on a middle school bathroom stall.

My suggestion? "Eat shit and die."

A classic. Pithy. Timeless. Also, it looked much better in ASL. I explained that all four words would sign near the face, so when they shot Anne's close-up, the whole phrase would read clearly. That's something people often forget. What works on set isn't just about what sounds good, but what looks good, too.

They were relieved that I understood how to play the camera: wide, medium, close. And the signs worked for every angle.

On my last day in Majorca, my luggage finally arrived. The suitcase finally showed up at my door. It was a bit beaten up, but intact. I figured a lone bag would've been detonated at the Tel Aviv airport, but nope, mine made it, complete with a pair of

TSA inspection gloves left inside. It felt a bit creepy. How many hands rummaged through my things?

A bit invasive, yes. But I got my stuff back.

Anne couldn't have been lovelier. Every day, she asked if I'd gotten my bag yet, and every day I'd say, "No, Anne. Remember this shirt? Does it look like I got my bag?" We'd laugh, me in my now-iconic shirt, her in couture, and it became our running joke for the week.

We wrapped up with a hug. A real one. No Hollywood air-kiss nonsense. Just two people who'd survived a strange little movie on a beautiful island, trying to teach the world how to tell someone off, in style.

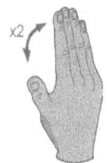

Transitions & Reflections

The Desert Shift

By 2017, I had been living in Los Angeles for 38 years. That's almost four decades of dodging traffic, and breathing air that I could see. I'd tried Portland, and I gave Italy a go.,

But Southern California had a gravitational pull I couldn't ignore. I just didn't think that "Southern California" meant LA anymore. I kept buying places and selling them, and I wasn't sure what I was looking for, but I knew I hadn't found it yet.

To make matters worse, I was slowly developing a rage problem every time I tried to drive to the grocery store. Flipping off grannies in their car really wasn't my style, and I knew I needed to make a change.

The Sign Language Company had grown to the point where I wasn't needed for daily interpreting. That's a good problem to have. And with Ann's help staying in LA, I realized, possibly for the first time ever, I could live anywhere and work remotely. The world had gone digital, and I was ready to hit refresh.

I had a discussion with Todd, and we both agreed that moving to Palm Springs would be the best plan. We'd had a weekend house in the desert since 2009, a little escape hatch from the grind, and we began to wonder if it could be more than just a weekend fling. Could we make it our full-time address? Only one way to find out.

It was just a couple of hours from LA if you timed it right (which you never do), so we sold our place and made the leap. Ann, who had long been the soul of the office, agreed to work from home, and since most of our friends were already too busy to hang out anyway, we left quietly.

Change is a good thing. Or at least that's what people say when they're in the middle of doing something mildly terrifying.

There were a few bumps as we adjusted, like trying to figure out how to avoid calling 911 when you see a lizard the size of your forearm in the backyard, but soon, things smoothed out. The business ran like we were still across the desk from each other. The phone system worked like an intercom, and with one button I could reach Ann, like magic. Or science. Same thing.

About a year before packing up and moving to the desert, I had an idea to help new interpreters to the world of interpreting. I kept interviewing eager interpreters, and many of them weren't quite ready for working in the real world. Many of them had graduated from ITPs (Interpreting Training Programs), but their skills and confidence were lacking.

My motto had always been "If you want to swim, you gotta get in the pool", but many of these young people weren't really ready for the pool.

So, I came up with the idea of creating a program for recent ITP grads and I called it SLICE. Sign Language Interpreters Continuing Education. I wanted a place where they could come and feel safe, once a month, free of charge, and practice their skills and get answers to their many questions.

I called it SLICE because I felt we were all a piece of the PIE - the Professional Interpreting Environment.

The first session had a handful of interpreters in the room. I was able to borrow a classroom from a local Community College and I always brought cake or pie so that everyone would get a "slice".

This was all gratis because I knew it would benefit me (and other agencies) in the long run to help these people and boost their interpreting skills and confidence.

I invited special guests each month - a Deaf CPA to talk to interpreters about how to manage their income and taxes; seasoned interpreters to tell their stories of their careers; various Deaf friends to help them practice in real time.

After the first session, word got around and the room was packed each month with eager interpreters wanting and needing to soak up as much material as possible.

The sessions started with everyone standing in a line facing me (where they couldn't see each other, so no "judging" would be possible), and I would read a speech so that they could all practice interpreting. We then split up into small groups to help each other with their expressive signs, voicing, fingerspelling, etc.

SLICE was a huge success and I only wish I had thought of it earlier. I envisioned it taking off and being adopted in other cities so interpreters in Atlanta, Dallas, DC, Miami would be able to continue their studies in a safe and welcoming environment. But, for the year that it existed, I would like to think it really helped and made a difference.

As for The Sign Language Company, the contracts kept coming in. I found myself collaborating with more production companies, one of which was none other than Ryan Murphy's. They reached out about a mini-series centered on Jeffrey Dahmer. You know, just your everyday light and breezy topic.

I was in negotiations and helping in the early stages when the entire world decided to shut down. COVID.

Everything stopped. Schools closed. Businesses shuttered. And sign language interpreters, along with basically everyone, were told to stay home and contemplate their new careers as bread bakers or TikTok dancers.

I remember thinking, "How exactly are we going to survive this?" Many agencies didn't. But we pivoted, quickly, and found ourselves relying on Zoom and other virtual platforms to keep interpreting alive. It wasn't ideal, but it was something.

Sign Language is a three-dimensional language. You need space, depth, angles. A computer screen is two-dimensional, and trying to interpret that way sometimes feels like trying to waltz inside a phone booth.

Also, Deaf people are social by nature. Connection is part of the language. Now we were separated by Wi-Fi with only a camera to keep us company.

One of my first Zoom jobs during that time involved a Deaf client giving me his bank account number to voice to the hearing person on the other end. Because there's no depth of field on screen, I couldn't tell if he was signing the letter "d" or the number "1", a pretty important distinction when dealing with a bank account.

I stopped him to clarify. He was not amused.

Everyone's patience was fried during COVID. I signed, "Sorry, but it's your bank account number, and I'd rather not accidentally route your paycheck to a scammer in Nigeria." He didn't laugh. I did. Internally.

That's when I realized just how attentive we had to be in this new virtual reality.

Shifting Sands and Surprise Sparks

The nature of my relationship with Todd had begun to change. After twelve years together, we had entered what I'd call a holding pattern, not quite crashing, not climbing, just circling. And then COVID arrived, which has never been known to breathe life into a relationship. Quite the opposite.

At the same time, something unexpected happened. I met someone. Someone who sparked something in me that I hadn't felt in a while. Enter: Nigel Sanches. He was thirty years my junior, from Brazil, and the relationship took me by surprise, just as it did everyone else.

Let's pause for a moment and acknowledge the obvious. Yes, thirty years younger. Yes, Brazilian. Yes, you have questions. No, I probably won't answer them.

When you're in a relationship, it's never just with one person. You inherit the whole family. Todd's family, his three siblings and especially his parents, had become my own. I adored them. And thanks to years of experience, I already spoke fluent Canadian.

Then came Nigel's family, equally lovely, equally warm, and surprise, I assumed my years of speaking Italian would make Portuguese a walk in the park. Nope. Portuguese is hard. Even Brazilians say so. I'm trying, but the brain cells don't bounce like they used to.

Todd, to his credit, seemed to recognize that we'd both reached the end of our chapter. He shared that he wanted to pursue a new career in the medical field and had been accepted to a school in Pennsylvania. Of course, everything was in a holding pattern until the world reopened, or at least figured out how to go outside again without gloves and a face shield.

Meanwhile, life threw us all into a completely unexpected situation.

Nigel's sister, Karol, was on her way to Australia to begin her Ph.D. studies in Melbourne. She had a layover in LA and was planning to spend a day with Nigel before continuing on. So far, so good. But then, the world learned that Australia had just closed its borders, so no more incoming flights.

Nigel called me from LAX. "What do I do?"

"Bring her to Palm Springs," I said. "We'll figure it out." And just like that, we had ourselves a little reality show.

For six months, our house became something between a sitcom and a social experiment. Under one roof was me, Todd, Nigel, Karol, our dog Jesse, and Rosie, Nigel's dog. No cameras, but definitely worthy of syndication.

We all survived. Somehow. Honestly, I think we deserved medals. Or at least a group rate for therapy.

Eventually, the Ryan Murphy project resumed, and I was back to commuting between Palm Springs and Los Angeles. Many meetings remained virtual, but there were plenty of times I had to be there in person. Hollywood may flirt with technology, but it still prefers sitting around the old-fashioned conference room table.

The production went smoothly. Ryan hired us again for another one of his series, The Politician, and just like that, we were off and running again.

Along with TV and film, I found myself working on commercials for companies like Apple, AT&T, and Microsoft. Each shoot was its own world, but one of the standouts for me was working with a young Deaf actress named Sarah Clifton. Sarah had that rare thing which was an undeniable presence, a kind of energy that lit up a set. Fresh, vibrant, incredibly talented.

When Sarah was cast in something, I made it a priority to be there. I didn't want to miss it. We had a bond. I was like a second father to her, and she respected my years in the business. I told her, "All I ask is that you mention my name when you win your Emmy. Or Oscar. Or both. No pressure."

There were so many incredibly gifted Deaf actors I had the privilege of working with, aside from the icons like Marlee and Phyllis.

John Maucere, a friend from a Deaf family, became part of ABC's newly formed Talent Development Program. He was the first Deaf actor selected. It was a big deal. ABC was ready to groom young talent for network television, and John had the chops. Plus, he had an advocate in actress Emma Samms, who just happened to be starring in General Hospital and Dynasty simultaneously.

I ended up interpreting for John during meetings, photo shoots, and back on The Home Show! Host Gary Collins greeted me like an old friend, recalling I had previously been on the show with Terrylene. Hollywood may be vast, but relationships can be tight and can last a very long time.

Cruise Control and Camera Moments

Not only did I work with Ty Giordano in the Ashton Kutcher film

A Lot Like Love, but we also teamed up again on a sitcom called Out of Practice, starring Henry Winkler, Stockard Channing, and a then-unknown Ty Burrell, who later found his groove on Modern Family.

I had met Henry a few times through Marlee. In fact, Marlee and Kevin were married in Henry's front yard! Later, Henry and I ended up working together on stage in Montreal. Marlee and Henry both do public appearances followed by Q&A sessions, and when Jack (Marlee's longtime interpreter) wasn't available, I'd travel with her to those gigs. Sometimes, it was a double bill with Henry and Marlee on stage. You can imagine the fun. And yes, it was exactly that much fun.

Another great talent I worked with was Anthony Natale. He played Richard Dreyfuss' son in Mr. Holland's Opus. Anthony and I also teamed up on His Bodyguard, a TV movie with Mitzi Kapture. Filmed in Toronto. In November. I hadn't been that cold since Jimmy Carter's inauguration. It was during that shoot that I had to fly back to LA for contract signing for the ill-fated Damon.

Anthony was part of the fantastic Deaf cast of CSI alongside Marlee and Phyllis, and he had a recurring role on Switched at Birth. Any set was better when Anthony was around.

But the most memorable time I worked with Anthony was on the film Jerry Maguire.

Jerry Maguire. Starring a little-known actor named Tom Cruise (I know, I know) and a newcomer named Renée Zellweger. When I got the job, the director, Cameron Crowe, asked me to help the casting office find a young Deaf man for a brief elevator scene, with his Deaf girlfriend, Tom Cruise, and Renée.

The auditions were held at 20th Century Fox, and a lovely young actress named Andrea Ferrell was cast as the Deaf girlfriend. I had recommended a talented new actor in town for the boyfriend role. He was a terrific stage actor, but unfortunately, something about him didn't translate on film. Cameron didn't quite buy the chemistry between him and Andrea, so I suggested they see Anthony.

One look at Anthony and they were sold. Now, here's the part where I make my most bold Hollywood move to date. I introduced myself to Tom Cruise… in the men's restroom.

Tom Cruise in the men's room, and Johnny Depp on a closed toilet lid. I told you that my career has taken me to many exotic locations!

I figured I should let him know who I was and why I was there. And well, there we were. No time like the present, even if that present involves fluorescent lighting and urinals.

To his credit, Tom couldn't have been more gracious. He welcomed me to the team, and after washing our hands, we both headed up to Cameron Crowe's office for a meeting.

And here's where I put my foot directly into my mouth.

The line "You complete me" was to be signed by Anthony's character and then interpreted by Renée's character to Tom. Now, I hadn't yet read the entire script (which, in hindsight, was probably a mistake), so during the meeting, I asked, complete-ly innocently, "Does it have to be that line? 'You complete me' doesn't really translate well in ASL. Can it be another line?"

Dead silence. Cameron Crowe looked at me and said, "No, Bill. It cannot be another line. It has to be that line. Figure it out." Lesson learned. Read the script.

But Anthony did figure it out, and the day came to shoot the scene. Twelve hours in a cramped elevator with Tom Cruise, Renée, Andrea, and Anthony. Tom is a perfectionist, in the best possible way, and he wanted to try every angle, every nuance. What Tom wants, Tom gets. Especially in an elevator.

Another favorite of mine is Shoshannah Stern. Sho had just graduated from Gallaudet and moved to LA when she walked into an audition for the sitcom Off Centre. I already knew most of the usual faces who showed up for auditions, it was always a mini-reunion, but then Sho walked in and just… owned the room.

She was cast immediately. A total pro from day one. We ended up working together on Weeds and she went on to star in many other projects. Most recently, she directed the first documentary about Marlee Matlin, which premiered at Sundance. Shoshanna shines her talent both in front and behind the camera.

I also worked with Troy Kotsur on an episode of Scrubs. Troy was a phenomenal stage actor, well known for his work with Deaf West Theatre, and had already made it to Broadway in Big River alongside Ty and Phyllis. Scrubs was his first on-camera experience, and he was such a natural that no one believed it was his first time.

He kept at it, and eventually, history. Troy won the Oscar for Best Supporting Actor for CODA. I couldn't be prouder.

And keeping it all in the family, I also worked with Troy's wife, Deanne Bray, on two different occasions, first on Heroes, starring Milo Ventimiglia, and again for the audition for 2 Broke Girls. Deanne is so talented that she starred in her own series, Sue Thomas: FB Eye.

Milo liked working with me so much on Heroes that he personally asked if I could come back on his new show, The Company You Keep. I worked on the pilot, tutoring both Milo and actress Sarah Wayne Callies in sign language for their scenes with Shaylee Mansfield, another remarkable young Deaf actress.

It's moments like these, where artistry and advocacy intersect, that make everything worth it.

Auditions, Prosthetics, and a Southern Side of Grits

Then there was Grounded for Life. I was brought in as a technical advisor because the producers wanted a Deaf character for an episode. Fine. Great. I helped them find Jody Stevenson, who absolutely nailed her audition. She was authentic, talented, and ready to go.

Then came the classic Hollywood pivot. "We're probably going to cast a hearing actress instead. Could you teach her to sign the lines?" Cue the dramatic pause. I looked at them and said, "No. I can't. And I won't."

Sure, you can teach a hearing person to sign, but you can't teach them to be Deaf. You can't teach life experience. You can't teach nuance. Jody brought something real to the table, and I wasn't about to let that go unnoticed. I gave them the ultimatum and if they didn't cast Jody, they would have to find someone to replace me.

They finally did the right thing and cast Jody. Then, as a cherry on top, they asked if I could play her father in the final scene. I half-joked that no one would believe I was old enough to be her father. I was. (Sigh.)

Now, let's move on to two fabulous women I call friends: Vae and Vikee.

Marsha Vae Goeken, just Vae to her friends, was one of the original actors in the Deaf cast of Beauty and the Beast with Terrylene. Vae had a certain sparkle, and she was a mainstay in Deaf theater circles in LA. If something cool and Deaf-related was happening on stage, odds were Vae was involved, and having a blast.

At one point, Marc Cherry (Desperate Housewives' Marc Cherry) wrote a new series for ABC starring Reba McEntire. The show was called Red Blooded. There was a role written for an older Deaf woman, sort of a Granny-from-The-Beverly-Hillbillies type. The casting director, Scott Genkinger, called and asked me to help.

During my pre-casting meeting with Marc, he told me he really wanted Marlee for the part. Don't get me wrong, Marlee is stunning, talented, iconic. But "craggy" isn't exactly an adjective used for her. The role needed a much older, rough-around-the-edges character.

I told Marc that there were other Deaf actresses worth seeing for this role. So we brought in a handful, including Vae and Vikee. Vikee gave a terrific audition, honestly, better than we expected. But the character was supposed to be thin and wiry, and Vikee, lovely as she is, didn't fit the physical mold Marc had in mind. I gently suggested they consider changing the look of the character to fit the performance.

But… I had already used up my "Can we change the line?" card with Cameron Crowe. Probably not wise to push my luck twice.

Then Vae walked in. She looked the part to a T. Marc loved her energy and presence, but the role demanded quick adaptability, and Vae, like many great stage actors, needed more time to develop a character. On film, you often don't have that luxury. That's why people like Laura Linney and Meryl Streep are who they are. They can shift gears on a dime.

In the end, Marc cast Marlee.

Her time in the makeup chair rivaled Ron Perlman's transformation into the Beast for Beauty and the Beast. They applied prosthetics to age her face, neck, and arms, yellowed her teeth, and topped her with a grey wig that screamed "witchy elder."

When she walked on set, no one gave her the usual starstruck attention. Not even a glance. It was jarring, and oddly perfect, it helped the character come alive.

Sadly, ABC passed on the pilot. Something about American Idol eating up too many days of the week. Their loss. It was a fantastic script and an amazing story that deserved to unfold. The pilot was filmed in Atlanta.

How I missed sweet tea and grits!

As for Vae, she got her moment in the sun with an episode of 911. The plot was a Deaf woman trapped in her burning apartment building. Vae wowed everyone at the audition with her panicked screams and all-too-believable performance. She was cast, and she crushed it.

And now, Vikee. Her moment came on the HBO series Getting On, starring Laurie Metcalf. I don't know how many Emmys Laurie has, but it's not enough. The show followed nurses caring for the elderly in a hospital, and Vikee played an overweight, elderly Deaf patient. The casting was spot-on.

The cast table read was one of the hardest things to sit through, not because it was bad, but because it was so funny we could barely breathe. Laurie's delivery was flawless. Vikee was incredible in the role. Every day I came to work on that show, I felt like I'd hit the jackpot.

And then, in classic fashion, the producers asked if I could play the interpreter signing to Vikee at the foot of her bed in the final scene.

"Throw me in, Coach."

I had another Marlee adventure that was pure fun. It wasn't a film, but an adventure for sure.

As I mentioned before, whenever Jack wasn't available to travel with Marlee for a speech or event, I would go. Marlee called and asked if I was available for a quick, one day trip to Las Vegas - all on David Copperfield's dime.

World famous magician, David Copperfield, had gone on a date with Marlee one time a long time ago. Marlee said that what she remembers most vividly about their evening was that she had to drive. David doesn't drive. When they arrived at their destination and gave the keys to the valet, David took out a wad of cash that looked like thousands of dollars. The world of interpreting affords me a modest home and car. Maybe I should've gone into magic!

Anyway, David asked Marlee to join him with a group of Deaf, amateur magicians traveling from England to meet with David and to see his private museum. He thought it would be fun to have Marlee there and he knew the Deaf Brits would be thrilled to meet her. So, Marlee asked me to come along.

Arriving in Las Vegas on Southwest (what? No private jet?), we were greeted by one of David's staff in her...Prius. Prius? Again... no limo?

We were driven to the MGM Grand where David performed his show and where he lived while in Vegas. After a bit of security clearance, we were permitted to enter a private elevator that took us up to David's penthouse. Upon entering, we saw a lavish spread of bagels, cheeses, fruit, danish, coffee, tea and soft drinks - all for us. David finally appeared (magically!) and we all three sat for a chat and to discuss the plans for the day.

We took the elevator down to the casino level and walked through the casino with no one noticing the two stars in their midst. People were too focused on gambling to take notice. We were on our way to where David's Rolls Royce (that he didn't know how to drive) would whisk us away to his museum.

As we walked past all the slot machines, I asked David to pull the lever after I deposited a dollar. I said, "prove to me how good a magician you are!" The look he gave me made me instantly realize he had probably been asked to do that a million times. So much for originality!

David's museum is a nondescript building in the desert. No signs. Nothing. You'd never know what it was when driving past. David was our personal guide and the pride he had of its contents just oozed out of him.

It's called The International Museum and Library of the Conjuring Arts. It's filled with his collection of everything from his first magic trick as a young boy, to most everything owned by Houdini. All of Charlie McCarthy's dummies were there, too, and I expected one or two of them to start talking to us as we walked by.

The Brits were in awe (as Marlee and I were) and were so appreciative of the day spent with David at the museum.

David had to get back to prepare for his show, so Marlee and I were driven from the museum directly to the airport. David took the Rolls, we had the Prius.

Two flights, a ride in a Rolls Royce, breakfast with David Copperfield, and a private tour of a place not open to the public. All in all…another "magical" day.

Looking Back, Leaning Forward

I found myself taking stock of my life. It snuck up on me, really. After so many years of showbiz sets, studio lots, and Zoom squares, I looked around and realized, I was in my 60s. How did that happen? (And more importantly, does AARP know where I live?)

The truth was, I was feeling restless again. I had achieved so much. Worked in film and television, traveled the globe, rubbed shoulders with celebrities, politicians, and even royalty. I mentored a whole generation of interpreters. That's a resume you don't just stick in a drawer.

And still… I wasn't quite ready to hang it all up.

I considered selling the business. I thought, "Maybe it's time to slow down, let go, kick back." But I had this gut feeling, The Sign Language Company still had more to do. And so did I.

Ann started talking about retirement. I could tell she'd grown a little weary after years of showing up, day in and day out. She loved coming into the office when I lived in LA. But now, working from home felt… different.

So, in anticipation of Ann's well-deserved exit, I had a conversation with Nigel.

Nigel had worked for a company in Brazil managing close to 100 employees. The man had a serious work ethic, a mind for detail, and nerves of steel, three things you need to work in this business without losing your hair or your humanity. I thought, "Could we live together and work together?" Risky. But we were willing to try.

Turns out, it worked beautifully.

The transition was as seamless as we could make it. Ann bowed out with grace. Nigel stepped in with professionalism. Of course, it took some time for clients and interpreters to get used to his style, but everything fell into place.

Over the years, The Sign Language Company has provided countless hours of pro bono work. One of our biggest partnerships has been with the National Association of the Deaf (NAD), where we've sent up to 25 interpreters to support their national conventions, at no cost.

Whenever an event touches me personally, AIDS walks, breast cancer fundraisers, I work for free. Always have. My mom battled breast cancer before passing from bone cancer, and that stays with you. If I can't convince interpreters to donate their time, I pay them myself. I get it, this is a job, and not everyone has the same personal connection. But when I do have that connection, I act on it.

And now, here's the part every writer dreads. The wrap-up. The "How do I end this?" question that has loomed since chapter one.

Let me tell you what I've learned.

The incredible thing about interpreting, after doing it since I was 17, is that it's never the same. Never. Every job is different. Every client brings a new energy, a new story, a new reason to be there. After 50 years, I'm still surprised. I'm still learning. Still showing up curious. Still counting my blessings especially when I have the good fortune of working with new interpreters. I continuously learn from them.

And so, dear reader, I want to say thank you. Thanks for coming along for this ride. I know my life has taken some twists, turns, and U-turns. It's been a path not unlike the Yellow Brick Road, with side quests and scenic routes I never expected. But those detours led to lessons. They led to joy. And I hope, maybe, they gave you something, too.

I'm still on that path. Still waking up every day wondering who I'll meet next, what story I'll hear, what moment will surprise me.

And if reading my journey has inspired you to share your own, I hope you do. I'm still the sponge I was at 17, soaking up every bit of humanity I can before I reach that Emerald City.

I'm grateful that Mary Anne lives down the street. I'm thankful for FaceTime so I can still talk to Evelyn and Welby. And if I could have one more dinner with Mom, Dad, and Jeffrey, just one, I'd listen even more closely to what that 17-year-old version of me was dreaming up back then.

I may not be the youngest in the room anymore, but here's the funny thing– I don't feel done.

Looking back, I see I have done a lot. But looking forward…

…I feel like I'm just getting started.

The End?

Bill lives in Palm Springs with his partner, Nigel, and their dog, Rosie.